Columbo

This book is dedicated to all the teachers I encountered at Highcliffe, Stonehill and Longslade Schools. My heartfelt thanks especially to: Mrs Val Almond, Mr John Bence, Mr Paul Kelly, Mr Richard Lawrence, Mr Peter W. Mans, and Ms Jill Smith. Thank you for your dedication, so often beyond the call of duty. Thank you for your belief in my potential, especially during my A-level years. Thank you for your kindness, generosity, time and immeasurable patience. My goodness, you were patient! I owe you so much, so many of us do. I hope this may be a fitting dedication, especially as I spent so many happy hours as a teenager in the UK watching *Columbo* when I should have been doing my homework: thank you for teaching me how to learn.

Columbo

Paying Attention 24/7

David Martin-Jones

EDINBURGH
University Press

Edinburgh University Press is one of the leading university presses in the UK.
We publish academic books and journals in our selected subject areas across the
humanities and social sciences, combining cutting-edge scholarship with high editorial
and production values to produce academic works of lasting importance. For more
information visit our website: edinburghuniversitypress.com

Edinburgh University Press Ltd
The Tun – Holyrood Road
12 (2f) Jackson's Entry
Edinburgh EH8 8PJ

Typeset in 11/13 Monotype Ehrhardt by
Manila Typesetting Company, and
printed and bound in Great Britain

A CIP record for this book is available from the British Library

ISBN 978 1 4744 7979 0 (hardback)
ISBN 978 1 4744 7980 6 (paperback)
ISBN 978 1 4744 7981 3 (webready PDF)
ISBN 978 1 4744 7982 0 (epub)

Contents

Figures

Acknowledgements

This book took several years to write, and many people kindly contributed. My thanks to John Caughie, Sofia Bull, Dimitris Eleftheriotis, Lucy Fife Donaldson, Andrew Jarvis, Matthew Holtmeier, John Trafton, and all the anonymous peer reviewers for helpful feedback on drafts. To John Caughie especially, whose initial intervention was instrumental in shaping the text in many ways. Thanks to Lucy and James Walters for pre-publication sight of a draft of *Television Performance*, and similarly to Yannis Tzioumakis for a chance to read the proofs of *Acting Indie*. A huge thank you, especially, to Toby Neilson, Oliver Kroener and Kathi Kamleitner for brilliant research assistance – I would never have reached the finish line without you guys (maybe not even the starting line!). The amazing Lee Grant also generously spoke with me about starring in *Columbo* – a charming, unforgettable experience for which I shall be forever grateful.

Research and archival work was conducted at various locations, on and off site. Firstly, at the British Film Institute's Reuben Library (in 2019 and 2020), and BFI Special Collections at Berkhamsted. Thanks to all the helpful staff at these locations, especially Nina Bishop and Nicky Clarke for all your help remotely prior to the second visit, and Nigel Good at Special Collections for helping when I had a tight schedule during the first. Secondly, extra special thanks are due to several incredibly helpful professionals in archives in the USA. Thank you to Mary K. Huelsbeck, Assistant Director, Wisconsin Center for Film and Theater Research, University of Wisconsin-Madison. Your assistance with locating information on audiences for the NBC Mystery Movie, at a distance, was very much appreciated. Thank you also to Josie Walters-Johnston, Reference Librarian, Moving Image Section, at the Library of Congress. Your diligence in unearthing the sponsors and commercials of the early seasons, at a distance, was invaluable. Thanks to Genevieve Maxwell, Reference Librarian, Academy of Motion Picture Arts and Sciences, Margaret Herrick Library, for pursuing my questions and offering further directions to explore, and, similarly, to Maya Montañez Smukler at the Archive Research & Study Center, UCLA Film & Television Archive, for helpful advice on where to search for specific details. The book would not be what it is without the generosity of these archives and their courteous and professional personnel, in enabling off-site research. I will remain extremely grateful for this. Closer to home, this work was made possible by the University of Glasgow Film and Television Studies audiovisual collection, for which my thanks to Michael McCann, and current and former colleagues for your hard work in building this invaluable archive. Likewise, to the University of Glasgow library, and especially its lifesaving original 1988 copy of *The Columbo Phile*.

In terms of the intellectual shaping of the argument, thank you to all those at *Film-Philosophy* in Brighton who gave valuable input and asked insightful questions: Jane Stadler for being supportive and suggesting key texts to research especially, John Mullarkey also for drawing my attention to the important place in my argument of the functioning of the unusual narrative structure, and David H. Fleming for suggesting Franco 'Bifo' Berardi. Thanks to everyone else who spent time talking through the ideas with me, suggesting helpful directions and things to read, including (in no particular order), Robert Burgoyne, Colin Gardner, John Drabinski, Greg Singh, Mel Selfe, William Brown, Belén Vidal, Tim Bergfelder, Ian Garwood, Lucy Bolton, Eirini Nedelkopoulou, Laurence Kent and Carl Lavery. Thanks especially to Gillian Leslie for being so positive as always, but especially for believing in the project. I am not sure this book would be here without your help. Thanks are also due to the various *Columbo* fan sites and social media groups that keep the series alive. Thanks finally, and as always, to Sol and Elena, and all my family, for their patience with me around the attention I pay to work. Thanks especially to Ro and John for access to your private literature collection which helped shape the argument. Thanks most of all to Sol for the *Columbo* DVDs, not to mention the T-shirt and poster, and your forbearance as I watched them . . . amidst all the hours and hours of other marvellous seventies cop shows which you enjoyed so much.

A note on episode notation. Some ambiguity surrounds which seasons the last episodes of *Columbo* belong to. They were infrequent towards the end, and some are as well considered stand-alone television movies. Rather than denoting episodes by season or series (even though an online database like Internet Movie Database does so), all episodes are denoted by title and year.

Introduction:
Fifty Years of *Columbo*

Something is '*bothering*' Columbo. There is this one little detail about the case he is working which he just cannot let go. It stays with him even when he is at home with Mrs Columbo, long after the end of the working day. It interferes with his appetite and it won't let him sleep. This detail is on Columbo's mind so much that he even makes a special trip back out to the chief suspect's home, the very next morning, just to ask him (or occasionally it is a her) about it. This little persistent niggle, this 'just one more thing', is what will eventually crack open the case for Columbo and convict the murderer. This is a detail which none of the Lieutenant's fellow police officers in the LAPD. notice, even though they are all professionally trained to look for clues. Curiously, as he is so often distracted, Columbo has spotted it. Why? Because Columbo has an almost superhuman ability to pay attention. Not to his wardrobe, evidently, or where his pencil might be, but to his work. The cost of this, though, is that the detail will keep on bothering him, night and day, until the case is solved. Until then, Columbo must pay attention to the case, 24/7, his work as a detective being an all-consuming attentive labour.

As the above summary condensation of so many *Columbo*s indicates, this book argues that analysis of this extremely popular television show uncovers its sustained engagement with attention. There is nothing particularly mysterious about this term, *attention*, although to be fair it does have some interesting connotations one might not immediately expect. On the one hand, this is attention in the everyday sense. Precisely as it is meant in the expression 'pay attention' which parents are forever saying to their children. There is, then, something incredibly *ordinary* about the engagement with attention in *Columbo*, as perhaps befits this much-loved show about the down-at-heel 'everyman' detective. On the other hand, as might be expected of a book-length study, there is a little more to it than this.

The analysis of attention in *Columbo* in the pages that follow stems from the (oft-noted) understanding that television is itself an attention-seeking device. Indeed, that television plays a powerful role in shaping the manner in which we, its viewers, pay attention to the world around us. This is to engage with the idea that what we pay attention to is shaped by external forces, and that this shaping is an integral aspect of how society functions. Attention, some argue, may even be a key factor in driving the economy. These thoughts have occurred to scholars across numerous disciplines, from Art History to Business to Television and Film Studies, and the relevance of this deeper meaning to the term is unpacked in a dedicated chapter on attention later on. For now, though, it is enough to realise that what the exploration of *Columbo* reveals is how our manner of paying attention to the world was shaped in the later decades of the twentieth century in ways that continue even to this day.

In its simplest expression, then, this is a book about how, when watching *Columbo*, we are all encouraged to be (or even, learn how best to be) attentive labourers like Columbo. What is useful about such an interpretation is that it can help us understand more about our everyday lives in the early decades of the twenty-first century. This is especially so in our quotidian roles as attentive labourers, with many of us now typically paying attention to screens for much of our lives within what many now consider the attention economy (an idea that I explain and qualify in Chapter 2).

This contemporary life of attentive labour, *Columbo* shows us as though in a flashback to our recent past, was determined by the historical changes of the era in which the show emerged. *Columbo*'s commencement as a series in 1971 coincided with US involvement in Vietnam and was bracketed on either side by US-backed coups in Indonesia (1965–1966) and Chile (1973) which removed left-wing political opposition to capitalism and ushered in an era dominated globally by neoliberal ideology (Harvey 2005; Klein 2007; Westad 2007). Neoliberalism, which considers a self-regulating – ideally, deregulated – market to be the best distributor of wealth, seeks to reduce the state's role in governing society. In the USA, it was the Reagan years, during which *Columbo* was off the air (the show's return coinciding with the fall of the Berlin Wall at the end of the Cold War), which saw neoliberal economic policies transform the country. The society which then emerged in the USA and across much of the globe was (and remains) polarised by wealth inequality. This has led many commentators to conclude that neoliberalism is a form of nihilistic and permanent class war pitting all against all to the benefit of the super-rich (Harvey 2005: 16–17; Shaviro 2011: 77; Berardi 2015: 104).

These historical changes form the *backdrop* against which Columbo's paying of attention plays out across the many decades during which the show was on the air. As such, over its thirty-five-year lifespan, *Columbo* indicates the shift in emphasis with respect to what it means to pay attention that emerged along with the contemporary world. Put another way, whilst the manner in which Columbo pays attention to his work does not change much from its first pilot in the late 1960s to its final episode in the early 2000s, what *Columbo* indicates regarding the ramifications of this *does change*. The shifting socio-historical terrain of the era and the changing role of attention within it thus become evident to the attentive observer looking back with hindsight. Hence this is a book as much about what *Columbo* means for us, now, as it is about what *Columbo* meant for viewers then: its negotiation of how attention should be paid, I would argue, thus going a long way towards explaining the continuing popularity of the show today.

Columbo at Fifty

Columbo began fifty years ago. After two pilots[1] (February 1968 and March 1971), episode one of series one was shown in September 1971. The first seven series (1971–1978) aired on NBC. After a ten-year break the show was rebooted in 1989, running, intermittently, on ABC until 2003. Over the thirty-five-years there were sixty-nine *Columbo*s in total.

Immediately popular, Peter Falk's performance as the rumpled, rain-coated detective, cigar in hand, remains iconic. This is not the case, of course, for any number of other television shows before or since. *Columbo*, in this respect, is one of a rare number of television shows in history which has sustained public interest for so long, both during and after its initial years on-screen. Five decades on, reruns still air, for instance on the US network ME TV (Memorable Entertainment Television), Sundays at 7 pm, whilst Sundance Television runs *Columbo* marathons over the mid-winter festive season. Online, Peacock streams the entire back catalogue on demand for US viewers. In other countries *Columbo* likewise remains

---

[1] Whilst 'Prescription: Murder' (1968) was not necessarily intended as a pilot, it generated the network interest to have become one if Falk had then been interested in developing things. When 'Ransom for a Dead Man' (1971) was later proposed as a *Columbo* pilot, Levinson and Link initially felt it unnecessary because they considered 'Prescription: Murder' to already be one (1981a: 85–86). Thus for ease of discussion I refer to both precursors as the show's (two) pilots.

popular, with repeats still showing on ITV4 and 5USA in the UK, as just one example. In addition, Amazon Prime has added the first two series to its online streaming content provision, and DVD box sets remain on sale. As a result of *Columbo*'s continued presence on people's screens, online fan communities clamour for a Hollywood movie or another series reboot starring Mark Ruffalo (after his performance in *Zodiac* [2007]), or Natasha Lyonne (following the Netflix series *Russian Doll* [2019]).

Columbo also remains in the news. The British television writing and producing duo of Mark Gatiss and Steven Moffat – who created *Sherlock* (2010–2017) – have looked into securing the rights to produce a new version of *Columbo*, albeit unsuccessfully thus far (Cremona 2019).[2] In 2018 *Rolling Stone* placed *Columbo* first in their 'TV's Top 10 Detectives' (Sepinwall 2018), and in the same year a Los Angeles Superior Court Judge (allowing a lawsuit against Universal filed by the series creators William Link and Richard Levinson, the latter deceased[3]) even joked about 'passing out cigars' (E. Gardner 2018) so central is *Columbo*'s place in US, even global, cultural memory.[4]

In this respect, *Columbo* has a cultural centrality which makes it perhaps a little more than just a cult favourite with fans. If we search for *Columbo*'s continuing influence in the contemporary cultural milieu we find: an online locations map; a band named after the show; a quiz book; a cookbook; a colouring book; YouTube channels; innumerable references to *Columbo* peppering contemporary television shows (not to mention acknowledgements of *Columbo* across other media, such as Japanese *manga*); newly created fan-oriented products ranging from T-shirts to mugs to cushion covers; vintage memorabilia including the original 1970s board game and Italian language promotional posters on sale on online auction sites; and numerous *Columbo*-related online podcasts, fan sites and social media groups. These latter fan groups indicate the 'aliveness' of *Columbo* to this day, as they organise online watch parties, and detail and debate everything from the real (as it were) life of Columbo's Peugeot to the theories surrounding whether Mrs Columbo 'exists'. As

---

[2] See further clarification from Steven Moffat on the incredibly helpful *Columbophile* website (Columbophile 2019).

[3] Richard Levinson died in March 1987, William Link in December 2020.

[4] News of the two-year lawsuit would sporadically reappear in publications like *The Hollywood Reporter* until a settlement was reached in 2019. Link and Levinson were awarded just over US$70m in back profits and interest from the show's estimated US$600 million profits (Cullins 2019; Patten 2019; and see also Pedersen 2017). Just over a month later the same judge overthrew his own judgment. The case will be tried again (Patten 2019).

recently as 2010, one of Columbo's two creators, William Link, published *The Columbo Collection* of original short stories, a work preceded by Falk's *Columbo* anecdote-packed autobiography (2008) and followed by Richard A. Lertzman's and William J. Birnes's Falk biography of 2017.

The conflation of Falk with Columbo, whilst perhaps a little unfair on Falk considering his varied acting career, is not insignificant when considering the ongoing popularity of *Columbo*. Falk carried with him the legacy of Columbo throughout his life and the association continues long after his death. For example, YouTube immortalises the times when the Lieutenant (Falk in costume and largely in character as Columbo) cameoed on Johnny Carson, and again for the hilarious Dean Martin-hosted roast of Frank Sinatra. As Falk continued to act in movies around his shooting commitments to *Columbo*, he likewise traded on the character as much as his own undeniable talents. Not only did he play Bogart-styled detectives in *Murder by Death* (1976) and *The Cheap Detective* (1978), he also effectively appeared as himself, as the Peter Falk who plays Lieutenant Columbo, in the internationally lauded art film *Der Himmel über Berlin / Wings of Desire* (1987). As recently as 2019 a French documentary by Zed Television exploring Falk's different roles was provocatively entitled, *Peter Falk versus Columbo*. In this way, Falk, the star of *Columbo*'s back catalogue, keeps the show alive both in the minds of fans and in society's cultural memory banks more generally.

Two specific indicators of *Columbo*'s afterlife most clearly emphasise how the show's legacy is not only globally widespread but also culturally integral. The most heart-warming story of *Columbo*'s heritage is surely the bronze statue of Falk as Columbo in Budapest – with raincoat, cigar, thinking-hand-on-head pose, and faithful basset hound Dog. The statue was unveiled in 2014, three years after Falk's death, making the most of the US actor's Hungarian ancestry. Alternatively, the most impressive legacy is the naming of the 'Columbo Phenomenon' after the show – in which, at the close of a session wherein a patient has told their doctor everything *except* that which has been bothering them, they suddenly come to this point just as they are leaving (Frolkis 2013). These indicators of *Columbo*'s continuing widespread appeal demonstrate the show's ability to resonate with contemporary societal realities, both then, and now, both in the USA, and elsewhere. This begs the question, then, of why this enduring cultural appeal?

This book attempts to account for this by exploring *Columbo* as a product of its historical context first and foremost, but one which still has meaning for audiences today. This relevance is, very precisely, due to the continuation of the forces of change which shaped this context into the contemporary era. In line with Janet Wasko's observation that 'many have called television a storyteller, if not THE storyteller for society' (2010: 3), this book considers *Columbo* as though an artefact from the very recent past uncovered in a television archive. As such it can help to illuminate how the 'story' of the twentieth century was understood by 'society'. More precisely, it can indicate how viewers were encouraged, at the drawing to a close of the twentieth century, to understand two specific things: firstly, the role which attention plays in their society, and, secondly, the manner in which they should pay attention. Thus *Columbo*'s enduring fascination, I argue, pertains to the continuing relevance of this engagement with attention to today's world. *Columbo* reveals the manner in which attention has been shaped under what has become known as late capitalism (the post-war era, effectively),[5] and in particular during the era of neoliberalism's global dominance which begins to emerge in the 1970s and continues to this day. It reveals, then, the recent roots of how attention is shaped in the contemporary world.

To add a degree of depth to this argument, which will build throughout the rest of the book, it is useful to briefly step back and illuminate something of what the character Columbo may have represented for viewers, around the world, towards the close of the twentieth century. To do so, it is instructive to do something counter-intuitive, and examine Falk's rather curious appearance as himself in German *auteur* Wim Wenders's famous art film, *Wings of Desire* (1987). Here Falk plays a US actor – in fact, it transpires, a fallen angel – arriving in Germany to act in a movie being made in the still-divided Cold War Berlin. There, Falk is recognised by people on the street, including one he speaks with – Marion (Solveig Donmartin) – who addresses him as 'Lieutenant' because she identifies him from his appearance in *Columbo*.

To further emphasise that Falk is recognised as both himself and the character Columbo, he appears on a television set in a shop window, and his lengthy internal monologue strays to the contribution he made, of his own raincoat, to create Columbo's costume.

---

[5] There are various ways of defining or describing late capitalism. Influential in recent decades have been the writings of Fredric Jameson (1984) and David Harvey (1990) on postmodernity. In this instance I use the term to broadly indicate a post-war shift towards a more globalised model of capitalism which would be boosted by the emergence of neoliberalism in the 1970s and spread rapidly as the Cold War came to an end. As Harvey indicates, summarising Jameson, the cultural logic of late capitalism is such that advertising and the role of media like television in disseminating it are key to the perpetuation of the rapidly churning trends upon which the system has maintained itself since the 1960s/1970s (1990: 63).

Figure I.1 A fallen angel working in the ruins of a divided post-war Berlin, Peter Falk is addressed by Marion (Solveig Donmartin) as 'Lieutenant' in *Wings of Desire* (Wim Wenders, 1987).

Just what on earth is Falk, so specifically rendered as Columbo, doing in *Wings of Desire*? Wenders stated shortly after the film's release that he did not watch television, but even so he considered the best thing on television ever to have been *Columbo* (Wenders 1992: 77).[6] Is the appearance of Falk in *Wings of Desire* just an act of fandom on Wenders's part? No, there is something deeper than this involved which helps us understand what Columbo may have represented for viewers at that time.

Many existing interpretations of *Wings of Desire*, if they attempt to understand Falk/Columbo's presence at all, indicate his role in the film as one foregrounding the movie's blending of reality and fiction (Vila and Kuzniar 1992: 59). Such interpretations may focus on his ability to insert a level of 'popular art' into an otherwise elite format, the art film (e.g. Ehrlich 1991: 244). Alternatively, they may contextualise his presence in terms of Wenders's ambivalent feeling towards US popular culture, which arose due to the mixed success of his immediately preceding period directing in the USA (*Paris Texas* [1984] was a success, *Hammett* [1982] a failure). Other readings emphasise Falk's Jewish heritage, with regards to the resonances it would have had with *Wings of Desire*'s original script's greater focus on Berlin's Nazi past (e.g. Rogowski 2019: 15–16 and 47–48).

---

[6] Albeit, for Wenders, alongside *The Fugitive* (1963–1967).

Yet, there is another way to understand what Falk is doing in *Wings of Desire*. David Harvey famously discussed *Wings of Desire* when developing his seminal analysis of postmodernity in *The Condition of Postmodernity* (1990). For Harvey, Falk's arrival by plane into Berlin, along with the various languages coexisting in Berlin, the fragmented and alienated lives of many of the city's inhabitants, and what he calls the film's ubiquitous 'references to the international space of the media', together indicate the time-space compressions of late capitalism (pp. 314–315). Even at the time of *Wings of Desire*'s release, then, some commentators were attuned to its resonances with globalisation. To rack focus more precisely onto the argument developed in this book, Thomas Elsaesser, writing of Wenders's films more broadly, observes how they often use characters to investigate 'the cultural and national opposition between Germany and the United States'. Specifically, the US character in *Wings of Desire*, Falk/Columbo, represents a German experience of 'America in its dual role as resented but also emulated liberator' (Elsaesser 1989: 230–231) It is here that a productive way of conceiving of the Falk/Columbo character for this work offers itself: Falk/Columbo as representative of capitalism's US-led global expansion.

It is fairly unusual for an art film to introduce such a cameo, one which intentionally blurs the boundary between the real-life actor Falk (performing in a film-within-a-film) and the television character he was globally famous for playing (Graf 2002: 41). Importantly, it is not only that the characters in Berlin recognise Falk as Columbo, but also that *the viewers of the movie are also able to*. Falk's/Columbo's appearance, then, illustrates how strong the character's popularity was, internationally, even without a new episode having been produced for nearly a decade.[7] For this to work, Falk/Columbo had to be globally recognisable it is true. But more than this, for the appearance of Falk/Columbo to have *meaning* in a film such as this it has to also be a representative of something which everyone can 'recognise'. This something is not just 'America', as we might be tempted to conclude if we were to take Wenders and Elsaesser quite literally. Rather, by making just a little more explicit the global dimension of what Elsaesser was implying in 1989, and Harvey indicating in 1990, Columbo can be seen as the spirit of its time, or *zeitgeist*, of this particular moment of late capitalism's global reach.

For Franco 'Bifo' Berardi, the term *zeitgeist* specifically suggests a 'perception of imminence' (2015: 207). This is more than being prescient, then.

---

[7] *Wings of Desire*, emerging just prior to the return of *Columbo* with ABC two years later, is sometimes considered to be a contributing cause of the show's return (Patten 2019).

Rather, the spirit of the time is understood as something intangible, but something which can still be glimpsed in *zeitgeist* figures embodying its forever-coming-into-being-at-that-moment. It is for this reason that *Columbo* is so usefully analysed looking back in time from the present moment. What was coming-into-being globally at that time was specific to the late twentieth-century's shaping of attention. For Jonathan Crary, one of the most influential writers on attention, the Second World War swept away much of the pre-modern world which, until then, had coexisted with the modern. The ruins of Europe in particular offered a 'tabula rasa . . . for the latest phase in the globalization of capitalism' (Crary 2013: 66–67). In *Wings of Desire*, then, Falk/Columbo is pictured visiting the border zone of capitalism's continued post-war global spread. Appearing in the context of the divided Berlin of the ongoing Cold War, Falk/Columbo fulfils the need for a righteous but 'down to earth' (figured literally as an angel who has voluntarily given up his wings) engagement with a world moving out of the shadow of the Second World War under the leadership of the USA. 'Memories' of the war, portrayed using footage of the past, frequently interrupt the film's present-day world, and the presence of the Berlin Wall and the ruined wasteland in its vicinity serve as reminders of its legacy in the ongoing Cold War. But, as scholars noted in the early 1990s, *Wings of Desire* indicates a Berlin, if not a world, looking to move on from the Cold War to the era we now inhabit (Caldwell and Rea 1991: 46). Historically, the divided Berlin of the film would be united again two years later, propelling the expansion of neoliberal globalisation in the post-Cold War world. Falk/Columbo as *zeitgeist* figure thus presaged the global expansion of neoliberalism that would soon follow.

To consider *Wings of Desire*'s depiction of a divided Berlin with respect to the complex geopolitical shifting of global history is, admittedly, a little easier to do with thirty years hindsight. It is understandable that *Wings of Desire* might typically be interpreted with respect to its engagement with German *national* history (Cook 1997: 181–187). But the global dimension is key to understanding what Falk's/Columbo's appearance in *Wings of Desire* implies for how *Columbo* negotiates the post-war shaping of attention. With Berlin reunited, one of the last examples of the post-war ruination observed by Crary could be rebuilt in precisely the way he describes: by the free flowing of global capital across its spaces once the wall fell and the markets beyond it were opened up. In light of this we might interpret the Falk/Columbo character's attempts to reach out to the angels watching over Berlin as symbolic of a 'welcoming' spirit of the time. Typically, Falk tries to shake hands and welcome the angels into the everyday world, describing himself as a friend. This is, as Elsaesser indicates, a welcoming hand for Germany, but also we might add for many other parts of the world – equally ambivalent about, but also intrigued by, the role of the United States in the post-war world – Falk's/Columbo's gesture of welcome is strangely appealing. The handshake suggests something of an equal footing for any possible future relationship. The gesture of friendship, also evocative of a deal being struck, offers a chance to communicate in a personable way with the world's capitalist superpower: the possibility that there can be an 'us' in a relationship with the USA. Figured against the landscape of a divided Berlin representing the border zone of capitalism's post-war global expansion, Falk/Columbo thus stands as the *everyman figure of late capitalism* welcoming those as yet outside its borders to join in.

For this reason the analysis herein seeks to explain both what *Columbo* reveals about how attention is shaped in late twentieth-century society, and indeed how it participates in this shaping of attention. Put more comprehensively, by focusing on attention specifically, it is possible to illuminate how *Columbo* reveals the societal changes brought on by this historical transformation of the global economy, and the forms of attentive behaviour it requires. Simultaneously, *Columbo* also participates in shaping how viewers of the show behave attentively within this changing sociohistorical environment (in the USA and across the globalised world).

Thus, understanding Columbo as an everyman figure of late capitalism provides the grounding to an analysis of *Columbo* as exemplar of how the

Figure I.2 Falk/Columbo extends the hand of welcome to restless angel Damiel (Bruno Ganz), a future friend of US-led late capitalism in *Wings of Desire* (Wim Wenders, 1987).

late twentieth century shaped the manner in which we – to this day – pay attention to our world. The ways in which attention is regulated, after all, can greatly influence how economically productive a society may be (see Chapter 2). Television, as noted, an attention-seeking machine, is integral to this economic process. It looks to regulate how viewers attend to it amidst the everyday distractions of life, not least in its role as deliverer of advertisements. Hence, analysing *Columbo*'s exploration of how attention functions in society across this period illuminates the recent history of how attention has come to be regulated. To analyse Columbo, the everyman of late capitalism, the *zeitgeist* figure, is thus to analyse *Columbo the attentive labourer*.

Understanding how attentive labour is learned in this way is highly pertinent nowadays due to the importance of such attention-regulating devices as the internet and accompanying social media, on one hand, and, on the other, state surveillance's impingement on the public sphere if not our private lives. *Columbo*, predating the internet for most of its lifecycle, was nevertheless very engaged with how the public and private sphere were being reshaped by new technologies. Hence this book sets out to uncover *Columbo*'s charting of the emergence of our contemporary reality in the latter decades of the twentieth century. In particular, its negotiation of the societal functioning of attention under neoliberalism, and how this shapes our roles as attentive labourers.

Whodunnit?

This Introduction is designed like the start of a *Columbo* episode, to give the game away from the get-go. The 'murderer' has already been revealed: attention. The rest of the book, like Columbo's investigation, sets out to reach the same destination. In so doing, by following the clues that enable us to piece together the bigger picture, the requisite explanatory detail can also be filled in. In other words, the chapters which follow are the equivalent of Columbo's recreation of the murder to reveal how it was committed.

Chapter 1 provides an overview of *Columbo*'s genesis, its origins in literature and other popular cultural forms. This is a story often related in a certain way in existing publications on *Columbo*. However, this time the oft-told story is placed alongside another story, rarely related, of the show's emergence at a specific point in the development of the US television industry. These two complementary takes on the show's commencement indicate why a different interpretation of *Columbo* is now required. As this new interpretation is not about *Columbo*'s relative merits or failings, but its significance for our contemporary world, precisely how we understand the show's emergence within the television industry is crucially important.

Chapter 1 also situates the book in terms of the academic intervention it looks to make at the interdisciplinary intersection of Film Studies, Philosophy, and Television Studies. What is stressed is that any too universal an approach to our understanding of how audiovisual media shape attention needs to be tempered by acknowledging media specificity. In particular, the several decades of work on attention in Television Studies must be recognised alongside the perhaps more famous works on the subject from different disciplines (those of Crary and others). Related to this, the method of analysis is also outlined, indicating the four key questions arising from watching *Columbo* that determine the themes for the four chapters of analysis. Finally, *Columbo* is seen to offer something of nuance for existing debates surrounding the functioning of cult television. This is due to its rather unique narrative structure and, especially, the 'inconsistency' of its narrative world. With so much covered, Chapter 1 is the longest, but this groundwork is essential for positioning the argument in terms of existing scholarly debates and in defining its manner of analytic approach.

Chapter 2 begins in earnest the exploration of what *Columbo* does, on-screen, with regards to its engagement with attention. Initially, the chapter explains the importance of the idea of attention for our understanding of *Columbo*. This includes two dedicated sections which are crucial in outlining the book's central thesis. One examines how *Columbo* shapes the way we attend to it through its somewhat unusual narrative structure. This structure is found to function in the manner of a memory game, testing and honing our abilities to pay attention like a more complex version of 'Kim's Game'. The other section introduces the interdisciplinary area within which the study of attention sits, including works describing the attention economy. It unpacks thereby what it means to study *Columbo*'s engagement with the shaping of attention in the late twentieth century.

To help explain the usefulness of these ideas for the chapters which follow, Chapter 2 then provides a brief comparative analyses of two exemplary *Columbo* episodes: 'Identity Crisis' from 1975 and 'Columbo Cries Wolf' from 1990. Viewed comparatively these very different episodes indicate how the regulation of attention shifted during this period. Broadly speaking: the former episode illustrates how attention was shaped during the Cold War due to the machinations of state security and that particular conflict's global geopolitics. The latter indicates the monetisation of attention promoted in and following the Reagan years, as ideas surrounding the so-called attention economy began to emerge. It is not that what Columbo does is any different across the two episodes. He typically pays attention to his work in the same ways, he just gets older. However, the changing socio-historical backdrops which the very different episodes reveal do change. They thus illuminate the shifting historical agendas which influenced the purposes to which the shaping of attention was attuned (or rather, re-attuned) during this specific historical moment of late capitalism.

Both episodes foreground the same four areas through which *Columbo* brings into focus the way attention is shaped: firstly, the acting out or performance of identity in a world constantly surveilled (performing); secondly, humanity's interface with technology (learning); thirdly, the complexities that surround which classes do, or do not, have a say in how history is recorded by new technologies (policing); and, fourthly, exactly where a city like Los Angeles is situated under globalisation (locating). Analysis of the recurrence of these same four key areas in two episodes many years apart starkly reveals the socio-historical shift that has taken place in the interim, and, accordingly, the way in which the shaping of attention has transformed across the decades.

Thus, the concluding section of Chapter 2 offers a sort of 'in miniature' take on the book. The analysis of each of the four characteristics at this point is brief and introductory by design, to provide clear entry points for what follows. Chapters 3–6 then each provide a much fuller analysis of the four characteristics so that together they can illuminate how late capitalism requires the attentive labourer to act, learn, police and locate themselves so as to be a productive part of neoliberal society.

In Chapter 3, Falk's performance as Columbo is the central focus. This chapter uncovers the many different acting styles which intersect in his performance. These include not only a theatrical style akin to method acting, but also: stylistic characteristics of the acting which developed with live television; the influence of the time Falk spent collaborating on US independent films with John Cassavetes and Ben Gazzara (who also work with him on *Columbo*); and a form of slapstick reminiscent of earlier Hollywood comedic greats, such as Buster Keaton. By melding aspects of these diverse styles together, Falk as Columbo is found to embody, rather literally, the process of paying attention 24/7 necessitated by late capitalism. But what is important about this, the chapter argues, is the manner in which this performance can be very effectively deployed to catch criminals. The ability of the police to scrutinise all aspects of a suspect's everyday life, to pay attention to them in both public and private spheres, also opens up the question of whether the law under late capitalism still presumes innocence, or simply assumes guilt. On this view, Columbo seems a rather Orwellian character, a representative of the all-seeing surveillance state.

Chapter 4 explores why Columbo is perpetually involved in a process of learning about new technology in order to solve crimes. Or, put another way, why constant learning is necessary for Columbo to keep up with the demands of his job. His attention to his own self-advancement is seen to be that of the neoliberal subject as entrepreneur of the self (after Maurizio Lazzarato). Columbo's learning about new technologies, moreover, also has a didactic function. Columbo stands in for the viewer, as their every-man surrogate, in the learning process. There is a reassurance offered by *Columbo*, then, regarding the ability of everyone to keep up with the bewil-dering pace of technological change that is shaping our propensity to pay attention. However, along with this intended reassurance, an ambivalence also emerges. With the reach of technology omnipresent, and the world so closely monitored by security cameras that peoples' lives are lived – or rather, performed – as though they are on television (a world in which, *Columbo* emphasises, the innocent are those who simply sit and watch), it is debateable how reassuring it is to think of the police as such complete masters of this technology. Once again, then, an Orwellian Columbo.

Chapter 5 considers the idea that *Columbo* has class conflict at its heart. In spite of initial appearances, Columbo does not police class per se, but rather, history. Or at least, he attempts to reveal the truth behind how the past is retold, when this truth is twisted or altered by the murderer – as one might edit video footage, for example – to create a false alibi. The fact that the murderers are typically from the elite, in fact, is actually only indicative of their greater access to the technological means necessary to falsify history in this way. To combat this, Columbo deploys an older form of representation, theatrical restaging of the past. This he does to correctly realign the way in which the story of the past is told and to thereby catch out the murderer in their attempt to falsify it. This is akin to the notion of 'revenge' from the theatrical tradition of the tragedy, as in Hamlet's famous expression, 'The play's the thing wherein I'll catch the conscience of the king' (Shakespeare [c. 1599–1602] 1980: 121) Suddenly Columbo seems less like the invasive operative of Orwellian state surveillance of Chapters 3 and 4, and more of a representative of surveillance from below: common people using technology to watch the watchmen. Paying atten-tion 24/7, then, is now seen to be necessary to ensure the elite do not 'get away with murder', that is, get away with falsifying the historical record to their advantage at the expense of everyone else. Less Columbo as Orwellian 'Big Brother', more Columbo as defender of social justice.

Chapter 6 ponders where, precisely, *Columbo*'s LA is located in rela-tion to globalisation. Whilst *Columbo* often depicts Los Angeles as a city integral to the US nation (in episodes about election campaigns, or the West Coast's national defence industries), on other occasions LA is figured more as a gateway for interaction with the Pacific Rim. Historically, this latter was the result of the city's transformation during the 1970s into a gateway city designed to make the most of globalisation by interfacing with the rest of the world. Yet this transformation of the City of Angels led to vast wealth inequalities. Columbo is ultimately aligned with those at the lower end of this scale, especially the homeless. Columbo, on this view, again seems a more positive figure than in Chapters 3 and 4. Now he is associated with what Giorgio Agamben calls 'bare life', positioned as a champion of the right to life for all, not just the wealthy few (1998). The importance of the film and television industries in Los Angeles, which feature heavily across the show's history, is thus seen to be due to their role in shaping the manner in which we pay attention to those included and excluded from society's riches.

Finally, the Conclusion reveals how *Columbo* indicates the challenges that surround Columbo's obsessive, 24/7 attention to work. Especially the generalised anxiety which may attend to the role of attentive labourer. It recaps the various manifestations of Columbo which have been uncovered in the preceding chapters, ultimately finding, through comparison with the contemporary television show *The Purge* (2018–) that in spite of his seemingly moral/amoral approach to the law, Columbo is a defender of the democratic right to life for all.

From time to time the analysis also returns us to the present (as though in a retrospective flashforward from the time of *Columbo*'s run to now) to see what insights *Columbo* offers our understanding of contemporary television programmes. Detective series like *CSI: Crime Scene Investigation* (2000–2015), *Monk* (2002–2009), *Luther* (2010–2019), *Sherlock* (2010–2017), *Elementary* (2012–2019), *The Fall* (2013–2016), *Death in Paradise* (2011–) and *Bosch* (2014–), are variously seen to continue aspects of the negotiation of attention and attentive labour previously seen in *Columbo*. More broadly, *Columbo* is compared with recent cult favourites like *Mad Men* (2007–2015), *Game of Thrones* (2011–2019), *The Americans* (2013–2018), *Black Mirror* (2011–), *The Man in the High Castle* (2015–2019), *Mindhunter* (2017–), *American Gods* (2017–) and *The Purge* (2018–). These very different shows are yet like *Columbo* in that they negotiate different dimensions of the impact of attention on society: how we act, learn, police and locate ourselves in contemporary society.

At times, Columbo seems like the bad guy, an operative of the state security apparatus (Chapters 3 and 4). At other times, he seems like the good guy, the policeman of history and the guardian of a right to a meaningful citizen's life for all (Chapters 5 and 6). Television, of course, is known for holding such contradictory positions in play as part of the pleasure it offers (Mellencamp 1992: 149). Rather than evaluating 'good' or 'bad', then, grasping how attention is shaped is key to understanding the ramifications of *Columbo* for just how we pay attention nowadays. This seems exceptionally important for a contemporary 'post-truth' era concerned by Orwellian rewritings of the past, and the use of new technologies (the internet, social media) to propagate 'fake news', in ways which threaten to undermine democracy. Viewing *Columbo* as historical artefact, then, illuminates much about how we got to this current state of affairs. Like a good crime drama, though, there are lot of twists and turns to enjoy before we reach the end.

CHAPTER 1

Blueprint for Murder

This chapter establishes the context for the analysis in the chapters which follow. It begins by exploring *Columbo*'s genesis, twice. Firstly, by briefly rehearsing the well-known story of the show's development as a concept, its initial iterations on small screen and stage, and its production by Universal for NBC. Then, secondly, an alternative version of this story is offered, or rather, more context is provided that paints the usual story in a slightly different light. This is done by situating the show's commissioning in the broader context of some of the US television industry's chief concerns of the late 1960s and 1970s: around feature-length made-for-television films; the level of investment felt to be appropriate for them; the eschewal of violent content; and target audience demographics (including ratings, market shares, and advertisements). This new perspective on the oft-told story is informed by historical sources and makes it possible to both acknowledge the importance of *Columbo*'s origins in the work of Richard Levinson and William Link, and yet to also realise it as a product of the industrial conditions within which its commissioning was possible. The issues covered indicate the shifting societal terrain which the industry was integrally connected to (and reacting to) in its decision-making, and how *Columbo* meshes neatly with the agendas of the era. Together, then, these two different 'takes' on *Columbo*'s emergence offer a new ground upon which to build a different kind of analysis focusing on attention.

Following on from this, the book's argument is situated in relation to existing scholarly fields in which the issue of attention has been of growing interest over the past several decades. What is key, it is argued, is that whilst interdisciplinary areas like film-philosophy are now increasingly growing interested in attention, due regard should be paid to the much longer heritage of examining the topic of attention in Television Studies. This existing body of work can greatly inform the analysis of how *Columbo* reveals the late twentieth-century's shaping of attention, a process in which it was, as a television show, integral.

Finally, the chapter concludes with a transition towards the chief concerns of the next, regarding how *Columbo* works to attract and shape the viewer's attention. This is done by exploring how *Columbo*'s 'inconsistent' narrative world throws up challenges to some of the seminal theories which define cult television, due to its very specific way of appealing to its loyal fans. These challenges to our understanding of how cult television programmes usually 'work' reveal much about the memory game that *Columbo* encourages us to play: a game designed to hone our attention, which is detailed in depth in Chapter 2.

Columbo's Genesis I: The Oft-told Story

The story of *Columbo*'s genesis typically charts the progress from its origins in literary inspirations to theatrical and televisual originals, and two pilots, before the series proper began (Levinson and Link 1981a, 1981b; Dawidziak 1988, [1988] 2019; Catz 2016). Although the march of time has rendered many original sources out of print (including interviews with Levinson and Link), numerous fan-maintained online sites keep this history alive. This story usually focuses on the show's writers and its commissioning, often drawing on the aforementioned interviews with Levinson and Link published in the early 1980s (including Levinson and Link 1981a; Dawidziak 1988, [1988] 2019). As this story is not difficult to access, a brief summary is all that is needed. Then an alternative perspective can be offered which considers the emergence of *Columbo* within the shifting landscape of the US television industry of the time. This latter approach can flesh out the usual tale in a manner which, without detracting from the undoubted artistic genius involved in the show's creation, nevertheless provides a more multidimensional sense of *Columbo*.

Columbo was officially created in 1971, when Universal convinced NBC that they should produce a rotating, three-show formula, the *NBC Mystery Movie*. This 'wheel' concept, which had previously been attempted in the 1960s (Perry 1983: xiii; Snauffer 2006: 65–67), alternated a different detective show weekly. Initially this wheel was formed of an existing show *McCloud* (1970–1977), *McMillan & Wife*, starring Rock Hudson (1971–1977), and *Columbo* (Levinson and Link 1981b: 27). Columbo the character, however, existed long before this.

Columbo's creators, Levinson and Link, were long-time friends and collaborators from Philadelphia. They wrote together from junior high school through to college at the University of Pennsylvania (Levinson and Link 1981a: 9–11; Dawidziak [1988] 2019: 15). As they grew up they graduated from homemade radio plays, musical comedies and private eye novels to short stories in *Playboy* and television scripts (Levinson and Link 1981a: 10–13). They wrote for *The Fugitive* (1963–1967), *Dr Kildare* (1961–1966), *The Man from U.N.C.L.E* (1964–1968), *Alfred Hitchcock Presents* (1955–1962) and *The Alfred Hitchcock Hour* (1962–1965). They also created the show *Mannix* (1967–1975) which played for eight seasons on CBS. During this same period, dividing their time between California and New York to take advantage of opportunities to write for both television and theatre, they penned the successful play *Prescription: Murder*. It featured the detective Columbo, originally played by Thomas Mitchell, and toured the USA and Canada for twenty-five weeks (Levinson and Link 1981a: 15–16; Dawidziak [1988] 2019: 21). In fact, the character Columbo had been created earlier, in a former version of the same story, in a script entitled 'Enough Rope' which aired as part of the *Chevy Mystery Show* (1960). The very first Columbo, then, was played by Bert Freed on television (Levinson and Link 1981a: 86; Dawidziak [1988] 2019: 20).

Prescription: Murder was the script which Levinson and Link pitched to Universal, who were looking for longer-form television shows, and which became the first *Columbo* pilot. It initially attracted the attention of Don Siegel, as possible producer, before being passed to Richard Irving. Irving suggested the location be Los Angeles, and that Peter Falk play Columbo. Ultimately the pilot, which aired in February 1968 starred Falk, albeit because neither of Levinson and Link's preferred actors – Lee J. Cobb or Bing Crosby – were available. It received successful reviews and ratings and not long afterwards the writing duo signed for Universal (Levinson and Link 1981a: 17–19). After a second pilot, 'Ransom for a Dead Man' in March 1971 (a Levinson and Link story, scripted by Dean Hargrove, directed by Irving just like the first pilot), a series based on the two pilots was part of Universal's pitch to NBC which garnered Universal the *Mystery Movie* wheel (Levinson and Link 1981a: 86–87).

The first series of *Columbo* was produced in an incredibly short time. This was due to Falk's diary commitment to act in Neil Simon's play *The Prisoner of Second Avenue* commencing rehearsals that September (five months from *Columbo* receiving the green light) (Levinson and Link 1981b: 27). Numerous difficulties were faced. Although Steven Bochco was quickly secured as story editor – because producer Irving felt that such a dialogue-oriented show required his talents (Dawidziak [1988] 2019: 43) – very few writers wanted to participate. From a screening for sixty freelance writers, only two showed any interest. In addition, NBC were unimpressed with *Columbo*'s unorthodox elements: the late appearance of the star in each episode, the emphasis on dialogue over action, the lack of possible romance due to the spoken presence of Mrs Columbo, or at least the lack of a young, handsome sidekick. There were also running struggles for control between perfectionist Falk and Levinson and Link (Levinson and Link 1981b: 66; Dawidziak [1988] 2019: 44). Miraculously, as the legend goes, the first series of seven episodes was created in the time they had.

The NBC *Mystery Movie* format, with its Henri Mancini-composed theme, its wonderful stars of stage and screen, and its array of beautiful extras, was a success. In 1972 it moved from Wednesday nights to Sundays at primetime, as the NBC *Sunday Mystery Movie* (8.30–10 pm). Over the years, shows from the wheel which attracted significant audience figures, including *Columbo*, were extended from a ninety minute to a two-hour run (allowing for more commercials [Perry 1983: xiv; Snauffer 2006: 72]). Some were later taken from the wheel to stand alone (for example *Quincy, M.E.* [1976–1983]). In 1977 the *NBC Mystery Movie* wheel came to an end. The 1976–1977 season saw the number of *Columbo* episodes reduced due to Falk's other acting commitments (Dawidziak [1988] 2019: 263). Five *Columbo* specials were produced in 1978 but a decade's hiatus then followed before its return in 1989 with ABC, with Falk as a producer. This rebooted period saw three (shorter) series, and then single episodes running until 2003. Across the decades, which included changes to a huge number of personnel (Levinson and Link departed after series one, as did Bochco), Falk provided the show's continuity on- and off-screen.

So ends what might be considered the usual version of the oft-told story, or at least the version which focuses very specifically on the show's televisual origins. A more literature-oriented version can also be found, which tends to dig further into the background of the show's creators, as follows.

The deeper origins of *Columbo*, indicative of Levinson's and Link's love of literature, explain the show's 'inverted' formula, in which the viewer witnesses the murder then enjoys seeing the detective figure it out retrospectively. This formula can be traced to the English author R. Austin Freeman, especially the 1912 short story collection, *The Singing Bone* (Levinson and Link 1981b: 27; Freeman [1912] 2011). Here the idea that the behaviour of the murderer gives them away early on to the observant detective is evident, even if the attention which Columbo gives to interrogating his suspects is not.

Accordingly, the distinction is commonly made between a 'whodunnit' (e.g. Arthur Conan Doyle's Sherlock Holmes mysteries) and a 'howdunnit' (Freeman's Dr Thorndyke adventures), to indicate that *Columbo* is the latter. Columbo himself describes one case as a 'howhedidit' ('Columbo Goes to College' [1990]). Freeman, though, preferred to think of his stories as unfolding how the detective came to realise what has happened. Not quite a 'howdunnit', then, but: 'how was the discovery achieved?' ([1912] 2011: iii) The most accurate description of Columbo's formula, accordingly, is somewhere between 'howshegonnafigureitout', if we follow Freeman, and, as Mark Dawidziak notes, 'howzhegonnacatchhim' ([1988] 2019: 28).

Yet, it is questionable whether Freeman provides the most accurate literary precedent for *Columbo*, either in terms of narrative structure or character. After all, television crime drama emerges from what Sue Turnbull describes as the 'primordial soup' of its various origins in literature, theatre, radio and cinema (2014: 42). Likewise, *Columbo*'s originary influences are legion. Levinson and Link themselves note that they wanted to pay their 'respects' to writers they had read when young, including Ellery Queen, John Dickson Carr and Agatha Christie (Levinson and Link 1981b: 27). Unsurprisingly, then, *Columbo* follows a classical detective format in other respects, being an, as it were, 'transplanted' country house mystery (Levinson and Link 1981b: 27; Turnbull 2014: 25). This is a practice which continues today with the mansions of Bel Air and Beverly Hills that featured in *Columbo* being replaced with, for example, the idyllic (fictional) Caribbean island of Saint Marie in *Death in Paradise* (2011–). It is a generic trait of the country house mystery, after all, for a detective (perhaps complete with cigar like Carr's Dr Gideon Fell) to arrive and solve a puzzling murder committed amongst the rich and powerful. Moreover, Levinson and Link indicate that Columbo's character was also inspired by G. K. Chesterton's Father Brown, and Porfiry Petrovich from Fyodor Dostoevsky's *Crime and Punishment* (1866) (Levinson and Link 1981b: 66), precursors which will become key in later chapters. For now, though, so ends the more literature-focused version of the oft-told story.

The question arises of why this story is so often told in this way? Jane M. Shattuc helpfully observes the drawbacks in thinking which typically lead to its repetition in this format:

> Seemingly, we need an inspired source to make sense of American television. Commercial producers consider themselves 'creators' as they continually speak of holding onto their 'original idea.' But one might wonder: why should this be the case? American television is mass-produced; a series of stages serve as the assembly line where workers put together a similar product weekly with the production of over 200 like-products in the case of a successful series. This process is organised along rationalised lines, with as many as 300 people having some influence over the production of one program. So why do we need to have the agency of an individual, a source, or a creator to understand television? (2010: 142)

Taking up Shattuc's closing question in the rhetorical manner in which it is posed, the usual narrative describing *Columbo*'s creation seems very much a product of this kind of thinking. Such thinking is very specifically of its time, which was also *Columbo*'s time. As Shattuc notes, it was in the late 1970s that the idea of the producer as a creator emerged. Hence the examples she gives include famous writer-producers like Steven Bochco and Michael Mann (Shattuc 2010: 144). The emergence of this idea within the industry coincided with a certain type of narrative in 'magazines, newspapers, and academic books in the United States', of '"man-and-his-work" criticism' (2010: 144). Critics isolated 'TV "heroes" fighting for the originality of their vision over the network's constant drive for profit. Meaning was no longer the result of only a program (a product), a network, or a star, there was now a maker' (2010: 144). Coinciding as it does with the explanations given by writer-producers Levinson and Link in the early 1980s as to the show's genesis, this discourse may explain why *Columbo*'s particular oft-told narrative of origin has always held such sway.

For example, part of the *Columbo* chapter of Levinson's and Link's book, *Stay Tuned*, was published as an article in *American Film*. Both appeared in 1981 (Levinson and Link 1981a, 1981b). The full title given to the article was: 'How We Created Columbo – And How He Nearly Killed Us' (1981b: 27). This is followed by a prominent heading, before the text commences, which states: 'It was a detective series with a twist – no mayhem, no chases. What went on behind the scenes was another story – one that exposes the inner workings of network television' (1981b: 27). As expected, then, what follows in the article is an exposé of a seemingly valiant struggle between art and commerce. This is undoubtedly a true story, but the way it is framed is as per Shattuc's incisive critique. The story which is told is one of how an artistic vision struggled, and ultimately won out, against seeming 'compromise' (the realities of working in the industry, in essence), on the way to its emergence in commercial form (as a television show). These challenges are precisely those usually stated in the oft-told story, namely: most of the possible writers were not interested in participating due to the unusual narrative structure; the network executives did not appreciate the artistic vision and felt the star should appear earlier, not have a wife (so he could be romantically involved), but should have a regular work 'family' or at least an attractive sidekick, and that there would be more action and less talking; Levinson and Link had to threaten to quit to maintain their vision against such proposed changes; the overly controlling star Falk threatened to wreak havoc with the already too-tight schedule; and that they had to hide their scripts and dailies from Falk to protect the integrity of their stories.

Shattuc's work also reminds us that the persistence of this particular narrative of an against-the-odds origin was a feature of the emergence, around this same historical moment, of the discipline of Film and Television Studies in the university sector (at least in the USA and the UK). Scholars of these popular cultural forms often emphasised exceptional individuals (e.g. the film director as *auteur*) as they sought to legitimise their emerging subjects within elite establishments uncertain of the merits of popular forms. Hence the recourse to the Romantic ideal of the solo artist or maverick author at odds with the system (which seems to so compellingly 'explain' how *Columbo* emerged), which can be crafted by focusing first and foremost on its creators (Shattuc 2010: 144–145).

With this in mind, what the usual narrative of *Columbo*'s genesis evidently needs is a degree of rebalancing. The next section of this chapter will shed new light on this story, rendering it richer in implication for its socio-historical context. Without detracting from the undoubted genius and hard work of Levinson and Link, if we shift focus away from the authors, with the *broader* industrial landscape in mind (Feuer 1984: 6–7), what other factors may have played a role in the commissioning and development of *Columbo* at that specific moment?

Columbo's Genesis II: The Role of the Broader Industrial Context

Commercial television by the era of *Columbo* had become a medium for the delivery of ads (Feuer 1984: 2). As Levinson and Link pithily put it, 'the purpose of American television is to deliver an audience to an advertiser at the lowest cost per thousand. That's the American system of network television' (1983a: 26). *Columbo* emerged during a shift from broadcasting (aiming for the largest possible audience) to narrowcasting (targeting shows at specific niche demographics to provide focused delivery of adverts). This meant that television's potential to construct cultural consensus, as per the network era when most people were tuning into the same shows, instead became refined to a 'particular network and its typical audience member rather than . . . society in general' (Lotz 2007b: 40).

Exploring the emergence of *Columbo*, then, is to flash back to the peak of the network era (which spanned approximately 1950–1980) when television was still predominantly a fixed domestic medium around which the family might congregate (Lotz 2007b: 9–12; see also Spigel 2004). This was still the time of television as 'cultural hearth', as opposed to what is now the case, an 'electronic newsstand' (with television following a publishing model to target specifically identified demographics) (Lotz 2007b: 5). By the late 1960s when *Columbo* emerged an average US household was already consuming around 5–6 hours of television a day

(MacDonald 1990: 145). As Muriel G. Cantor and Joel M. Cantor summarise of this historical moment, the role of the networks in providing this content was substantial:

> Network television was at its pinnacle in the late 1960s and early 1970s. More than 80% of the audience was turning on at least one of the three networks each night. Together the three of them shared a virtual monopoly of the prime-time schedule in 1971. (1992: 16)

Columbo's original primetime slot with NBC, then, was on one of the three major networks which together in the mid- and late 1970s enjoyed a more than 90 per cent share of the primetime evening market (Gitlin 1983: vii; MacDonald 1990: 195). In its prime (and primetime) position of influence on NBC, *Columbo* resonated with and helped shape cultural consensus for a broad national audience. In such a context we can begin to understand *Columbo*'s origins a little differently. Firstly by considering the role of the feature length primetime show.

Small-screen features

The 1970s proved something of a turning point for the industry with regard to its provision of films for television. As cinema-going audiences began to dwindle, domestic television consumption rose (along with the growth of suburbia), making space for more movies on the small screen (Williams 1990: 61). There was also a shift in emphasis from rural shows of the 1960s – like *The Beverly Hillbillies* (1962–1971) and various westerns – to the city-based detective shows of the 1970s. This shift took place as television courted a more lucrative target audience for advertisers, one affluent, urban and young (Moore et al. 2006: 121). The fact that *Columbo* is movie length is part and parcel of this shift. In 1961, NBC's *Saturday Night at the Movies* (1961–1978), showing Hollywood films of recent vintage (including in colour as colour television sets rose in number), proved so popular that it ran until the late 1970s (Moore et al. 2006: 165–166). This was indicative of the collaboration between the movie studios and the television networks during the 1950s, especially the production of the 'telefilm' in Hollywood (Anderson 1994; Curtin 2004). By 1960, 40 per cent of 'network TV programs were being produced by the major movie studios' (Moore et al. 2006: 166). However, as the number of former Hollywood movies to screen on television began to be exhausted, and in the interest of producing substitutable content more cheaply, in 1964 the networks began to commission their own made-for-television movies

(Moore et al. 2006: 166). By 1973 they screened nearly twenty hours of movies per week (Moore et al. 2006: 212).

In this context, the emergence of the NBC *Mystery Movie* wheel provided a way to appeal to a younger, more affluent and more urban market for advertisers. Hence it initially incorporated *Columbo* in LA alongside its two other middle-aged, handsome detectives in New York and San Francisco. *Columbo*, for all its complex literary and theatrical origins and its untypical narrative structure, also clearly aligns with the epoch's advertising agenda. The idea that it was created *in spite of* the limitations of the industry, then, begins to seem overstated. The opposite, in fact, seems the case.

Investment

Understanding something of this broader industrial context is also illuminating with regard to the investment which went into *Columbo*. This is an aspect of the show which cannot really be assigned to its writers, nor exactly to a battle won by creatives against an apparently cost-cutting studio. Often television is thought to reflect low budgets and rapid production times (Moore et al. 2006: 213). Critical appraisal of its aesthetic merits may, as a result, be negative. For example, for John Thornton Caldwell, *Columbo* is a typical product of the Universal Studios lot, a 'systematized film-based telefilm production with uniform settings, lighting, looks and cutting' (1995: 57). Caldwell continues, of shows ranging from *Columbo* to *Knight Rider* (1982–1986):

> These MCA-style shows were shot in 35mm feature-film style. Due however to television's inevitable pressures – the less than feature-scale budgets, rigid series scheduling deadlines, and union rules – such programs were notable for sharing and perpetuating a proficient, but very neutral, B-film style from the lot. (1995: 57)

Caldwell may have a point to an extent. The above description does accurately describe something of *Columbo*'s numerous recycled interior locations, sparse or non-existent action sequences and emphasis on character interplay as the central audiovisual attraction. All such features are reminiscent of the B-movie. Even so, there is quite a difference between a B-movie and a television show like *Columbo*, and Caldwell's critique, in fact, should be taken with a pinch of salt.

Columbo was a multi-award-winning primetime show which attracted large audiences. It was initially shot in Technicolor, and although the first series was made rapidly this was as much due to Falk's other acting commitments as the inevitable pressures of the industry. Budget-wise, it is true that this was far from infinite. For example, when Falk directed 'Blueprint for Murder' (1972) to close out the first series he personally paid for more extras so that the active building site that features in the narrative would look more realistic (Dawidziak [1988] 2019: 85). Even so, the original director of the two pilots and later executive producer, Irving, pinpoints *Columbo* as the programme which prompted the setting in of the rot as 'the studios lost control of their shows', resulting in excessive production spend (Mann 1984: 8). For Irving, this was due precisely to Falk's famous perfectionism, with extra rehearsals and takes mitigating against rapid production. Rather than the usual five to seven pages of filming a day, Falk might manage two, thereby ensuring more days of filming, and extra costs (1984: 10; see also Dawidziak [1988] 2019: 276). This was in addition to the high salary Falk demanded, which gradually rose until, in 1976, Falk was the highest paid actor in television, on US$300,000 per episode (Armstrong 1976: 21; Dawidziak [1988] 2019: 194). Viewed in this light, then, the B-movie comparison seems reductive, as the many extra costs involved in shooting *Columbo* increased its quality. This clearly paid off, as is evidenced by both the popularity of *Columbo* and the numerous awards it received. There may have been battles with the studio, but ultimately *Columbo* was a particularly well-resourced programme. The B-movie comparison, then, seems a little off-pitch.

We can add that *Columbo* drew on significant established production talent behind the camera. In this it is again distinguishable from what might be expected of a B-movie. Of course, there were many industry personnel who worked on *Columbo* before moving on to greater things, as personnel did with B-movies. After all, in the 1970s, Universal Television produced more crime drama than the other studios and made opportunities available for perhaps 'rawer' talent, comparative to the lesser risk-taking of its competitors (Buckland 2006: 54; Snauffer 2006: 65). Alongside Levinson and Link, who later wrote and produced numerous shows such as *Murder She Wrote* (1984–1996) (with Peter S. Fischer, also a writer on *Columbo*), we might mention the writer Stephen J. Cannell (who later wrote *The Rockford Files* [1974–1980] and *The A-Team* [1983–1987]), alongside producers like Dean Hargrove (*Matlock* [1986–1995], *Diagnosis Murder* [1993–2001]), amongst others.[1] Most famously of all, *Columbo*'s first episode, 'Murder by the Book' (1971), was directed by Steven Spielberg, working from a

---

[1] On-screen, numerous actors similarly played small parts in *Columbo* before becoming more famous later in their careers (Kristen Bauer, Kim Cattrall, Blythe Danner, Jamie Lee Curtis, Pat Morita, Katey Sagal), or even appeared as extras (Jeff Goldblum).

script by Steven Bochco (Bochco 2017: 28–29),[2] both of whom were up-and-comers who would, each in their own way, later become giants of the film and television industries respectively.

Yet a number of established figures also wrote, directed and starred. For example, writer Jackson Gillis worked on several of the *Columbo* episodes of the 1970s – he also returned in the 1990s – having previously written for *Perry Mason* (1957–1966) amongst other shows. Across its lifetime, directors included Edward M. Abroms, Robert Butler, Jonathan Demme, Vincent McEveety, Leo Penn, Boris Sagal, Nicholas Colasanto and Sam Wanamaker. Numerous respected actors from stage, silver and small screen also featured – from Vera Miles to William Shatner – far too many, in fact, to list here.[3] There were even cameos, like that of the multi-Oscar-winning Hollywood costume designer Edith Head ('Requiem for a Falling Star' [1976]). Altogether this stellar line-up in front of and behind the camera confirms the position taken by Gary Edgerton, that the television movie should not be understood as a B-movie was in the film industry (as providing a training ground for crew members ultimately moving on to

---

[2] Spielberg signed a contract at Universal Studios aged twenty-two. He directed several television episodes, including the first of *Columbo*, before his television movie *Duel* (1971) began his propulsion to stardom. Bochco joined Universal Television straight out of college in 1966, spending twelve years there, getting promoted from writer to story editor, producer and creative producer (Bochco 2017: 20–27). On *Columbo*, Bochco notes that he wrote seven episodes, whilst Levinson and Link note that he wrote the first draft of the scripts for series one, which they had plotted (Levinson and Link 1981b: 28; Bochco 2017: 28; Dawidziak [1988] 2019: 44). Bochco left Universal Television in 1978, to join MTM Enterprises. Bochco is typically credited with his role in the invention of the format now known as 'Quality TV', commencing with his role as co-creator (and writer-producer) on *Hill Street Blues* (1981–1987) for NBC. *Columbo* has fun referencing these famous alumni. In 'Mind over Mayhem' (1974), we meet a child genius named Steve Spelberg (Lee Montgomery), whilst the Universal Studio Tour (including the shark from *Jaws* [1975]) features in 'Fade in to Murder' (1976) and 'Murder, Smoke and Shadows' (1989). The latter is an episode about a murderous young director with a penchant for special effects, another nod to Spielberg. In 'Ashes to Ashes' (1998), Columbo questions a suspect over who his cryptic use of the initials S. B. might refer to. The suspect responds, 'Sonny Bono, Sandra Bullock, Steven Bochco'. Columbo, smiling, replies: 'Bono, Bullock, Bochco, wow, there you really get the big ones. The crème de la crème, sir!'

[3] For example: Anne Baxter, Tyne Daly, Faye Dunaway, Ruth Gordon, Lee Grant, Deidre Hall, Mariette Hartley, Kim Hunter, Janet Leigh, Myrna Loy, Ida Lupino, Julie Newmar, Jeanette Nolan, Martha Scott, Don Ameche, Jack Cassidy, Jackie Cooper, Robert Culp, Emilio Fernández, George Hamilton, Wilfred Hyde-White, Sam Jaffe, Patrick McGoohan, Ian McShane, Leonard Nimoy, John Payne, Vincent Price, Martin Sheen, G. D. Spradlin, Rod Steiger, Dean Stockwell, George Wendt.

better things). Rather, it should be recognised that there was *already* quality talent involved (1991: 116–118). As such, Caldwell's choice of the term B-movie as a pejorative benchmark against which to measure *Columbo* ultimately seems erroneous.

The broader industrial context, then, adds depth to our grasp of why *Columbo* should not be understood as *solely* a work of creative genius, but, also, why it should not simply be dismissed as a substandard work churned out by the studio's production line either (even if it was, naturally, industrially produced television). The investment the show received, the extra money and time along with the presence of key creative personnel which together made *Columbo* so successful, reaffirms that it was not a popular show in spite of the industry, but because of it.

Violence

The broader industrial context also explains why *Columbo*'s non-violent approach to crime-busting – a conscious decision by Levinson and Link (1983b: 150) and often mentioned as an unusual feature for a detective show – is not actually so strange. Rather, once again, it is in line with industry norms of the era.

It is true that there was an increase in crime and law enforcement programming in the 1970s, with '40 percent of prime time schedules given to crime shows in 1975' (Carlson 1985: 29). Yet *Columbo* takes a rather sanitised, often oblique approach to the depiction of its opening murder. For example, when a chess grand master is pushed into a trash compactor in 'The Most Dangerous Match' (1973) this brutal attempt at murder is signified without any visual trauma. The victim is pushed through double doors into the hotel basement where the compactor is located. The edit provides the point-of-view shot of the victim as a coat is pushed into his face. Then there is a close-up of a sign on the door they have passed through, reading 'DANGER NO ADMITTANCE', and an amplification of grinding machine sounds along with dramatic music on the soundtrack before a sudden cut to black. Nothing is seen of the actual grisly event. Not even the man's fall into the compactor. This avoidance of any too-frontal a depiction of violence, coupled with the fact that Columbo never (or, hardly ever) carries a gun, again suited the overall shifting industrial landscape. Coinciding with *Columbo*, after 1968 the major networks turned away from violent content (Cantor 1971: 161). In this era the major networks practised 'least offensive programming', in the hopes of maintaining the largest possible audiences (Curtin and Shattuc 2009: 37). The sign on the door, stating 'DANGER NO ADMITTANCE' summarises perfectly this deliberate eschewal of on-screen violence. This broader industrial context thus illuminates more about why Columbo, in spite of his occasional aggressive behaviour towards suspects or their accomplices, and his questionable array of other crime-fighting devices – from entrapment to planting evidence (see Chapter 5) – is hardly ever violent.

Even in crime shows of the era where there was violence, it was often contained within stagey norms of a familiarly generic kind. For instance, in *The Rockford Files*, recurring fist fights appear as though straight out of the western bar room brawl, evoking James Garner's former role in *Maverick* (1957–1962). Again, in the *Mystery Movie* wheel's western *Hec Ramsey* (1972–1974) the occasional horseback shoot-outs and careering out-of-control wagon stunts spectacularly evoke the western's heritage in the wild west show and rodeo traditions. This is in stark contrast to, say, the lingering on death of a bloody western movie like Sam Peckinpah's *The Wild Bunch* (1969) made only a few years previously. Again, in *McCloud* (1970–1977), *Kojak* (1973–1978) or *The Streets of San Francisco* (1972–1977) even whilst criminals may fire guns wildly, the police reply, when it finally arrives, is minimal, measured and precise: one carefully aimed bullet often only wounding the criminal judiciously without taking their life.

Columbo's eschewal of violence, then, whilst indicative of great writerly skill on the part of Levinson and Link, nevertheless also corresponds exactly with the working practices and content agendas of the (transforming) industry of the time. Although it was undoubtedly a genuine artistic move to focus Columbo's investigative skills in the cognitive rather than the physical realm, nevertheless it cannot have hurt in securing the show's commissioning for primetime during the era of 'least offensive programming' (Curtin and Shattuc 2009: 37).

Target audience (ratings, market shares and advertisements)

Columbo's eschewal of violence also speaks to the show's targeting of a primetime audience more generally. Behind this decision lie various agendas concerning the demographics which such a show would have been thought likely to appeal to. At this point in time it seems impossible to calculate *Columbo*'s lifetime audience, due both to the show's wide international reach, especially at the time of its release, and its longevity over the decades. Just to give some sense of the problem, how can we gauge lifetime audience size or demographic/s when reruns of what was primetime viewing have, over the years, become considered safe for daytime television consumption? There are now also many generations of fans involved and from all around the world. Even today, *Columbo* DVDs often include the option of viewing with dubbing or subtitles in numerous languages. The research involved in charting such a complex terrain seems hardly feasible. Nevertheless, it is possible to consider a little of *Columbo*'s original domestic target audience by noting its primetime place in the scheduling, and, indeed, certain aspects of its content.

Columbo initially screened in a primetime slot, 8.30–10 pm as part of the *Mystery Movie* wheel. As such it can be considered to target as wide a range of adult viewing demographics as possible (Blum and Lindheim 1987: 2; Cantor and Cantor 1992: 1). Take, for example, Columbo's class, which is emphasised from the second pilot onwards once the dishevelled, chilli-and-crackers-eating, extended family-referencing Columbo first emerges. Columbo's 'everyman' character seems carefully crafted to enable recognition of (and perhaps even identification with) Columbo on the part of both working-class and lower middle-class viewers. Such a strategy of straddling class boundaries ensures an extremely large potential viewing demographic as together these two categories account for over half of the US population (Thompson and Hickey 2011: 209; Gilbert 2017: 13–15 and 246–251).[4] Admittedly, Columbo is often thought of as working class, or blue collar, and indeed this designation seems accurate in terms of many of the usual defining characteristics. For instance, Columbo never speaks of or otherwise indicates a college education, he has no pretensions in terms of taste, and his wardrobe, car and conversation indicate that he has to be very careful with money. However, other features often used to define working class are not so closely aligned. Noticeably, Columbo's seemingly blue-collar familial origins aside, having attained the rank of Lieutenant in the LAPD, Columbo does belong to a certain stratum of middle management. He leads a team, and although he often evokes the officious demands of his superiors as the reason for his nagging insistence on bothering suspects he clearly enjoys a large degree of unsupervised autonomy in his work. Moreover, the work itself is far from repetitive or unskilled (see Chapter 4). Finally, whilst Columbo's wardrobe may be dishevelled, this is not the case of his sergeants (who are typically neatly besuited, indicating a decent salary and professional expectation in terms of dress code), with whom Columbo shares a literal white collar (as distinct from their literally blue-collared uniformed colleagues). In all these aspects Columbo seems to align more with definitions of the lower middle classes.

---

[4] Albeit Dennis Gilbert only differentiates between working, middle and upper middle classes, nevertheless the distinctions between working and middle he offers are close to those which William E. Thompson and Joseph V. Hickey delineate for working and lower middle class. It primarily seems a slight difference of terminology.

Columbo's class ambiguity is not solely the result of class categories being themselves inconsistent (or at least, distinct to the measures used by different scholarly definitions). Rather, in terms of class, Columbo's ambiguous status evidences the character's potential to appeal to the broadest possible audience. After all, the boundary between these two particular classes grows increasingly blurry due to the 'declining income differential between them' (Gilbert 2017: 249). Hence, for the purposes of this book I refer to Columbo as lower middle class out of respect for the Lieutenant's professional status (perhaps in a rather British way, admittedly), whilst acknowledging that it could equally be stated as working class without the argument being necessarily different (see further on class in Chapter 5).

For the network, however, of equal if not greater importance were specific age groups, and viewers from both rural and urban areas. NBC immediately celebrated the *Mystery Movie* in terms of its ability to attract consumers with disposable income: people aged 18–49 in general, including, and in particular, those 25–49 (and most especially in this last niche, men). In a report released on 5 October 1971, on the two weeks ending 26 September, NBC stated:

> NBC's MYSTERY MOVIE is the top rated new programme of the 1971–72 season in terms of adult and younger adult audience delivery. NBC's MYSTERY MOVIE was viewed by more than 22 million adults 18+ and 13.7 million adults 18–49 per average minute . . . Further highlighting MYSTERY MOVIE'S impressive performance is its fourth place ranking among men 25–49. Only two front loaded Sunday Movie packages and Football outrated it. Finally, MYSTERY MOVIE delivered 10,770,000 adults 25–49 ranking seventh among all shows in this category. (NBC 1971a)

This self-assessment is entirely consistent with NBC's positioning of itself as the network most likely to reach precisely these sought-after adult consumer demographics (Alvey 2004: 48–49). However, some nuance is beneficial here, as the picture is known to be more complex than this.

Whilst 'young married and upwardly mobile professionals' were a key demographic target for the networks in this period, and whilst for a time primetime hoped to lure them by programming more works on 'controversial and serious themes' (including such shows as *M*A*S*H* [1972–1983]), *Columbo* does not engage with issues of social relevance in the manner of *M*A*S*H*, or even, say, *Kojak* (Blum and Lindheim 1987: 3). Rather, *Columbo* seems to have a broader range of viewers in its sites. This is perhaps unsurprising for, as Mark Alvey delineates, whilst in the early 1970s the three major networks did try to deliver to advertisers the most lucrative market of the younger, affluent, urban middle classes, nevertheless 'the networks continued to programme by and large for the masses, trying to garner the upscale audience as part of the bargain, all the while hoping for the breakout hit' (2004: 60).

The networks, for Alvey, would have been aware of voices in the industry pinpointing older demographics (such as fifty-plus age groups) as lucrative markets being forgotten in the race for the younger middle-class viewers and their (maybe to some degree fabled) greater disposable income (2004: 59–60).[5] In fact, the breadth of the original possible audience for *Columbo*, whilst it undoubtedly included the 18–49 age bracket, seems to also stretch to younger and older viewers on either side of that particular demographic. Let us firstly consider the latter of these: older viewers.

Commencing with the 1970s' episodes, apparent in *Columbo* is an appeal to older viewers that will have included those fifty-plus. That is, viewers able to appreciate the nostalgia which the show revels in when pairing up former stars of the silver screen as murderers mentally duelling with Columbo (see further in Chapter 6). Moreover, although Falk was in his early forties when the show commenced, the original plan had been to cast Bing Crosby or Lee J. Cobb in the lead. During this era other cop and detective shows did cast older actors, such as Karl Malden (who was sixty when *The Streets of San Francisco* commenced), Buddy Ebsen (mid-sixties in *Barnaby Jones* [1973–1980]) and Mildred Natwick and Helen Hayes (aged sixty-seven and seventy-two respectively when *Snoop Sisters* [1972–1974] joined the *Mystery Movie* wheel on a Wednesday night). Falk was not particularly young, of course. Comparatively speaking, Michael Douglas was in his very late twenties when *The Streets of San Francisco* aired, as one for instance. But Falk was much younger relatively speaking than the other actors considered for *Columbo*. Perhaps unsurprisingly, then, Falk's performance of Columbo's old-school, folksy charm manages to speak to a respectability a little out of step with the latest attitudes of the 1970s (even if loveably so). This does not seem to be accidental. The attractiveness of the older viewer was not lost on NBC, who in 1971 also advertised itself as having 'more programs in the top twenty among adults 25–64 than any other network. According to the Nielsen report for the 1971–72 season, NBC placed nine programs, almost half, in this list' (NBC 1971c). The

---

[5] Alvey notes that NBC had been paying attention to audience composition in its daytime scheduling since the 1950s (2004: 45). Prior to the 1970s it might typically emphasise demographics when discussing a show which was failing to attract a mass audience and when market share was not available as a way with which to promote its potential to advertisers (2004: 49).

third-highest rated of these nine shows was the *Mystery Movie*, coming in behind only *The Flip Wilson Show* (1970–1974) and *The Bob Hope Show* (1950–1979) (NBC 1971c).

Whilst the three shows initially included in the NBC *Mystery Movie* wheel did all feature attractive urban-based professionals, their age, and indeed the full extent of their urbanity, is worth considering carefully. Sam McCloud (Dennis Weaver) in *McCloud* (1970–1977), a show which was already running when the wheel commenced, played a New Mexico law-man fish-out-of-water in New York. As such he retained his rural roots and country ways in the big city. Noticeably, the actor playing McCloud, Dennis Weaver, took with him his association with rurality from the role of Chester in the western *Gunsmoke* (1955–1964). *McCloud*'s credits fore-ground this rural heritage, featuring the eponymous hero in his trademark cowboy hat incongruously riding a galloping horse through traffic down the middle of a busy New York street. Indeed, in the episode 'Manhattan Manhunt' (1970), McCloud tackles a fleeing suspect by leaping from his horse after chasing him through Central Park, a sequence evocative of the rodeo and wild west shows on which the western drew as a genre.

More obviously, *Hec Ramsey*, the fourth show to be added to the *Mystery Movie* wheel, in 1972, was a western. Its lead, Richard Boone, formerly the star of *Have Gun – Will Travel* (1957–1963), was in his mid-fifties. This was older than Falk in *Columbo*, Weaver in *McCloud* and Rock Hudson in *McMillan & Wife*, who were all in their forties when the wheel com-menced. An older demographic, then, was certainly not forgotten in the wheel and nor was a rural demographic judging by the presence of the west-ern. The latter demographic, in particular, helps explain the appearance of country star Johnny Cash as the murderer in the *Columbo* episode 'Swan Song' (1974). This before we mention detective shows on other networks in which rurality featured. On CBS, for example, in *Cannon* (1971–1976), Frank Cannon (William Conrad) reprised the post-war western-cum-thriller format of *Bad Day at Black Rock* (1955) in its pilot, his business travel outside of LA in the series thereafter taking him to various inhos-pitable small rural towns. Again, in another Quinn Martin Production, *Barnaby Jones* – as Buddy Ebsen transitioned from *The Beverly Hillbillies* and various westerns to an urban cop show – the private detective returns from retirement on his ranch to resume his career, bringing with him the potential for rural spectacle (for example, scenes of a horse that performs tricks to his whistle ['Sunday: Doomsday' (1973)]).

The sponsor participations which *Columbo* attracted from the advertis-ing world can add further depth to the audience demographics that this

primetime show was thought likely to draw.[6] Both Mark Dawidziak and
Shelton Catz, in the two existing books on *Columbo*, note that as *Columbo*'s
popularity increased the show was lengthened to enable more ads to be
included. Each author considers the extent to which advertisements were
detrimental to the quality of the show (Catz 2016: 136–139; Dawidziak
[1988] 2019: 95–96). The drive to include more advertisement is unsurprising, considering that commercial television, as noted, is a delivery system for ads. Even so, especially for Dawidziak – who draws on the views of
Levinson and Link, Bochco and Falk – this padding out is thought to have
led to redundant or drawn-out scenes, or to having reduced the effective-
ness of the programme's pacing. Yet there is another way to approach this.
Television Studies has long acknowledged the importance of analysing ads
for our understanding of the full meaning of programmes. For example,
Raymond Williams seminally observed the wholistic nature of televisual
flow (of adverts, trailers, and so on) within which shows are embedded,
and which accord them cultural meaning and value (Williams 1990: 86–96
and 118). Accordingly, it is worth realising how *Columbo*'s content inter-
mingles with its ads in a manner which reveals its target demographics at
primetime.

When the NBC *Mystery Movie* wheel commenced on a Wednesday
night it attracted over 100 sponsors, primarily, as might be expected,
manufacturers of packaged goods, white goods and automobiles. These
included numerous household names. Whilst too many to mention in full,
the spread is amply illustrated by considering just some of those clustered
under C: Canada Dry, Carnation, Chevrolet, Chanel, Coca-Cola, Colgate,
etc. (NBC undated-a). If we focus in on *Columbo* specifically, the range
of commercials which accompanied, for example, 'Death Lends a Hand'
(1971) on WNBT/WNBC on a Wednesday night help illuminate the
show's wide target audience. They included well-known brands of instant
coffee, washing machines, cat food, hair spray, cola, fabric softener, fried
chicken and deodorant (NBC undated-b). Interestingly, though, by 1972,
with the wheel now showing on a Sunday night, the episode 'Dagger of
the Mind', whilst including many similar advertisements – tinned soup,
cars, cameras, cold and flu remedies, tumble dryers, men's slacks, insurance, disinfectant spray, cheesy puff snacks, razors, colour televisions,
cake, drinks mixers, typewriters and soap – also indicates the anticipated
presence of women viewers. This demographic is recognised by a range of

[6] For an explanation of the history of television sponsorship in the US industry, from 'single sponsorship' of a dedicated show to the 'magazine sponsorship' model, in the 1950s,
see Jason Mittell (2003: 44–49).

advertisements for ladies' shavers, compacts, make-up and perfume (NBC undated-c).

Thus, *Columbo*'s manner of squarely addressing key adult audience (and consumer) demographics, whilst also engaging with older viewers, as well as with both urban and rural viewers, is apparent. This is, one might argue, the broad appeal of a country house drama, as per this aspect of the show's literary origins, but, equally, it is the ideal type of show for primetime in the broadcasting (as opposed to narrowcasting) era. To recap Alvey: programming for 'the masses' but including 'the upscale audience as part of the bargain' (Alvey 2004: 60).

We can add to this illumination of *Columbo*'s broad appeal the seemingly counter-intuitive idea that a younger viewer might also be attracted to this cop show. On reflection, this is not actually such a strange idea, considering that *Variety* reported as early as 1972 on the importance of the combination of Disney and *Columbo* to NBC's success in attracting primetime audiences relative to its competitors (Anon. 1972: 33). Indeed, *Columbo* is a very sanitised cop show which might enable family viewing to an extent. Historically, *Columbo* emerged prior to 8–9 pm being officially designated, for a period, the 'family hour' (Carlson 1985: 30; Brooks and Marsh 1995: xix). Even so, this idea of who this slot is suitable for can be said to be apparent in Columbo's scheduling there. For example, on its move to Sunday night, in 1972, *Columbo* immediately followed NBC's airing of *The Wonderful World of Disney*, indicating the degree to which *Columbo* might offer some households a continuation of sufficiently sanitised family-oriented viewing, albeit in which parents might be joined by older offspring than all those youngsters previously enjoying Disney (Brooks and Marsh 1995: 1193). Observing various editions of the *TV Guide* for the era[7] we find *Columbo*'s particular time slot to indicate something of a possible changeover moment in terms of familial viewing demographics: the point where younger children go to bed, but older children can perhaps watch a little longer with parents. Or at least, one could argue that the 8–9 pm slot holds fairly safe shows like *Bewitched* (1964–1972) (when the first series of *Columbo* aired in September 1971, on a Wednesday) in comparison to a more racy movie like the James Bond spy thriller *Goldfinger* (1964) starting at 9 pm.[8]

---

[7] Various *TV Guide* editions of the early 1970s and late 1980s were consulted at the British Film Institute (including 15 September 1971, 17 September 1972 and 6 February 1989). Also consulted were editions of *Television Index* from the same periods.

[8] September 1972.

Admittedly, such a distinction is less clear if we emphasise other shows. The sense that there might be a difference between a darker comedy like *M*A*S*H* in the 8–9 pm slot (when the second season of *Columbo* commenced, on a Sunday evening, in 1972), or indeed the sitcom *The New Dick van Dyke Show* (1971–1974) commencing at 9 pm, and *Columbo*'s opening on a murder in the 8.30 pm slot, is far less clear-cut. Even so, that children might be in control of the dial at that specific time was certainly the case. On 11 October 1971 NBC celebrated the NBC *Mystery Movie* (then on a Wednesday night) becoming a 'Top Rated New Show', not long after it launched with *Columbo*'s 'Murder by the Book' on 15 September. They stated that the 'NBC Mystery Movie's performance was particularly impressive considering that the first half-hour faced a strong Charlie Brown Special rather than its usual Carol Burnett competition' (NBC 1971b). Indeed, during the 1960s and 1970s generally, across the three networks, shows to commence at 8 pm included *I Dream of Jeannie* (1965–1970), *The Man from U.N.C.L.E* (1964–1968), *The Brady Bunch* (1969–1974), *Happy Days* (1974–1984) and *The Waltons* (1971–1981), and even at 8.30 pm could still be found such family-safe fare as *The Flintstones* (1960–1966), *The Beverly Hillbillies* (1962–1971), *Star Trek* (1966–1969) and *The Six Million Dollar Man* (1974–1978) (Brooks and Marsh 1995: 1181–1200).

Within the drama itself, as *Columbo* progressed there were also occasions when a younger viewer, presumably watching with a parent, seems to be acknowledged. Otherwise, what can we make of Columbo's humorous engagement with a child character, the knowingly named Steve Spelberg (Lee Montgomery), alongside Robby the Robot (from *Forbidden Planet* [1956]) in 'Mind over Mayhem' (1974)? Or again, the intelligent young adult women who Columbo sometimes interacts with, one of whom is even integral to solving the case with him ('Ransom for a Dead Man' [1971])? This seemingly direct appeal to much younger viewers would recur later in the show's lifetime, especially when it returned in the late 1980s and 1990s. For example, consider the sudden hiatus in 'Sex and the Married Detective' (1989) created by Columbo's tuba playing for a group of young children. His melody accompanies a playful montage of a fountain moving independently outside, before the children join Columbo's tuba march. It is hard not to notice the shift of address towards a younger viewer in such a standout moment in what is otherwise a *noirish* and somewhat steamy episode (for *Columbo* at any rate).

Even so, and whilst only a couple of decades later *Columbo* reruns would appear in daytime slots where they could more easily be viewed by younger audiences, there is little doubt that its primary target initially was older viewers. Even if the potential to appeal to a younger viewer was not forgotten, it was typically adults who would have seen Columbo's tuba playing, and adults who would have enjoyed the nostalgia value of Robby the Robot nearly twenty years after his debut in *Forbidden Planet*.

In any case, when *Columbo* was brought back by ABC in 1989, its appeal to a wide audience – including both older and younger viewers – was retained. *Columbo* aired on a Monday night, initially, before moving to Saturday night a year later. It was, again, part of a *Mystery Movie* wheel, initially alongside programmes like *B.L. Stryker* (1989–1990), and later with dedicated *Kojak* television movies, amongst other shows. The ABC *Mystery Movie* wheel was scheduled a little later at 9 pm, at the same time as shows like *Lonesome Dove* (1989) and *The Golden Girls* (1985–1992). Falk was by now in his early sixties, and so was paired off against younger murderers. They were often in their forties, as murderers tended to be in in the original seasons, but also included much younger actors. For example: a youthful movie director in 'Murder, Smoke and Shadows' (1989); two students in 'Columbo Goes to College' (1990); a disturbed, young, kidnapping ambulance driver in 'No Time to Die' (1992); and a trendy nightclub owner (and television actress girlfriend) in 'Columbo Likes the Nightlife' (2003). In the first season, by contrast, the actors playing four of the seven murderers were born within three years of Falk (Jack Cassidy, Robert Culp, Roddy McDowall, Patrick O'Neal) whilst Ross Martin was only seven years older, and the youngest of all, Susan Clark, was sixteen years younger. The change which occurred with the passing of time, from middle-aged Falk typically sparring with another actor in their forties, to an older Columbo investigating murderers twenty to almost forty years younger than himself, indicates how the adapted new *Columbo* ensured that many different demographics could still engage with the show.

Finally, regarding *Columbo*'s attempts to appeal as broadly as possible at primetime, something similar can be said of its international audiences. *Columbo* was a popular export product in the UK, Japan, Italy, Iran, the Netherlands, France, Romania, Mexico and Hungary at the very least (Dawidziak [1988] 2019: 309–310). Famous Italian *auteur* Federico Fellini is said to have departed dinner parties to catch *Columbo* ([1988] 2019: 309). In Japan, *Columbo* reputedly challenged baseball for popularity (Levinson and Link 1981b: 68), and Falk was twice invited to formal dinners at the White House when first the Japanese Emperor, and later the Prime Minister Masayoshi Ōhira, asked to dine with Columbo (Falk 2008: 179). Indeed, the most repeated anecdotes about *Columbo* involve its international audience. For instance, Falk was asked by the American ambassador to Romania to be filmed reassuring the Romanian people that the limited number of episodes available annually was not due to their government imposing a quota on their beloved US show (Falk 2008: 221–224). Again, when Falk was filming *Vibes* (1988) in Ecuador, in an isolated Incan village in the Andes he was recognised as 'Tenanté Columbo' by delighted children (Falk 2008: 149–150). Even though it is beyond the scope of this work to provide an exhaustive verification of this audience reach, at least one indicative example can be given, from the UK.

Columbo was screened on several terrestrial channels in the UK, including on ITV, which (unlike BBC One and BBC Two) shows commercials. On ITV, *Columbo* appeared sporadically across the year, alternating with other films, or adaptations of best-selling novels, usually at primetime. Episodes appeared in the top twenty shows by viewing figures in 1979, 1988, 1989 and 1991 (Gambaccini and Taylor 1993: 97). All were weekend primetime slots, on Sunday in the 1970s and on Saturday in the 1980s and 1990s. All started just shortly before the 9 pm 'watershed' (after which content would be thought unsuitable for younger viewers), at either 8.15 pm or 8.40 pm, with the exception of 'Murder, Smoke and Shadows'. This last, one of the first of the new episodes when *Columbo* returned after a decade's hiatus, aired in 1991 at 7.40 pm, clearly with a much fuller family audience in its sites.

The episode which drew the largest audience was 'Murder Under Glass', from the last series of *Columbo* in the 1970s, on Sunday, 15 April 1979. The *TV Times* for that week does not declare the episode's arrival with any significant fanfare, suggesting that by then viewers were familiar with *Columbo*. When aired on ITV, typically, *Columbo* would compete with more highbrow fare on BBC1, such as the Sunday film, play of the month or other feature length dramatisation, followed by *That's Life* (1973–1994). On this occasion, however, it was Easter Sunday, and BBC1 was screening a film version of the rock opera *Jesus Christ Superstar*, factors which may also have contributed to the larger audience for *Columbo* in an era of limited choice between three terrestrial channels.[9] Thus, *Columbo*'s broad audience appeal, and tailoring to the primetime slot both in the USA and elsewhere internationally,[10] are far from inconsequential in understanding

---

[9] Channel 4 launched in 1982.

[10] In Germany, RTL negotiated a deal to bring *Columbo* back to German screens and reported 6.5 million viewers for *Columbo* in 1991 (Kingsley 2004: 8; Koehl 2004; see also Meza 2004). In France, in the mid-1990s, TF1 was screening *Columbo* as part of a cop double bill (following French *policier*, *Navarro* [1989–2005]) during primetime (Anon. 1995: 46). France even made Falk a Knight of the Order of Arts and Letters in 1996 (Anon. 1996: 16).

its origins, emergence and success at this particular point in the history of the television industry.

Overall, what this broader industrial view of *Columbo* emphasises, first and foremost, is the need to understand the show's origins in a different manner than in the oft-told story. But there is also more to be gleaned than just this. If *Columbo* is more than just a work of great creative genius (even if it is most certainly that as well) but is also an industrial product in tune with a time when primetime television helped people understand their lives – to return to Janet Wasko, television as 'THE storyteller for society' (2010: 3) – what is *not* needed is an evaluation of whether it has aesthetic worth or not, or of which episodes are better than others. This is still the usual next step after recounting the oft-told story, to weigh up episodes in terms of quality. Instead, what *is* now needed is a way of grasping what *Columbo means*. This book therefore argues that it is in the shaping of attention that this meaning is to be uncovered. For this, a very different approach is required. From the television industry, then, let us shift our attention to the scholarly understanding of the medium in relation to attention.

An Interdisciplinary Approach

The approach to *Columbo* which this book takes emerges from the interdisciplinary field of film-philosophy (scholarship at the intersection of Film Studies and Philosophy), which has also recently begun to explore television. It is from here that the inspiration to focus on attention was obtained, and, indeed, it is here that this book looks to make its intervention.

Historically, there has been engagement with television and philosophy under the broad banner of critical theory, especially with the thought of Martin Heidegger during the mid-1990s (Fry 1993; Dienst 1994). In some ways a precursor for this book, Richard Dienst's *Still Life in Real Time* (1994) drew on the works of Heidegger, Jacques Derrida and Gilles Deleuze to explore, broadly speaking, the world through television and television through the world. What is a little different now is the gradual emergence of a groundswell from a different quarter. Very recently, film-philosophy has belatedly begun to turn to television (e.g. Sanders and Skoble 2008; C. Gardner 2012, 2018; Nannicelli 2016; Stadler 2017; Graham and Sparrow 2018).

A useful example indicating what is at stake in this turn is Steven M. Sanders's and Aeon J. Skoble's *The Philosophy of TV Noir* (2008) which explores 'the philosophical ideas presupposed and reflected' in television noirs from *Dragnet* (1951–1959) to *The Sopranos* (1999–2007) (Sanders and Skoble 2008: 1). Sanders argues that: 'noir television is particularly valuable in dramatizing situations and experiences that raise philosophical questions about how to live, what kind of person one should be, and what, if anything, gives meaning to life' (Sanders and Skoble 2008: 1). This is very much in line with the way in which film–philosophy is often described, as exploring how films 'do' philosophy, or, put another way, considering how films can 'think'. Television, then, like film, can be said to have, or expound, a philosophy or philosophies. After all, if there is a 'philosophy of TV noir', then there are presumably many more philosophies, or ways of philosophising, amongst television's various offerings.

It is in the historical moment of this shift of emphasis in film-philosophy, towards television, that this book on *Columbo* examines attention. Specifically, it looks to intervene at the intersection of, on the one hand, Television Studies's long-standing interest in television's mediation of attention, and, on the other, how various critical thinkers consider our contemporary world. The last of these includes both philosophers and cultural theorists, particularly through foregrounded engagement with several contemporary Italian minds: Giorgio Agamben, Mauricio Lazzarrato and Franco 'Bifo' Berardi (along with passing discussions of the ideas of their countrymen Omar Calabrese and Umberto Eco). The Italian 'flavour' to the theory involved seems perhaps fitting, considering Columbo's Italian-American heritage. The reality is, though, that the overarching theoretical influence on the analysis of *Columbo* is informed by Gilles Deleuze's and Félix Guattari's famous critiques of capitalism. This heritage, in particular Guattari's thinking, is evident in the work of the Italian thinkers referenced throughout.

This book's theoretical dimension also draws upon an interdisciplinary range of ideas about attention, including work within Film Studies as epitomised by Jonathan Beller's *The Cinematic Mode of Production* (2006). This latter text is indicative of an interdisciplinary convergence with Art History (Beller is influenced by and develops seminal works by art historian Jonathan Crary [1999, 2013]), and various other fields in which attention is being explored. Work on attention will thus require a dedicated discussion in Chapter 2, wherein the different areas which intersect to make this intervention (work in Television Studies on attention, theoretical ideas of attention) are explored together. An intervention at this particular intersection seeks to broaden the scope of our understanding of how ideas like that of attention (and its intertwined societal and economic functions) can be fruitfully explored in relation to a specific television show that has maintained a huge global following over the decades.

Crucially, this type of analysis can happen in a more pinpointed manner in relation to television than it can if applied to film, due to the differences between the two media: their different industrial conditions and markets, narrative structures, viewing experiences, longevity, societal functioning, and so on. It is what is medium-specific to television which can help advance understanding of a theoretical subject like attention. In particular, the qualities which television offers that film does not, which film-philosophy now has to grapple with, are often noted to be both television's longevity across time (which is integral to *Columbo*'s cult status, as I discuss further below), and also its potential for liveness (which I touch upon in Chapter 3) (Caldwell 2019: 23). To elucidate the nature of this intervention, the remainder of this chapter examines how this work exists in relation to film-philosophy's turn to television, as well as certain existing debates within Television Studies like that surrounding cult television.

Television-philosophy (?)

The manner of approach to *Columbo* which this book takes can be clarified through engagement with one of the most sustained examinations of television philosophically, Ted Nannicelli's *Appreciating the Art of Television* (2016). Nannicelli's in-depth exploration of television as art approaches it rather as an art historian might when assessing the results of the labour of a painter (2016: 122–208). This book shares Nannicelli's concern with understanding a show like *Columbo* as at once a product of authorial agency and yet also an industrial product specific to the era in which it emerged. It considers *Columbo* an artefact in line with the direction that Nannicelli pursues when discussing television shows as:

> special sorts of artifacts – the results of human agential activity performed within a tradition of television-making . . . as shaped, expressive, usually communicative objects whose natures, meanings and values all need to be conceived as standing in relation to the conventions, norms, aims of that tradition and its history. Furthermore, it is to approach them as attempts – often but not necessarily successful – to achieve various goals, such as communicating meanings, eliciting emotions, and expressing ideas. (2016: 5)

Thus, this book's analysis of *Columbo* contains discussion of both Levinson's and Link's roles as originators and creators of the show, of individual directors (Gazzara in particular, in Chapter 3), even Falk himself as producer and occasional writer. At its heart, though, and what differentiates my own approach from Nannicelli's, this book is more interested in how *Columbo* reflects, and reflects upon, the changing history of attention in its lifetime. This is visible in retrospect, even if we cannot expect its personnel to have always necessarily been in tune with it as they made individual episodes.[11] This approach makes sense in light of the show's employment of numerous creative personnel over the decades. *Columbo*, although created by Levinson and Link, is ultimately the product of many creative people. As such it reveals as much about its times (as an industrial product aimed at a certain audience, and, simultaneously, as a mediator of socio-historical change) as it does any particular authorial vision.

Importantly, this approach distinguishes this book from its two book-length predecessors.[12] The first, Mark Dawidziak's ground-breaking *The Columbo Phile* ([1988] 2019), has at time of writing been re-released for its thirtieth anniversary. It was based on interviews with key figures in the show's NBC years. These include *Columbo*'s creators, Levinson and Link, along with Falk and Bochco. For its part, Sheldon Catz's fascinating *Columbo Under Glass* (2016) covers the entire run, both the 1970s with NBC and the return of *Columbo* under ABC. There is no way to compete with the behind-the-scenes insight of Dawidziak. It is even said that Falk consulted with Dawidziak regarding the content of the earlier episodes when the show was reborn with ABC (Lertzman and Birnes 2017: 378–381; Dawidziak [1988] 2019: 384–388). Similarly, the encyclopaedic knowledge of Catz is not something this book can hope to match.[13] But, ultimately, this is a very different kind of book. Whilst, like these predecessors, I am also a fan of *Columbo*, what this book provides is a very different work of analysis.

What unites Dawidziak and Catz is an evaluative approach to *Columbo* – making a case for the higher quality of some episodes over others.

---

[11] In terms of authorial agency, this is also to balance out too strong a sense of its creative force giving birth to the work with the various counter-arguments which surround the Romantic figure of the artist or *auteur*: for example, that creative personnel may or may not always themselves be conscious of the historical forces which work through them, especially when they express themselves in generic forms with long histories. This, even whilst, contrariwise, granting that they may consciously foreground a distinctive authorial style, and be astute at manipulating well-worn discourses surrounding the supposed tensions between art and commerce to construct their star image (Stoddart 1995: 44–55). This is to gloss over several decades of work on the *auteur*, coming from various perspectives, structuralist and post-structuralist, including by Peter Wollen, John Caughie and Timothy Corrigan.

[12] Paul Hughes's interesting *The Columbo Case Files* (2018) is a compendium of his internet-based writings.

[13] Dawidziak and Catz helped keep alive *Columbo*'s legacy for fan communities (Catz 2016: 369), and this book owes a debt to their efforts.

However, this kind of evaluative approach has many challenges. As noted above regarding claims that the quality of some *Columbo* episodes suffered because of the lengthening of episodes to enable more advertising space to be sold, what can be a compelling point in terms of an evaluative approach can seem redundant from other perspectives. This is to touch upon a long-running argument about the nature of taste, and the role it plays in shaping the assessments of quality. As there are a range of audiovisual pleasures offered by any television show, some viewers may like a good narrative (convincing clues and a watertight case, as emphasised by Catz), but others may appreciate the pleasure of the spectacle (e.g. the sudden appearance of Los Angeles Lakers stars, Johnny Cash singing in close-up, a woman bossing her family business's male-dominated board of directors, or Columbo entertaining children on the tuba). In such evaluative writing there is the sense of a 'taste' hierarchy – of greater and lesser or preferred and less-preferred episodes – akin to the kind of rankings by 'quality' associated with Andrew Sarris's work determining a 'pantheon' of famous directors, or *auteurs*, in the 1960s (Sarris [1962] 2004: 562; Stoddart 1995: 42–43). Analysing and hierarchising episodes via quality, then, typically reveals subjective bias, whether conscious or unconscious, on the part of the critic.

Instead, to see *Columbo* as an artefact is to interpret it with a degree of authorial intention in mind but tempered by the realities of the television industry at the time as structuring milieu. This is the benefit of considering the additional dimensions to the oft-told story of the show's genesis which were outlined above. There is no real reason, then, to assert a qualitative judgement if the emphasis is placed instead on how the show relates to its socio-historical context.[14]

Such an approach also provides a wider lens through which to view *Columbo* than has previously been deployed by scholars – from various disciplines – writing on the show. This book hopes to offer more in terms of: *Columbo*'s negotiation of its socio-historical context than is possible when exploring one episode, 'Dagger of the Mind' (1972), for its provision of a 'fresh Shakespeare' (Jaster 1999); a more inclusive focus on the life of the show than an analysis of the friendship between Falk, Ben Gazzara and John Cassavetes on their collaborations on *Columbo* and American Independent

---

[14] In Paul Hughes's *The Columbo Case Files* (2018) he states that his intention is to explore *Columbo*'s 'place in American culture' (2018: 2). Yet his manner of doing so is essentialist. For example, he explores 'paying attention and asking questions' (p. 5) but only as 'deep practices not unrelated to love' (p. 4). Again, when Hughes attempts to contextualise socio-historically around the 1970s, he explores very generalising ideas like 'health and sickness' (p. 185) or 'pride' (p. 244).

movies (Hastie 2017); a greater breadth than a study of Steven Spielberg's contribution to the series as the director of the first episode (McBride 1997; Buckland 2006; Morris 2017); and more historical contextualisation than is found in studies of the function of variation in *Columbo*'s serial narrative form (Calabrese 1992: 39–40; Eco 1994: 83–100).

Finally, to begin to round off this discussion of the intervention this book looks to make, it is also worth clarifying why it does not aim to greatly influence the field of Television Studies. This is, after all, a discipline within whose distinctive history some particularly philosophical or theoretical approaches have been deployed (Gray and Lotz 2018: 8–33). The difference between the approach taken in this book and what might be considered more typical of the mainstream of Television Studies is evident if we look at the various ways of approaching television currently dominant in the field. For example, Janet Wasko's *A Companion to Television* (2010), whilst setting out to inclusively introduce the field's broad terrain, does so under headings which emphasise: 'History', 'Aesthetics and Production', 'The State and Policy', 'Commerce', 'Programming, Content and Genre', 'The Public and Audiences' and 'International Television'. Numerous other such texts reveal similar emphases, indicating that in the mainstream at present things theoretical may often tend to function in the background.[15] Or at any rate, they are not foregrounded quite as they are in film-philosophy, the area in which this book situates itself.[16]

With this discipline specificity in mind, we might consider that there are many more typical ways to approach *Columbo* as an artefact, or object of analysis in Television Studies, than the one undertaken herein. A television historian, for example, might be interested in the question of just exactly who watched *Columbo* over the decades – what was its audience from the 1970s until the early 2000s? They might approach this question

---

[15] Other examples reinforce this backgrounding of the theoretical. Wasko can be seen to follow Glen Creeber's *Tele-visions* (2006), in which, whilst half of the chapters deal with various ways of analysing television (including some theoretical directions), the second half indicates: audience, history, regulation, national and international, and convergence. Robert C. Allen and Annette Hill's *The Television Studies Reader* (2004) has seven sections covering television's institutions, spaces, modes, production, social representation, audiences and convergence. Jonathan Gray and Amanda Lotz's *Television Studies* (2018) divides the discipline into four key, often intersecting, approaches: programmes, audiences, industries, contexts.

[16] Harry Benshoff's 2016 introduction to film and television analysis, foregrounds theory throughout. Yet even here its final chapter, 'Contemporary Thinking on Nation, Race, Gender, and Sexuality', stops short of the concerns currently prevalent in film-philosophy (ethics, posthumanism, ecology, etc.).

by conducting archival research to seek out information regarding the show's sponsors over time, consulting the trade press, and by examining which commercials were scheduled during *Columbo*.[17] This chapter contains a degree of this type of work, informed by materials from archives in the UK and the USA, even if it is not the primary focus of the book itself.[18] A different type of Television Studies scholar might set up interviews with *Columbo* fans to ascertain what pleasures the show delivers, whether the emphasis was historical or contemporary. Doubtless there are many other ways of proceeding.

By contrast, this book explores *Columbo* by analysing the televisual text in its socio-historical context. Naturally, an act of interpretation of this kind is not in any way controversial. Film Studies, Television Studies and many other Arts and Humanities disciplines regularly conduct such hermeneutical work. In so doing, they follow broader shifts since the 1960s and 1970s, prompted by thinkers like Michel Foucault or Deleuze and Guattari, away from seemingly ahistorical theoretical approaches. Grounding hermeneutics in this way, analysing *Columbo* with regard to its socio-historical context, is thus not intended to be ground-breaking. Television crime drama, after all, is often interpreted with respect to its negotiation of socio-historical change. This is especially so in texts following in the wake of Charlotte Brunsdon's seminal work on the topic (2000: 195–200). Sue Turnbull, for example, in *The TV Crime Drama* (2014) emphasises the importance of understanding the genre 'at a specific moment in time and at a particular social and historical context' (p. 40). The same is true of scholarship on other televisual modes and genres, including dedicated books on discrete series like *Mad Men* (2007–2015) (such as the various collected essays in *Analyzing Mad Men* [Stoddart 2011]), as well as in work on long-running productions as diverse as the influential documentary, *Seven Up* (Bruzzi 2007) and the science-fiction children's programme (with cult following), *Doctor Who* (Leach 2009). Indeed, work on crime fiction per se, especially crime literature, also often approaches texts in this way (see Chapters 2 and 5).

The approach herein taken to *Columbo*, then, is not intended to be earth shattering, even if its recourse to philosophy is nowadays perhaps a little

[17] My thanks to the anonymous Reader 2 of an early iteration of this project, who indicated what they considered were the shortcomings of the book in this respect.

[18] On site in the UK, at the British Film Institute, London, July 2019 and January 2020. Off site in the USA, via correspondence with the Wisconsin Center for Film and Theater Research, University of Wisconsin-Madison, and the Moving Image Section at the Library of Congress, both January 2020.

unusual for the mainstream of Television Studies. *Columbo* is understood to be an artefact, the analysis of which reveals as much about the meaning of the programme as it does the shaping of attention in that era, the two being inextricably linked. The approach to this stems, though, from a rather different set of questions than those listed above regarding industry and audiences. The research questions propelling this work relate to attention, and stem primarily from considering the show's aesthetic aspect (i.e. what is seen on-screen). Specifically, they arose initially whilst watching *Columbo* episodes without any academic purpose in mind, simply for pleasure. In so doing, several things began to 'bother' me. I found that, like Columbo, I had 'just a few questions' to ask of the show. Accordingly, I began to watch and re-watch with these questions as my focus, analysing the entire run of *Columbo* chronologically, twice, with a critically engaged eye, to uncover the answers.

The key questions which emerged are: Why does Columbo act like he does? Why so many machines? What exactly does Columbo police? Where is LA? Together these questions inform an exploration of *Columbo*'s engagement with attention at the close of the Twentieth Century: its ability to reveal how it is shaped, and *Columbo*'s role in shaping it. Chapters 3–6 provide the answers to these questions, the Conclusion then pulling together the strands to complete the picture of *Columbo* and the transformation of attention which took place in the late twentieth century. It is in this way that the book offers something a little different in its recourse to theory. It indicates how one television show 'philosophizes' or 'thinks' this socio-historical shift in the shaping of attention. Hence we might tentatively consider this a work of television-philosophy.

Analysing a show with such a long lifespan in this way requires a flexible approach to the number of episodes explored in each chapter. Overall, the argument weaves though the entirety of the show's episodes (all sixty-nine are mentioned at some point). Some chapters focus in depth on only a couple of key episodes: providing a significant and clear comparative approach to *Columbo* across the decades and thereby illuminating the changing historical context it negotiates (Chapter 2). Others mention as many as thirty episodes as part of a wider ranging exploration of a topic like performance (Chapter 3). Some episodes may only be mentioned once, and briefly, whilst others – those which bring different aspects of the argument into clearest focus – may recur across chapters. In addition, *Columbo* is considered alongside contemporary detective shows from NBC's *Mystery Movie* wheel, including *McCloud, McMillan & Wife, Hec Ramsey, Banacek* (1972–1974) and *Quincy, M.E.*, as well as comparable shows of the era like *The Streets of San Francisco, Kojak* and *The Rockford Files*.

Thus *Columbo*'s longevity informs the analysis. It indicates one key way in which its medium specificity offers insights into how attention was shaped in the late twentieth century in a manner which a films or films could not.

As noted, the intention is not to intervene significantly in Television Studies. Even so, there is a minimal contribution to that discipline. This can be seen by briefly recognising what is specific about *Columbo* as a work of television. Its longevity on-screen, which is very different from what a typical film might manage (even most franchises), is only matched by its ongoing and vibrant cult afterlife. To round out this chapter, then, let us examine how this analysis of *Columbo* does offer a little something to Television Studies, through the show's problematisation of certain aspects of now seminal definitions of cult television. This will provide a springboard into the next chapter, on the role of *Columbo*'s somewhat unique narrative structure in its shaping of attention.

Columbo's Cult Afterlife

Columbo was, from its first airing, immediately popular. Both pilots performed well in the Neilson ratings, its first season placed in the top ten most watched shows, and its first four seasons helped the *Mystery Movie* wheel consistently place in the top twenty-five most watched programmes (Brooks and Marsh 1995: 1265–1266; Link 2010: 12; Lertzman and Birnes 2017: 184 and 187).[19] Falk as Columbo soon adorned the cover of *Time*. However, in contrast to *Columbo*'s popularity with the viewing public, *Columbo*'s initial reviews were lukewarm.

Variety, for instance, was doubtful about the initial pilot, 'Prescription: Murder', which aired on 20 February 1968. Their review considered it to 'come across more as a padded-out hour-actioner segment than as a feature film', that the script had 'soggy stretches' and that 'more distinctive dialog and characterization might have given it more substance'. It also criticised the acting, deemed the ending 'predictable and unconvincing', and overall condemned it as having the 'slickly expensive look typical of

---

[19] Measuring the success of *Columbo* thusly is challenging. The measurements are taken for the *Mystery Movie* wheel, rather than individual shows. We can tell that the first four seasons drew large audiences. In the sixth edition of *The Complete Directory to Prime Time Network and Cable TV Shows* (1995), Tim Brooks and Earle Marsh draw on the Nielson ratings to list the wheel as the 14th in the 'top-rated programs by season' for 1971–1972 (at 23.2 per cent of audience); then it jumps to 5th for 1972–1973 (24.2 per cent); at 14th for 1973–1974 (22.2 per cent); and at 22nd for 1974–1975 (21.3 per cent), after which it drops out of the top 25 (1995: 1258 and 1265–1266).

such endeavours' (Frie 1968: 38).[20] Yet this is curious indeed, as *The Film Daily* reported the following week that the pilot 'scored one of the most lopsided victories of the season when it more than doubled both the combined ratings and combined shares of its competition in the New York City Overnight Nielson Ratings', with a peak of a 53.6 audience share, and an average of 45.2, well ahead of the rival networks respective audience shares for their programmes (ABC had 22.2, CBS 14.7) (Anon. 1968: 3).[21] A similar disparity was evident when the first episode of the first series (the Spielberg and Bochco episode, 'Murder by the Book'), aired in 1971. *Variety* found Falk's acting 'overdone' and his style 'predictable and repetitive', and foretold the 'one-dimensional role' would 'wear thin quickly' (Bok 1971: 24). Only a year later, however, *Variety* reported that NBC had edged ahead of CBS in the fifth week of the season-to-date Nielsen ratings, with *Columbo* specifically (now in its Sunday night spot) cited as key to this success. It was rated second in the Nielsen's ranking of 'Network's Top Shows' (with a market share of 42) at that specific moment (Anon. 1972: 33).

To be fair to the critics, *Columbo* did, quite quickly, also become a critical success. The first series garnered Emmy awards for creators, Levinson and Link, and its star, Falk (Levinson and Link 1981b: 67). Ultimately four of Falk's five Emmy wins would be for *Columbo*, and over its lifetime the show would be awarded Emmys for supporting actor (Patrick McGoohan, twice), best guest actress (Faye Dunaway), editing (Edward Abroms), cinematography (Lloyd Ahern, Harry Wolf, Richard Glouner) and best limited series (Hyatt 2006: 265; Catz 2016: 364). What this initial disparity between *Columbo*'s popularity with its audience as opposed to the slightly-slower-to-catch-on critics indicates, then, is the manner in which the show resonated with viewers *in spite of* the parameters of expectation of critics. As this popularity remains in force today, what can we make of *Columbo*'s ongoing appeal to its fans with regard to existing definitions of cult television?

---

[20] *Variety* is known historically for publishing reviews under pen names. Frie and Bok, cited in this chapter, are presumably examples of this.

[21] The difference between market share and ratings is helpfully elucidated in Michael Curtin and Jane Shattuc's *The American Television Industry* (2009). Both are percentages. Ratings indicate a percentage of the total number of television-owning households which tune in to a particular show, whether the television is on or off. Share indicates a percentage of the total number of television-owning households which tuned in to a specific show, out of all those in which the television was turned on. This, then, can be understood as the difference between a percentage of what is hypothetically possible (ratings) and what is possible in the reality of the moment (share) (2009: 35).

Columbo both does and does not coincide with the seminal definitions of cult television. Key thinking on cult film and television initially looked back to Umberto Eco's work, from 1985, in which he argued that a cult show,

> must provide a completely furnished world so that fans can quote characters and episodes as if they were aspect of the fan's private sectarian world, a world about which they make up quizzes and play trivia games so that the adepts of the sect recognise through each other a shared expertise. (1985: 3)

From this starting point, and ensuing critique, grew initial calls in Television Studies for a more multidimensional analytic approach to understanding cult television at the intersection of texts, production context, distribution, audience reception and fan engagement (e.g. Hills 2002: 131–143; Gwenllian-Jones and Pearson 2004: x).

Immediately, it is clear that *Columbo* is neither fish nor fowl with respect to such a definition. As the show's global cult afterlife indicates, it furnishes more than enough of a complete world for fan engagement of the sort described: from quizzes to cookbook to touristic attraction statue to online watch parties (see the Introduction for the full panorama). However, what stands out from repeated consumption of *Columbo* is the *inconsistency* of this furnished world, a feature which has significance for how it shapes attention.[22] This might seem a slightly perverse point to make, considering *Columbo* is a generic cop show repeating a winning formula. However, it is clearly the case that such inconsistences appeal to fans. This is worth digging into further.

In a breakdown of the emerging ideas of cult television of the early 2000s, Matt Hills finds that, at a textual level, a 'consistent narrative world' (2004: 511) is often considered crucial to definitions of cult television. The fan community engages with an 'immensely detailed' and 'fantastic' world, of which they can only glimpse a fraction in the show itself. Around a show like *Buffy the Vampire Slayer* (1997–2003), then, we might find a 'hyperdiegesis' – an 'extended, expansive narrative world', or a 'Buffyverse' – emerging amidst the television programme, spin-offs (i.e. *Angel* [1999–2004]) and various forms of fan engagement (Hills 2004: 511). This is a function of seriality, and the consistency required when such a

---

[22] Even without conducting the kind of fully rounded research which cult television scholars indicate as best practice, it is possible to state that *one* aspect of fan engagement is also precisely that which keeps *Columbo* from aligning with existing definitions of cult television: *textual inconsistency*.

cult universe grows through ongoing viewing of a show. This, even if it must, to retain interest, *occasionally* play with its own narrative rules (e.g. Hills notes the standout episode of *Buffy* which was performed as a musical). Again, many cult shows are fantasy or science-fiction programmes, immersion in which reveals the complex rules by which this universe functions, and often include an 'endlessly deferred narrative' exploring this universe. This is apparent, for example, in the continuing 'voyages' to 'strange new worlds' of science-fiction shows from *Star Trek* (1966–1969) to *Farscape* (1999–2003) and beyond (pp. 511–513).

Yet, *Columbo* does not fit this model because, rather than the 'multiple time frames and settings' necessary to fuel a 'potentially infinitely large metatext' (Gwenllian-Jones and Pearson 2004: xii) as in the 'Buffyverse', *Columbo* offers a very different experience: no singular, coherent 'Columboverse', only a multiverse of infinite variations on *Columbo*. This is not a serial form, after all, it is an episodic format, and rather than occasional differences working to maintain interest (such as the musical episode of *Buffy*), here *inconsistency itself is the norm*. This is so even in spite of the formulaic nature of each episode – see the murder, watch Columbo catch the murderer. What shape does this inconsistency take?

Even whilst each episode begins anew, and is coherent to itself, episodes often create cognitive dissonance in the mind of the dedicated fan, revealing thereby the absence of any coherent and consistent fictional world encompassing the episode. For example, Mrs Columbo cannot possibly be the greatest fan of every single celebrity-murderer Columbo encounters. Columbo presumably does not have such a huge and interesting family as he describes. It is never clear if Columbo has children or not (he very occasionally indicates that he might, but on another occasion definitively states that he never did); can speak Italian or not (in some episodes he speaks Italian, in another he claims he could not master it); is aviophobic or not (sometimes afraid of flying, other times revelling in it); is happy to drink on duty or never does (he claims, and does, both); enthusiastically loves to read mystery novels or does not because he cannot figure them out (both of which he states); has had the top down on his convertible Peugeot before or not (in 1991 he claims it is the first time, but we have seen it previously in 1976); or even whether Mrs Columbo is real or not (we never see her, even if others do, and we see Columbo speak to her on the phone). Just at the narrative level, then, *Columbo* only really has coherence *within* each stand-alone episode. Across episodes it is, at best, enigmatic in terms of evidencing a coherent 'Columboverse'. Thus whilst seminal definitions of what characterises cult television tend to exclude episodic cop shows like *Columbo* (focusing instead on textual features more normal to the science fiction and fantasy genres), the show's cult appeal indicates that there is more to be learned here.

The recurring presence of several actors playing different roles across various episodes of *Columbo* only adds to this deliberate inconsistency. Sometimes *Columbo* episodes can appear a little like plays performed by an acting company or troupe, with roles rotating as they perform their repertoire. Actors like John Finnegan, Vito Scotti, Val Avery, Mike Lally, Fred Draper and Bruce Kirby play different parts in numerous episodes. The likes of Joyce Van Patten, Anne Francis, Mariette Hartley, Molly Hagan, Dean Stockwell, Ray Milland, Leslie Nielsen, James McEachin, Wilfred Hyde-White, Tim O'Connor and Patrick O'Neal join the show a couple of times, but again playing different parts each time. It seems unlikely that many people watching in the 1970s would have had an issue with respect to consistency of world, as the inconsistency provides enjoyment from recognition and familiarity within (generic) difference. Conversely, some less attentive viewers may simply not have spotted it at all, especially in this still just-pre-video era, consistency not necessarily being something a *Columbo* viewer may have sought in any case.

Nowadays, for dedicated fans like Sheldon Catz and Paul Hughes spotting these appearances seems to be a key pleasure, judging by the mentions that occur in *Columbo Under Glass* (2016) and *The Columbo Case Files* (2018) respectively. Similarly, on online forums, eagle-eyed *Columbo* fans have spotted numerous inconsistencies, including that the murderers in two different episodes of the first series drive the exact same Mercedes, down to its very license plate![23] This suggests that at least *one* of the cult textual pleasures which *Columbo* offers to fans is that of seeing how the formula repeats with this evident inconsistency, creating an incoherence and discontinuity *resistant* to the construction of a coherent 'Columboverse'. How else can we assimilate that Bob Dishy appears in different episodes playing a cop working alongside Columbo, but with a different first name each time? Or, that John Finnegan appears as a colleague or seemingly a former colleague (now bar owner) of Columbo's in some episodes, whilst in others as someone employed in a completely different career (such as, amongst other roles, a security guard, a foreman on a construction site, or as an assistant director on a television set)? Compounding this sense that continuity should not be expected (but rather, that inconsistency is

[23] This piece of trivia has appeared several times on the Lt Columbo Forum for fans (part of The Ultimate Columbo Site). For example: http://pub10.bravenet.com/forum/static/show.php?usernum=806565873&frmid=6&msgid=1298887&cmd=show (accessed 3 January 2020).

part of the fun), the NBC *Mystery Movie* wheel provided supporting roles for various actors across the different shows. Bruce Kirby, for example, played supporting roles in both *McCloud* and *Banacek*, not to mention his appearances in *Ironside* (1967–1975), *Kojak*, *The Streets of San Francisco*, *The Rockford Files* and *Delvecchio* (1976–1977). Many of these, of course, were made by Universal. Weekly viewing in the 1970s, then, may well have included the same kind of playful pleasure in recognition that fans of *Columbo* indulge in today.

In a certain sense, noting this playful inconsistency may not indicate anything more than the 'errors' which may inevitably creep in to long-running television shows (Nannicelli 2016: 137). As noted, Falk himself may have had to consult with Mark Dawidziak, the author of *The Columbo Phile*, once the second run began with ABC, due to details he himself could not recall from the NBC years. If anything, such inconsistencies (for example, perhaps of actor-character [Finnegan], or character name [Dishy]) simply re-emphasise the need to consider *Columbo* within its industrial context. *Columbo*, after all, was presumably not initially produced with a cult following in mind, something which has been argued for more recent programmes since the 1990s (particularly after fan intervention helped propel *Star Trek* reruns into syndication in the 1970s [Reeves et al. 1996: 28]). *Columbo*'s textual inconsistencies, we might argue, are just a product of the show's era of production, and in this sense there is nothing remarkable about them. Indeed, there were other shows of the time in which familiar actors appear playing different characters across various episodes, so who would really care if Dishy reappears as a colleague of Columbo but with the wrong first name? This is before we even think about how fans engage with soap operas in which characters may be played by different actors, or a storyline suddenly recast as just a dream as in *Dallas* (1978–1991). Thus the in-jokes which *Columbo* very deliberately indulges in, like the referencing of other *Columbo* episodes in a way that a dedicated viewer might pick up on, can be dismissed as just that, in-jokes, rather than a deliberate, foregrounded and tongue-in-cheek play with inconsistency.[24] In a sense, of course, this is all true.

---

[24] For example, in the first episode of series one, 'Murder by the Book' (1971), one of the writing duo responsible for the (fictional) Mrs Melville Mysteries gifts a signed copy of a book to a blackmailer who has realised his guilty secret (he has murdered the other half of the writing duo). The title of the book is *Prescription: Murder*, also that of the first *Columbo* pilot. See Chapter 4 for another example of such self-referential behaviour in 'Fade in to Murder' (1976).

Yet for many cult shows of more recent decades the consistency of the narrative world is crucial. When such an inconsistency was deliberately introduced into *Buffy*, with the sudden arrival of Buffy's sister Dawn (Michelle Trachtenberg) in season five, the 'Buffyverse' accommodated it by providing an explanation for it within the diegetic world. In *Columbo*, by contrast, revelling in such inconsistency – such as when Columbo verbally introduces yet more and more family members, including a nephew who enthusiastically practices both needlepoint and weightlifting – is all part of the viewing pleasure. On the one hand this could be seen as simply noting that seminal definitions of cult television are a little limited due to their emphasis on science-fiction serials. Yet on the other, as the next chapter will explore, these inconsistencies provide an access point for our understanding of the show's shaping of attention. Namely, *there is something strategic about the play with inconsistency which is made into a feature of the show, which helps shape how we pay attention in our everyday lives.*

Think, in particular, of Mrs Columbo's deep and pre-existing fanaticism for everyone famous whom the Lieutenant meets during his investigations. This would seem to deliberately indicate the illusionary nature of the hyperdiegetic world (the 'Columboverse') which Columbo verbally conjures up by referring so frequently to Mrs Columbo and his seemingly-impossibly-large family. It is here that the narrative inconsistency points to *Columbo*'s shaping of attention. Briefly for now, as the next chapter explores this in depth, it is as if each episode were a *game* which is fully reset each time a new episode starts. The next iteration of the game will contain mostly familiar content, but with some slight variations.[25] In this, *Columbo* is like any number of games, but an apposite comparison might be the board game *Clue* (*Cluedo* in the UK). In both *Clue* and *Columbo* we know that there will be a murder, murder weapon, location, and so on, but each time how we get to this knowledge will be different (see also Kim 2014: 1–2). Or rather, specifically in the case of *Columbo*, it is like *watching someone else* play *Clue/Cluedo* when you already know who the killer is, the fun being in seeing how the other players figure out what happened from the clues they find. The moments in which the inconsistency of the 'Columboverse' is revealed, then, become the running joke that validates

---

[25] This emphasis on variation is somewhat as was noted of the neo-Baroque nature of *Columbo* by Omar Calabrese in his influential book on that topic (1992), albeit he was not interested in the show's game-like quality.

this experience as being one of gaming. The viewer's attention can be distracted momentarily by the inconsistency, and this is very pleasurable, but this will likely not be for too long because what has been 'spotted' (the actor in a new role, the new reference to the family, or the fact that Mrs Columbo is the latest celebrity-murderer's biggest fan) is incidental to the process of investigation.

Thus the way in which *Columbo* offers visual pleasures to its fans sets it apart from, and illustrates something of the fault lines in, seminal definitions of cult television. A slightly different approach is needed, then, to uncover what is so appealing about *Columbo* as a cult show. Following the influential work on cult television of Jimmie L. Reeves, Mark C. Rodgers and Michael Epstein on *The X-Files* (1993–2018), *Columbo*'s shifting popularity across its lifetime and beyond – from primetime favourite, Emmy award-winning Nielsen's ratings high-achiever in the 1970s, to online streaming cult niche in the 2010s and 2020s – can be seen to reflect the industry's shift from broadcasting to narrowcasting that has occurred since the time of *Columbo*'s first appearance (Reeves et al. 1996: 24). Tellingly, this was part and parcel of the broader economic shift to post-Fordism under Ronald Reagan which occurred in the historical interstice between *Columbo*'s two runs, accompanying also a geopolitical 'displacement of cold war order by New World Disorder' (p. 24). This historical shift, taking place in the background to the last fifty years of *Columbo*'s popularity, then, also reveals how the show expresses the transformation in the way in which attention is shaped across this period (the subject of Chapter 2). *Columbo* undergoes the shift from a primetime show shaping cultural consensus to, especially after its run had finished, a cult classic for special interest audiences. Its changing role as a shaper of attention in ways which remain relevant even today thus illuminates the background socio-historical change very clearly. This is, specifically, *a change from attention in the service of national security during the Cold War* (when *Columbo* played on a major network during primetime, shaping cultural consensus nationally and even internationally), *to the increasing monetisation of attention for private gain as per Reaganomics, and the now globally prevalent understanding of neoliberalism* (as *Columbo* transfers to a more niche programming position enjoyed mostly by cult audiences as re-runs, DVDs, and through online streaming).

In arguing this, the cult status of *Columbo* is not insignificant. The longevity of the show's popularity, whilst related to the aforementioned industrial factors, is also testament to something else that is closely related to *Columbo*'s unusual structure: its game-like nature, and the importance of inconsistency (and perhaps nostalgia) in it.[26] This is explored further in Chapters 2 and 6. Yet, as noted, this foray into cult television is not an attempt to intervene in the cult television debate to any real degree. After all, many of the questions which can be asked of such seminal definitions have since been interrogated, often by these same scholars (e.g. Hills 2012; Pearson 2012). The findings of this book offer at most a curious footnote to that debate. Rather, then, much as the historical contextualising of *Columbo* with respect to the US television industry and audience above is schematically included to lay the ground for the critical analysis of *Columbo*'s shaping of attention which follows (not to add great archival depth), similarly, this book does not pursue in depth the kind of analysis proposed by Hills, Gwenllian-Jones and Pearson.[27] Detailed accounts of *Columbo* in the manner of television history or audience reception studies will have to await the labours of others.

Even so, to recap the start of this chapter, I am broadly in agreement with the emphasis in work on cult television that what might be considered the 'mythological' notion of a cult show's origins amongst fans should be tempered by realising both the importance of its written origins *alongside* the reasons why programmes emerge when they do, looking as they do, in a complex and often-shifting industrial and socio-historical landscape.[28] If we do begin thus – by contextualising the oft-told story – then the ground can be established for further interdisciplinary analysis of a show like *Columbo*: as though it were an artefact able to reveal much about how the shaping of attention has transformed along with *Columbo*'s changing socio-historical context.

In sum, that some aspects of this analysis of *Columbo* may contribute something of interest to Television Studies is to be hoped for. Nevertheless, the major intervention remains in and for film-philosophy, around our understanding of how television shapes attention. Crucially though, and

---

[26] Other ideas surrounding cult television similarly fall short of explaining *Columbo*'s cult cache. For example, it does not offer the same kitsch pleasures as Mark Jancovich and Nathan Hunt identify of *Columbo*'s contemporary, *The Six Million Dollar Man* (1974–1978). As Jancovich and Hunt note, this popular primetime show of the same era has latterly gained a cult afterlife on more specialist channels. Yet, *Columbo* does not share its kitsch appeal from 'production values [which] have come to appear hopelessly outdated' (2004: 29).

[27] For Hills: 'an approach that recognises how cult texts, their producers, and their fans are all institutionally located' (2004: 522).

[28] See Hills, on how the fan community is involved in the creation of the story of a show's origination or its, as it were, *auteur* (2002: 133).

the reason for the above engagement with key aspects of the interdisciplinary terrain, this intervention can occur precisely *because* of existing work on attention in Television Studies. Rather than this book advancing Television Studies, then, Television Studies advances film-philosophy. We might even say that it creates a further work, of television-philosophy. Just how this happens is tackled in the next chapter, which also commences the analysis of how *Columbo* shapes attention.

CHAPTER 2

Pay Strict Attention

In 'Identity Crisis' (1975), Columbo investigates CIA operative, Nelson Brenner (Patrick McGoohan) who has murdered a fellow operative going by the alias of A. J. Henderson (Leslie Nielsen). Brenner and Henderson previously worked in Latin America, covertly influencing the Cold War in Uruguay and Bolivia. Part-way through his investigation, Columbo is picked up by the CIA, and the Director of the Special Department, Washington, says to him: 'I want you to pay strict attention.' The Director then reveals that Brenner is one of his operatives. Taking this advice literally, Columbo listens carefully to the tape-recording Brenner uses to establish his (false) alibi and finds the clues that establish Brenner's guilt. Revealing the results of his detective work to Brenner, Columbo reiterates the CIA Director's advice: 'pay strict attention'. This episode from the time of the end of the war in Vietnam brings into focus how *Columbo* engages with the purpose, not to mention the value, of paying attention. Columbo pays attention to solve crimes, a matter which is seen – in the 1970s – as integral to a global geopolitical context in which the USA's national security is key.

When *Columbo* returns to the screen, as the Cold War draws to a close at the end of the 1980s, this same engagement with attention recurs but is given a very different emphasis. Fifteen years later, in 'Columbo Cries Wolf' (1990) the proprietors of a men's magazine trick Columbo into paying attention to their activities. The murder of one of the business partners by the other is faked, leaving a trail for Columbo to follow on CCTV. The magazine's owners use the scandal which surrounds the investigation, the publicity and global press attention in particular, to increase its monetary value. The emphasis on how attention should be channelled remains: again Columbo pays attention to solve a crime. This time, however, it is figured as part of a context in which the USA's economic prosperity, due to its global business connections, is key (the magazine sale involves a British media magnate, who conducts international business transactions with Japanese businessmen in LA). The monetisation of attention by the attention industries – seen in the value publicity can add to the financial worth of a magazine on the international market – has supplanted the Cold War era's dedication to surveillance in the service of national security.

With this difference in mind, this chapter has two purposes. Firstly, it outlines two complementary dimensions through which *Columbo* can be understood to negotiate the shaping of attention: textual and socio-historical. These dimensions bring together the two levels of theoretical analysis which inform the chapters that follow. Initially, Television Studies' engagement with how the medium actively works to attract our attention is outlined, enabling an exploration especially of how the unique narrative structure of *Columbo* (understood to function like a game) works to attract and shape viewer attention. Following this, theories of attention, especially those which focus on it being historically determined, are introduced. The brief survey of this field includes the identification of the notion of the attention economy (or, at least, the attention industries), which indicates the continued relevance of understanding how attention is increasingly monetised in the late twentieth/early twenty-first century. This first purpose takes up much of the chapter.

Secondly, the chapter provides a brief analysis of 'Identity Crisis' alongside 'Columbo Cries Wolf' to illuminate *Columbo*'s engagement with this shift in how attention is channelled societally during these decades, whilst neoliberalism emerged to prominence from the ashes of the Cold War. As noted previously, what Columbo does – paying attention in order to solve a crime – does not change. The four key ways in which he does this – how he performs, learns, polices and locates himself – are equally evident across both episodes. The ingredients, as it were, for being a good attentive labourer were thus already evident in the early 1970s as the world turned towards neoliberalism as a dominant economic ideology. What changes, then, is the backdrop to his actions. This change starkly reveals the historical transformation in how (as in, *to what ends*) attention was channelled during the end of the twentieth century: from attention in the service of national security to attention for individual economic prosperity. The introductory discussion of these four aspects of Columbo's attentiveness at the close of this chapter is thus intended to set up the more in-depth exploration of each in the subsequent chapters.

'Just One More Thing . . .'

Television is known for its ability to attract our attention and *Columbo* uses several devices to do so. It is worth unpacking the first of these points before focusing in on what *Columbo* does to attract our attention.

Since the early 1980s, Television Studies has explored the 'attention-seeking' nature of the medium. Intrinsic to definitions of television, then, are the typically domestic 'practices of looking' associated with it (Spigel 2004: 2). For example, as early as 1982, John Ellis famously noted that television works on the assumption that the viewer may not be giving their full attention to the small screen in the corner of the room. Because 'attention has to be solicited and grasped' by the television, various devices are deployed to attract the potential viewer's 'glance' its way. This may include a catchy theme tune, for example, or canned laughter (1982: 162–163). Nowadays, television is a device desirous of our attention amidst a distracting milieu increasingly full of competing screens (Morley 1986; Spigel 1992: 73–98; Lotz 2007b: 19–20 and 51; Modleski 2008: 90–96; Hassoun 2014).

This understanding of the function of television, especially within the domestic sphere in the twentieth century, opens out onto broader concerns which are helpful for this discussion of *Columbo*'s particular manner of attention seeking. As John Caughie observes, drawing on Jonathan Crary's work on attention (Crary's work is outlined further below), television's negotiation of the contrary pulls of attention and distraction – indicative of the 'instability of attention' – mirrors those of modernity more generally (2008: 13–14). Hence, back in 1986, Sut Jhally and Bill Livant posit that the act of watching television 'reflects the organisation of human labour in the economy as a whole' (1986: 124). Put another way, watching television can be understood as a form of work. It is a type of labour which mines our attention rather than our manual activities, and which demands long hours. Twenty years later, to bring the discussion back to the present, this is again stated explicitly by Jonathan Beller who, also developing upon Crary, argues that the act of looking has become a key form of labour in our electronically interconnected, global economy (2006: 2). Younger generations in the USA, for example, currently dedicate as much as seventy hours a week to paying attention to screens (Roda 2019: 7), the temporal equivalent of two full-time jobs. In such a context, *Columbo*'s soliciting of the attention of the viewer is not news. After all, this book sets out to demonstrate that there is something very televisual about the way in which attention is shaped, which can be uncovered by analysing this one particular show. Specifically, then, it is how (and to what ends) *Columbo* shapes attention which rewards further exploration.

Most apparently, there is Columbo's trademark catchphrase, 'there is just one more thing . . .'. This is typically delivered to attract viewer attention to the screen and is followed by a pregnant pause to give us time to focus on Columbo's latest revelation about his investigation. In terms of attention seeking, it is the *Columbo* equivalent of canned laughter. The pause in particular provides a clear prompt to the distracted viewer that something important is about to be revealed about the case, a turn of the screw in Columbo's pursuit of the criminal. The dramatic intent of the line becomes very evident if we remember that Peter Falk's accentuated delivery of it is so different from its more typical, and entirely unremarkable, use as a stock phrase in detective shows of the era. For example, the line, or a very similar equivalent, is delivered by both McCloud and Quincy in their respective eponymous shows in the NBC *Mystery Movie* wheel. Only, on those occasions, it is said without the same fanfare or dramatic purpose given to it by Falk.[1] Hence we can see how, whilst diegetically (in the narrative world) Falk's self-conscious performance of the line – milked so beautifully over the decades – is designed to make the murderer sweat, even so, extra-diegetically (beyond its function in the narrative world) this pause also has an important role to play in how *Columbo* attracts the viewer's attention to the screen.

In this direct appeal to the viewer we can also see how the show's theatrical and literary origins are adapted to the medium of television. *Columbo*, as is often noted, is a very talky show, with little of the action found in much crime drama – more Agatha Christie than *Kojak* (1973–1978), as Richard Levinson and William Link note was their intention when creating an 'English drawing-room mystery' focused on 'dialogue and ingenuity' rather than action (1981b: 28). We can thus consider the attention-seeking function of Columbo's catchphrase to be the equivalent to music in other, more action-packed 1970s television cop shows. Much as the pronounced guitar wah-wah and insistent trumpet punctuations of *The Streets of San Francisco* (1972–1977) seek to draw viewer attention to the visual pleasure of rooftop pursuits and speedy car chases through scenic streets, so too here Columbo's catchphrase attracts the viewer to its key selling point: Columbo's attention to the case. Indeed, there is nothing out of the ordinary about this emphasis on dialogue. Television is closely linked in its origins to radio and has been defined as more akin to radio with pictures than small-screen cinema (Ellis 1982; Corner 1999: 37). This emphasis on dialogue as a form of hail to the viewer is extremely apparent, for instance, in Levinson and Link's *Ellery Queen Mysteries* (1975–1976), in which the eponymous lead directly addresses the audience (breaching the fourth wall convention), challenging them to solve the crime before he

[1] In 'Somebody's Out to Get Jennie' (1971), season two of *McCloud* (1970–1977), McCloud says 'Just one other thing before I forget.' In 'Snake Eyes' (1977), season two of *Quincy, M.E.* (1976–1983), Quincy says 'One more thing, in case you didn't know it.'

reveals the answer. Hence, we should understand Columbo's catchphrase to function as a hailing device for potentially distracted viewers who might be eating, talking, or doing housework or homework.

Various other attention-seeking elements of *Columbo* can be similarly noted. For example, consider the rotating guest appearances by famous film and television stars playing the murderers. As Richard A. Blum and Richard D. Lindheim observe:

> Series often turn to special casting to attract attention during critical ratings periods. Casting of public figures, sports figures, movie stars, music performers, and other known personalities as special guest stars has proved to be an effective method of attracting attention. (1987: 154)

This explains both the numerous special guest stars of large and small screens on *Columbo*, but also the choice of famous country star Johnny Cash as murderer, and the standout cameos by Edith Head, selected stars of the LA Lakers, Ron Cey of the LA Dodgers, Little Richard and even Robby the Robot. Yet the catchphrase, star casting, cameos and other such devices are really just microcosmic elements of what takes place at the narrative level. It is *Columbo*'s distinctive structure – with the murder at the beginning, known to the viewer but not to Columbo – which is the big attention grabber. This could seem, perhaps, counter-intuitive. This revelation of the murderer early on might seem to remove the need to pay attention later. However, the opposite is true. The viewing experience, due to this particular structure, suggests a game of paying attention which we are invited to play. We know how the murder was committed, but have we paid enough attention to the unfolding investigation to realise how Columbo will figure it out? Put another way, we have seen all the clues, but can we realise their *relevance* before Columbo *reveals* them to us? Admittedly, this is not, in itself, a particularly outstanding revelation solely in terms of how *Columbo* functions. It has been stated by critics since the 1970s.[2] However, that this is like a memory game, a rather complex one designed to hone how well we pay attention, is not usually addressed.

As Raymond Williams notes, games are prevalent on television. Most apparently, physical games, especially televised sports, are incredibly

---

[2] In 1975, in *Films in Review*, Alvin H. Marill notes: 'We've seen all the clues, yet Columbo routinely confronts the murderer, after virtually annoying him to death, with one we've somehow missed. And that's it. Yet we're willing to come back for another serving because, for all of the Falk schtick and the incredible amount of padding, its great fun' (p. 41).

popular (Curtin and Shattuc 2009: 2). More than this, for Williams: 'Several parlour games which had in effect disappeared have been restructured as television shows, and use has been made of every kind of quiz and guessing game' (1990: 70). Games, it would seem, are good for engaging viewer attention as they require active involvement. This is also a feature of murder mysteries. The game-like nature of *Columbo*'s narrative structure harks back to the show's origins in the country house mystery. This literary genre has been considered, since John G. Cawelti's work in the 1970s, to reduce crime to 'a puzzle, a game' (1976: 105). As Martin Edwards notes, the 'pleasure of trying to solve a puzzle' goes a long way towards explaining the longevity of the popularity of the country house mystery, not to mention the leisure activity of related contemporary activities, like participating in a murder mystery weekend (2016: 7).

Yet there is a key difference. As noted in Chapter 1, *Columbo* follows the very specific tradition established in the mystery novels of R. Austin Freeman, of revealing the murderer initially. This is not a structure entirely typical of the country house drama, the puzzle in which is usually one of figuring out whodunnit before the detective does. Is *Columbo* most accurately described as a puzzle, then? Or rather, in *Columbo* is there much to be puzzled about, considering the narrative is entirely linear and the murderer and manner of death are known to the viewer?[3] In fact, *Columbo* is even more linear than a whodunnit, as there is generally no need for a suspenseful 'reveal' (after first gathering together all the suspects in the drawing room) as per the country house drama generically. *Columbo* does not typically require a flashback, for example, because we have seen the murder in the first place. As we already know the answer to the question of 'whodunnit?', there is no puzzle (about the past) to solve.

Rather, *Columbo* offers a slightly different kind of game for the viewer to play. Firstly, the viewer must pay close attention, honing their skills at observing what they do see during the murder, so as to, secondly, ascertain how Columbo can piece it together in his investigation. The game, then, is not to figure out who did it, but to figure out how Columbo will figure it out. And it is in this process that memory is key. There are three stages to this process. Firstly, during the murder, did we spot the clues that Columbo has to spot to solve it? Then, secondly, whilst remembering the murder itself, can we figure out how Columbo figures it out? Third and

---

[3] As a telling contrast, since the millennium there have been many 'puzzle films' which create giant narrative enigmas. Warren Buckland identifies these films as embracing 'nonlinearity, time loops, and fragmented spatio-temporal reality' (2009: 6). Paradigmatic films include *Memento* (2000), and on television, *Lost* (2004–2010).

finally, can we anticipate how he may trap the killer or otherwise secure a confession?

In the course of this complex memory game the viewer is both witness and investigator. *Columbo* begins with the murder, meaning that as viewers we become witnesses to a crime. The game here is to pay attention and log events in our memories. In tension with our apparently all-knowing position, though, is the role we must then play as investigator: the test of whether or not we can be as attentive as Columbo. Even whilst there is nothing that we, the audience, have not seen, *Columbo* also tests how alert we are, how well we were paying attention. We may initially have been witnesses, but now we are amateur detectives. It is in this way, then, that *Columbo* functions as a mental exercise, a complex memory game in fact, to hone our skills at paying attention as both witness and investigator.

In this respect, the importance of clues in *Columbo* cannot be underestimated. At first glance, Columbo often seems as though he is following his gut instinct when pursuing a murderer. However, as Sheldon Catz has shown in impressive detail, Columbo is actually always following a key clue or clues when he begins to hone in on the killer (2016: 141–187). For example, in the second episode of the first series, 'Death Lends a Hand' (1971), the murderer, the head of a private investigation agency called Brimmer (Robert Culp), lashes out at his victim with a backhanded strike. Columbo seems to focus in on the murderer with impossibly rapid divination on first meeting him. This seems purely instinctive at the time of first watching. Yet, ultimately, it transpires that Columbo, having noticed a bruise and a distinctive cut on the victim's left cheek, began immediately to seek a left-handed killer wearing a large and equally distinctive ring. This he quickly ascertains was the case with Brimmer by disingenuously feigning an interest in astrology and palmistry and giving Brimmer's left hand an impromptu reading. During this silliness Columbo takes the opportunity to examine the ring on Brimmer's left hand and finds the two diamonds which left the distinctive cut.

Columbo does not follow gut instinct, then, but clues, and thus the game of attention for the viewer is to realise what is motivating Columbo's investigative turns. We must try to remember the clues the murderer left behind, and then also to realise how they might be informing Columbo's thinking. There are any number of illustrative examples throughout the show's lifetime, a colourful one being the pink carnation absent from a conductor's lapel during the filmed performance of a concert at the Hollywood Bowl in 'Étude in Black' (1972). We see the carnation fall at the crime scene, knocked out of the lapel by the exertion of the deadly blow. This is not a subtle or hidden clue. Quite the opposite. The camera specifically provides a foregrounded and sudden zoom in on the flower, on the floor, as the killer departs without realising its loss. The first question this poses for the viewer is whether Columbo will realise its importance, which he does after spotting the murderer, maestro conductor Alex Benedict (John Cassavetes), retrieving it at the crime scene. The second, though, as important, is whether he will determine how to use it to convict the musical killer. This Columbo does by re-watching tapes of Benedict conducting the concert (carnation missing), which we also saw in the narrative, against the footage of him leaving the crime scene after retrieving the carnation (carnation back in his lapel).

During the concert, when Benedict realises that the carnation is missing from his lapel whilst in the midst of conducting, the zoom in on the carnation in the crime scene is intercut, along with the noise of the shrieking parrot which accompanied the murder, to visualise Benedict's realisation that he lost and must retrieve the flower from the crime scene. This jarring editing and sound combination, so out of place at the concert, leads seamlessly into an identical zoom in, plus an accentuating freeze frame, on the lapel where Benedict's carnation should be. Yet even with the pointed help of the editing, cinematography and soundtrack (the two matching zooms, the intercutting, the parrot shrieking and the freeze frame when Benedict realises the carnation's absence), remembering *and also realising the import for how Benedict will be caught by Columbo*, all together, is not easy. This challenge, indeed, is often what makes the memory game of *Columbo* so enjoyable.

This idea of *Columbo* as a complex memory game brings us back to the previous chapter's exploration of the show's inconsistent narrative world. *Columbo* is unusual in this respect, at least in contrast to other long-running cult series which create the impression that a coherent universe exists beyond the fraction of it seen in the show (e.g. *Buffy the Vampire Slayer* [1997–2003] and its 'Buffyverse'). This difference can be further explained by *Columbo*'s game-like function. Like many games of attention which test memory, with each episode *Columbo* deliberately resets to zero. The next time the game is played, its parameters will be the same but what transpires within them will be different. This is much as anyone playing tic-tac-toe will expect to see the same distinctive empty frame at the commencement of each game but will experience each game as unique. Or, more accurately, considering the role of memory in the viewer's 'playing' of *Columbo*, it is like in the electronic game *Simon*, from the late 1970s, in which the player has to remember and repeat the sequence of flashes of the coloured touch pad which is unique to every iteration of the game. With each new *Columbo*, then, the inconsistency of each iteration with respect to the broader Columboverse gestured towards (i.e. this week Mrs Columbo is the biggest fan of celebrity X, who Columbo happens to be investigating, whilst last week it was celebrity Y) indicates that there is not one but, rather, an infinitely multiple number of possible 'Columboverses'. Each episode pushes reset, creating a new iteration of the 'Columbomultiverse' within which our complex memory game will take place.

For this reason, whilst *Columbo* provides the same kind of mental practice as many games, like the card game Patience, or, a Sudoku puzzle, due to its emphasis on memory its closest correlative is Kim's Game. In Kim's Game, a series of objects are introduced to the observer, before being covered. Memory recall is then tested in the naming of as many objects as can be remembered. The game's name derives from its appearance in the famous novel, *Kim*, by Rudyard Kipling, in which it is known as 'The Play of the Jewels'. The game is used in the training of the novel's eponymous hero, Kim, in the arts of spying ([1994] 1901: 165–167). *Columbo* functions similarly to Kim's Game, albeit, as noted, it is more complex. *Columbo* asks us, what did you see (during the murder)? Then, it covers that up again, as it were, and introduces the detective. Now, finally, it asks, where is each of the things you saw, and what is its importance as it recurs in the investigation? Each time we play, of course, the game will be reset – new objects chosen, or, rather, a new murder committed and new clues revealed – which is necessary to make it effective as a complex test of memory that focuses attention.

The differences between *Columbo* and Kim's Game are instructive to consider. The most important of them is the added twist of the attentive viewer also having to realise the possible role of what they see during the murder in obscuring or revealing the guilt of the murderer. This is also what differentiates *Columbo* from other detective shows which could otherwise be said to function similarly. The distinction would be that in *Columbo* the actual crime is seen, rather than the first introduction to the murder being the crime scene, the murder having already been committed. As we see and understand more about motive, means and opportunity due to having seen the murder, there is nothing necessarily mysterious for the brilliant detective to reveal. Hence the detective does not know more than us, as is so often the case, but less. Indeed, in this respect the depiction of Columbo as a lower middle-class 'everyman' plays into the idea that at best he is the viewer's equal, but certainly not their superior (see Chapter 5). With nothing new to emerge, in *Columbo* there is a distinct emphasis on memory instead. This encourages viewers to labour attentively at 'solving' the case with precisely the same vigour as Columbo, only by using slightly different faculties.

Beyond the functioning of the text itself, the similarities with Kim's Game help further clarify what may initially appear perplexing about this discussion of *Columbo* as a game. After all, if watching television is, in fact, an act of labour, then how can *Columbo* be a game? Surely a game involves play and thus provides respite from labour? In fact, the evocation of a game is not intended to suggest that our daily lives should be understood as acts of play.[4] Rather, the complex memory game internal to *Columbo* is a way of training attention for attentive labour, much as Kim's Game is a mental exercise to sharpen attentive focus used by organisations like the Boy Scouts (after take-up in the early twentieth century) and even for military training (Hopkirk 1996: 157).[5] In terms of the act of looking being one of labouring, then, *Columbo* is a complex memory game which improves our attentive labouring functions. As will be discussed in Chapter 4, a feature of *Columbo* is that it focuses viewer attention on learning about the new technologies they encounter in everyday life. There is a sense, then, in which *Columbo* as game can be understood to act as a kind of (televisual) simulator (in the sense of, flight simulator) giving viewers a chance to practise the honing of attention required in a technologically-oriented world. *Columbo*, in effect, offers us *a gaming experience designed to enhance our ability to labour by looking*.

In this respect it is worth remembering that *Columbo*, along with the NBC *Mystery Movie* wheel, was quickly moved from Wednesday to Sunday nights. James Monaco, writing in 1977, notes that this is the moment in the week when the most 'innovatory and attractive' shows of the era screened (Monaco states only four such shows, in his view, including *Columbo*). Tellingly, for Monaco the weekend is 'the one period in the weekly schedule when audiences can be assumed to have enough energy actually to watch, follow and actively enjoy a programme' (1977: 160). Once again, then, what we might consider peak leisure time is, in fact, a period of intense, active (looking as) labour. Hence *Columbo* is like a game, but like Kim's Game it has serious implications for how people are trained to behave by television. After all, in terms of the labour of looking, the complex memory game involved in *Columbo* is the perfect tool for

---

[4] This position is typically advocated by scholars of computer games and may indicate their interest in making the case that the world be understood thusly (e.g. Zimmermann and Chaplin 2013; Sicart 2014).

[5] The UK's Royal Navy indicates that Kim's games are used as part of its sniper training, on a web page dated 2014 but still active in 2020, and with an updated news feed: https://www.royalnavy.mod.uk/news-and-latest-activity/news/2014/july/31/140731-royal-marines-sniper-training (accessed on 9 January 2020).

honing viewer attention to what some consider to be their real purpose at the screen, the consumption of the advertisements that the show delivers. Whilst the viewer is actively playing the game of trying to remember what they saw during the murder, and of figuring out why this will be important to Columbo's investigation, they are also involved in a similar memory game: recalling what they saw advertised so as to remember what they must now purchase.

When understood to be like a game, there is an evident pleasure in repeating the experience by watching an(other) episode of *Columbo*. But in this respect, what happens in *Columbo* is at odds with the findings of a body of work on the temporally elongated nature of our engagement with television. This includes long-running shows of different kinds, from sit-coms to soap operas to so-called quality television. This area of scholarship notes, in particular, the manner in which engagement with character is fostered, including through the longer-term nature of the viewer's shared history with a favourite show (e.g. Nannicelli 2016: 69–72). In this respect, a contemporary cop show like the BBC's *Luther* (2010–2019), although in part inspired by *Columbo* (each episode commences with the crime, for example), is in actual fact very different. *Luther*, unlike *Columbo*, engages the audience with the nuances of the personality of the eponymous character over several series, just as this literature tends to argue (Turnbull 2014: 147). *Columbo*, however, does not. It presses restart with every episode in every respect, including depth of Columbo's character. Repeated watching of *Columbo* is thus not pleasurable because it helps deepen appreciation of a consistent character any more than it helps us to navigate a coherent 'Columboverse'. If anything, Columbo's character is so engaging because of the enigmas and inconsistencies which emerge with each new repetition in difference (e.g. Mrs Columbo's fandom repeats, only with a different celebrity focus). Rather, it is pleasurable to watch an(other) *Columbo* because each episode tests (and improves) our attentive powers: *Columbo* as Kim's Game.[6]

---

[6] The cult appeal of *Columbo* may lie in the chance it offers of 'having another go' at a puzzle once attempted years previously, or, alternatively, reruns of *Columbo* may offer the opportunity to try a new puzzle (if you did not see the episode before, or have forgotten it), or, to try again to *recall* what were the clues that you missed the first time. This process can take place over a temporal distance which might stretch into years or decades. This is not the same as explaining cult success in terms of nostalgia. The idea that nostalgia may play a role, albeit without being the sole reason for a show's cult status, is sometimes evoked in discussions of cult television. Yet, as Angelina I. Karpovich notes of *The Avengers* (1961–1969), nostalgia does not provide a very full explanation of its, or any, cult following. Rather, Karpovich argues that 'contemporary and subsequent viewers

Hence analysis of the narrative structure of *Columbo* begins to reveal what the rest of the book will explore in depth: there is a link between its function, in enabling the practising of attentiveness as though it were a game, and the broader socio-historical context in which it emerged. John G. Cawelti's influential work is useful here. Cawelti notes that the genre of the country house drama, that which *Columbo* updates, typically offered a 'temporary release' from the 'cultural tensions' of the late nineteenth and early twentieth centuries. It provided a safety valve to rid readers of 'doubt and guilt, generated at least in part by the decline of traditional moral and spiritual authorities, and the rise of new social and intellectual movements that emphasized the hypocrisy and guilt of respectable middle-class society' (1976: 104). As we shall see in Chapter 5, in Cawelti's analysis of the cultural functioning of the classical detective novel we find very much the same reasons that are given for the emergence of *Columbo* in the 1970s, as the viewing public came around to the idea of watching white-collar criminals getting their comeuppance (Stephenson-Burton 1995: 135). This shift in public mood occurred due to the civil rights, feminist and hippy movements; to Watergate; to the Vietnam protests; and to the generally pervasive realisation that the USA's post-war affluence was not equally available to all.

For Cawelti, the classical detective story offered reassurance to readers who might be feeling the kinds of 'doubt and guilt' noted above in specific ways. Firstly, it reassured that crime was just a matter of 'individual motivations', and not the fault of the social order per se. Secondly, 'by reducing crime to a puzzle, a game, and a highly formalised set of literary conventions, it transformed an increasingly serious moral and social problem into an entertaining pastime' (1976: 105). This second feature, in fact, reaffirms the first. Together, both aspects reassured readers that crime is not something which the existing social order is to be blamed for. Instead, it is but a matter of a few rotten apples threatening to spoil the otherwise healthy barrel. As importantly, it is something which the current social order is equipped to, and indeed does, control.

---

recognise . . . a range and complexity of narrative and stylistic elements that distinguish it from, and make it more culturally significant than, most other television shows of its genre and period' (2010: 41). Equally, any attempt to reduce *Columbo*'s cult status to solely nostalgia does not provide a full enough conclusion. For example, the nostalgia offered by encountering former stars of the silver screen in *Columbo* cannot explain why *Columbo* has a much larger cult following than other shows offering the same pleasures, like *The Love Boat* (1977–1987). *Columbo*'s game-like nature and the inconsistency of the Columboverse together offer a fuller explanation for its cult longevity (alongside Falk's performance of the character of Columbo, as explored in Chapter 3).

The reassurance is thus that there is no need to question whether the appearance of crime might suggest that the barrel itself is actually rotten (a topic I return to in Chapter 5). This reassurance is integral to the role into which *Columbo* casts the viewer, as both witness to and investigator of the crime. The reassurance that society is not thoroughly rotten, but only a few of its bad apples, justifies the blanket call to participate in surveillance culture (as witness and investigator). Hence, playing the game of *Columbo* is to participate in the everyday paying of attention to all aspects of life as though it may reveal information that will be important in determining another party's guilt at a later date.

This channelling of the viewer's attentive labour naturalises the link between being attentive and the all-seeing (and all-seen) nature of the surveillance society that emerged during the period in which *Columbo* was on our screens. This Gilles Deleuze famously referred to as the late twentieth-century's emerging control society, in which we are no longer surveilled within contained institutions as we were in Michel Foucault's panopticon model for the disciplinary society of the eighteenth and nineteenth centuries (in schools, prisons, barracks, factories). Instead, we are increasingly subject to 'ultra-rapid forms of free-floating control' (1992: 4) which permeate society. Surveillance, accordingly, has become ubiquitous. As a key example, Deleuze discusses how the prison, an institution which exemplified the panopticon model in its manner of constraining criminals, is gradually being supplemented by measures for restraining people within society itself. These include 'the use of electronic collars that force the convicted person to stay at home during certain hours' (1992: 7). In the control society, we are discouraged from mass political actions, and, instead, set one against each other in competition, as per the atomising individualism of neoliberalism (p. 5). Policing, accordingly, becomes a matter of our perpetually policing each other, and, indeed, ourselves (see also Chapter 5).

To flashforward briefly, this is a situation which various contemporary television shows are currently involved in negotiating, as Colin Gardner illuminates when expertly analysing the BBC television series *Spooks* (2002–2011). The illustrative quote which Gardner chooses from Gilles Deleuze and Félix Guattari's *A Thousand Plateaus* (1987) very succinctly describes the situation in which *Columbo*'s channelling of viewer attention is also situated. This is a world in which peace is maintained via micro-fascisms, 'based on perpetual fear, "giving any and everybody the mission of a self-appointed judge, dispenser of justice, policeman, the neighbourhood SS man"' (2018: 141). The training which *Columbo* offers its viewers in how to pay attention, whilst itself a small cog in this huge machine, remains instructive of our grasp of the bigger socio-historical picture. *Columbo* as Kim's Game trains its viewers to be everyman policemen, like Columbo himself, perpetually labouring to pay attention.

To begin to consider the game-like nature of *Columbo* in context, how does this training of the viewer's attention sit within a broader panorama of the shaping of attention under modernity? In particular, in terms of the latter decades of the twentieth century when the show was on air.

From Paying Attention to Making Attention Pay

The idea that our attention is channelled so as to ensure that the emergence of society is shaped in a specific way and functions in a certain manner is not a new one. In *Suspensions of Perception* (1999) the art historian Jonathan Crary outlines how the way in which we pay attention is shaped by historical forces and will be particular to a given era. For example, in late nineteenth-century Western society, the madding swirl of modernity created rapidly expanding urban environments. This required a new regime of attention from the population as new visual media offered competing attractions for the eye (amusement parks, music halls, cinemas, and so on). What people are encouraged to focus their attention on, and what is left to occupy the background, is thus revealing of the emergence of historically specific forms of subjectivity (1999: 1–4). For film and media scholar Jonathan Beller, in *The Cinematic Mode of Production* (2006), it is enough to consider the famous idea about how national identity is created, Benedict Anderson's theory of the construction of imagined communities via the synchronicity created by mass transport and media forms in the nineteenth century. What this means, as Beller indicates, is that something as powerful as a nation can be constructed from reading national newspapers (2006: 6). If enough people are paying attention to the same news simultaneously, then it seemingly concerns them all. Thus our attention creates the borders of the community which mass media help us to collectively imagine ourselves a part of, and the idea of the self as a national subject. Indeed, with the post-Cold War rise to global prominence of neoliberal globalisation, the 'imaginary' which people feel they communally belong to may be as much global as it is national (Steger 2008: 179).

Nowadays, the mass use of, say, newspapers in cafes and on railway stations along with radio in the home (as per the early–mid-twentieth century) still exists. However, they have been supplemented by the more atomising use of portable electronic devices in coffee shops and airports along with

TV and the internet at home. As Waddick Doyle and Claudia Roda summarise in *Communication in the Era of Attention Scarcity* (2019: 2):

> The multiplication of communication channels and platforms, caused by the digital transformation of our media systems, generates increasing demands on our attention, to the point that often we do not know which way to turn nor even how to spend the attention we do have given the quantity of communication channels available.

Both of these historical moments, even though they require us to interface with different media, indicate how attention is channelled by modernity. What, then, of how attention was shaped in the late twentieth century precisely: the era of *Columbo* very specifically?

Coinciding with the start of *Columbo*, in seminal works from 1969 and 1971, Herbert A. Simon observed that with new technologies, especially computers, proliferating an abundance of information the attention needed to process it was growing scarce. Information, Simon argued, 'consumes the attention of its recipients. A wealth of information creates a poverty of attention and a need to allocate that attention efficiently among the overabundance of information sources that might consume it' (Simon 1971: 40–41). Put simply: if attention is scarce in an information-rich world then some information will be filtered out – lost, effectively – if no one pays it any attention. Hence, strategic decisions must now be made regarding how best to utilise the finite human attention available to process ubiquitous information (Simon [1969] 1996: 143–144).

By the late 1990s and early 2000s, with internet usage expanding rapidly, and especially in the wake of the dot.com bubble (and the Millennium Bug), there emerged into popular consciousness the idea that an 'attention economy' may exist (Davenport and Beck 2001; Lanham 2006). Like Simon before them, writers exploring this topic emphasise that attention has become a scarce commodity. However, now it is the online digital era which provides the informing context. Suddenly information overload is an issue for everyone who can access the world wide web, whether at home or at work (Lanham 2006: 6–8). Admittedly, it is debatable whether an attention economy exists, or whether we are actually discussing the changing ways in which attention is shaped: the ecology of attention, as it is increasingly being theorised.[7] After all, those who identified the attention economy were not entirely disinterested parties, the term being first coined in 1990 by a future Google CEO (Crary 2013: 75). It is perhaps

---

[7] A useful summary of some of the positions currently developing, especially relating to digital technologies, can be found in Roda (2019).

more accurate, then, to talk about the recent growth of certain attention *industries* channelling attention in specific ways. In *The Attention Economy* (2001), Thomas H. Davenport and John C. Beck, whilst outlining their argument regarding 'the business implications of attention' (p. viii), ultimately provide key examples from the 'attention industries' of 'advertising, movies, television and publishing' (p. 93). This more specific terminology makes more sense, especially in light of the developing role of television in the twentieth century as a delivery system for advertising, designed to grab the attention of viewers, and because of how such attention industries can be understood to contribute to the economy more broadly by channelling attentive labour (Davenport and Beck 2001: 93). Nevertheless, the term attention economy has taken hold, and is gradually becoming synonymous with scholarly explorations of the society which exists under neoliberalism: late capitalist or, increasingly, post-industrial society (e.g. Bueno 2017).

As noted, how attention is channelled in any epoch influences how subjectivity is constructed. This is true of *Columbo*'s epoch, but also today's. Crary, for instance, lucidly traces a historical timeline from Thomas Edison (the Kinetoscope of 1893) to Bill Gates (the proliferation of personal computers in the 1980s) to illustrate how the attention of consumers of visual media has been channelled over the course of the twentieth century. The commonality is these devices' rendering of people *socially isolated* in their consumption of images and sounds (Crary 1999: 32–33). This emphasis on isolation also involves a degree of hollowing out of subjectivity, with how well one pays attention being assessed against what is happening externally: how well one can keep up with the changing pace of modernity (Crary 1999: 81–84). As Crary summarises: 'Attention thus became an imprecise way of designating the relative capacity of a subject to selectively isolate certain contents of a sensory field at the expense of others in the interests of maintaining an orderly and productive world' (Crary 1999: 17). In other words, as Columbo learns, we are required to 'pay strict attention' at all times (as capitalism increasingly requires our engagement with attentive labour 24/7), but with most dedicated focus to our work as attentive labourers.

This longer historical perspective is worth exploring further to assist the analysis of attention in *Columbo* which follows. As observed earlier, not everyone is entirely convinced that there is an attention economy, or at least not in the manner in which it has recently been theorised. Exemplifying this helpful scepticism is Yves Citton's *The Ecology of Attention* ([2014] 2017). Citton positions himself in line with Crary and Beller in making the case that attention overload is not precisely a recent phenomenon relating to late twentieth-century information technologies but has been understood to exist for centuries. A clear example Citton gives (drawing on Ann Blair) is the seventeenth-century development of the now familiar Table of Contents page for books. This was designed to enable readers to 'oriente [sic] themselves in the overabundance of texts, in which they already feared they may drown' (2017: 12). Even in the twentieth century, many decades before the introduction of the computer, the consequences of the increased attention required of workers under industrialisation – in particular 'an "exhaustion of attention"' – was noted as early as 1902 by sociologist Gabriel Tarde (p. 5). So too did Tarde understand the manner in which the adverts for the new goods which industrialisation produced worked to attract and fix attention on the product advertised, arguing that the entire newspaper was, in effect, a giant advertisement. The echo of this is clear in more recent work on the role of television as a delivery system for advertising, a process which helps to construct the very audiences who then consume the products (p. 5) (see Chapter 1). The re-emergence of the discourse of information overload in the late 1960s and early 1970s works of Simon with regard to new information technologies, Citton astutely points out, may relate as much to the then-prevailing perception of that particular moment of the post-war context as it does to the emergence of a new attention economy. After all, it coincides with Daniel Kahneman's *Attention and Effort* (1973), on the capacity and limitation of human attention, and Alvin Toffler's *Future Shock* (1970), which argued that the accelerating pace of change, in that era, was palpable (Citton 2017: 6). This latter book was even mentioned in 'A Friend in Deed' (1974), in a manner which illuminates how this historical moment was perceived by those within it as uniquely overloaded. Lieutenant Duffy (John Finnegan) asks Columbo: 'Haven't you ever heard of future shock? The world's going to hell with itself. Believe me Columbo, times have changed.'

The role of television in this process is not difficult to determine, nor is it coincidental that television became a household norm from around the 1950s to the 1970s. Tellingly in this respect, Crary's observations of how isolation is fostered by the technologies of modernity echo certain earlier scholarly observations: such as Williams's view that television contributes to a broader social shift away from media which foster communities towards those which promote more isolated consumerism (1990: 88), or again, Anne Friedberg's insights regarding how television and the VCR brought into the private sphere the 'mobilized virtual gaze' of modernity that had previously been specific to the public sphere (1993: 4). Likewise, for Crary, in the twentieth century television 'emerged as the most pervasive and effective system for the management of attention' (1999: 71) and, therefore, of the socially isolated subjects it creates. Nowadays when we watch movies or television, or spend time on the internet, we are working: 'to look is to labour' (Beller 2006: 2). Richard Dienst is helpful in clarifying why this is:

> Just as factory machines helped to aggregate and abstract human labor (as labor power) in the steam age and thereby defined the metaphysical foundations of capitalist wages and money, so now television, as a late capitalist machine, makes possible another exchange system in which time is again aggregated and valorized en masse. We work at television, participating in the creation of value that appears to us in the form of images. (1994: xi)

Accordingly, the time we spend in front of the television, the attention we give it, is integral to how value is calculated. It influences the worth which attaches to certain prime advertising slots, for example, once the ratings indicate their popularity.

Further sense can be made of this seemingly counter-intuitive idea – that looking is labour, television the twentieth century's answer to the factory machine – if we consider the example that has become crucial to twenty-first century life: the internet. Companies like Google mine the attention of those surfing the net to determine what people will pay to see (Beller 2006: 302–303). Social media platforms analyse users' 'likes' to realise what people are paying attention to, like a vast consumer survey. Again, influencers pay attention to locations and products, posting images of them online for their followers to labour by looking at. Such attention given to our attention enables, in turn, the most targeted of adverts to reach us. This is a similar strategy to that of television's recent shift to narrowcasting (see Chapter 1). Crary traces this situation back, specifically, to the introduction of television into 1950s' US society. At this time, the private space of the home was penetrated by the market (television as delivery system for adverts), annexing leisure time in the service of boosting capitalism (viewing as a form of work) and transforming the (active) expectation of citizenship into (passive) 'viewership' (2013: 79).[8] As Michael Curtin

---

[8] For decades television audiences – or at least, their attention – have been understood as commodities which are bought and sold (Smythe 1981: 231–234). Audiences 'work' for the advertiser; ensuring demand for the products advertised – paying attention to what to buy, then buying it, is their job (pp. 243–244). A more complex idea than its original enunciation in the 1980s allowed (Caraway 2011), there is now a body of literature on how the 'marketplace of attention' (Webster 2014: 2) is formed at the intersection of: media, their users, the measurement of their interactions (Webster 2014), media content, their audiences, the interventions of advertisers (Napoli 2003), technology companies, policy makers and public interest organizations (Napoli 2010).

and Jane Shattuc summarise: 'Shows attract the attention of audiences and that attention is what TV executives sell to advertisers' (2009: 34). What does this mean for the seemingly 'leisurely' act of watching television?

In a later work, *24/7*, Crary argues that the always-operational nature of global capitalism has now re-aligned humanity with markets such that the distinction between work and non-work time has been eradicated (2013). Flexible online working hours dissolve boundaries between personal and professional spheres, and the success of corporations is 'measured by the amount of information that can be extracted, accumulated, and used to predict and modify the behaviour of any individual with a digital identity' (2013: 75). Our attention is thus monetised: bought and sold to increase sales, and by turns, production. At our computers, for Beller, we are the humans-cum-batteries of *The Matrix* (1999). Entrapped within the matrix, our attention to its fictional world keeps it running (2006: 7). A more accurate dystopian *televisual* re-imagining of our contemporary world is the episode 'Fifteen Million Merits' of *Black Mirror* (2011) – in which humans work exercise cycles to store energy, attention garners currency ('merits') and people are discouraged from closing their eyes before a constant barrage of all-surround screens. In reality, attentive labourers include those employed to influence or bias public opinion via their targeted online activities. This might include so-called Russian troll farms and Chinese water armies, or the Filipino 'cleaners' who moderate content on social media sites (Zuboff 2019: 509). In short, paying attention to influence how attention is paid can now be the extent of one's employment.

The new media which ensure that the attention industries are a major shaping societal force emerge along with the increasing electronic surveillance of society. This includes: CCTV technology in public spaces, electronic monitoring of employees, biometric identification cards and passports, and surveillance security measures policing the borders between wealthy gated communities alongside impoverished slums (Graham 2013: 12–13). Most apparently, there is the greater surveillance, especially dataveillence, enabled by the internet (Fuchs et al. 2012: 3). The whole world is now increasingly watched by the technological eyes paying attention to our every move: an era of 'surveillance capitalism' (as outlined by Shoshana Zuboff [2019]), in which behaviour is monitored so closely it may be possible to predict or even influence it (see further in the Conclusion).

The emergence of this situation is noted by Columbo in 'Make me a Perfect Murder' (1978). Speaking of a fifteen-year-old nephew who has sold his stereo equipment to make, instead, 8 mm films, Columbo says: 'When I was a kid in my neighbourhood we had heroes, DiMaggio . . . You know who he's got on the wall? Francis Ford Coppola.' For Columbo's nephew, the most exciting thing to be is no longer the spectacular draw who people pay to see (DiMaggio), but the one who makes the movies grabbing everyone's attention (Coppola). Such a view resonates with Franco 'Bifo' Berardi's argument that a new kind of heroism emerged in the late 1970s, supplanting that known previously. This is, for Berardi, a shift under financial capitalism from the hero as active subject to the hero as object, or more precisely, as image designed to attract attention. Berardi's exemplar, drawing on Hito Steyerl, is David Bowie, but Columbo's own example similarly indicates the same contrast: from active hero (DiMaggio) to the new hero who, without the same physical prowess, can nevertheless draw our attention to the image (Coppola) (2015: 3–4). Thus industrial capitalism gave way, for Berardi, to 'semiocapitalism', the buying and selling of signs (2015: 90), such that by the close of the second decade of the twenty-first century the construction of the self as image, as brand, has become ubiquitous (Berardi 2015: 41–44). With the spread of social media especially, everybody has become the great director, like Coppola, creating *themselves* as image. In this context, worth is determined by how many people pay attention to you. As Waddick Doyle and Claudia Roda summarise: 'Brands represent systems for the production, distribution, and consumption of attention' (2019: 5). To flashforward, the notion of the brand as an attention-attracting strategy is so ubiquitous that the contemporary television show *American Gods* (2017–) satirises this situation by conflating cinema, television and the internet with godliness. Nowadays even a deity is conceived of as a brand, and, as such, is only as powerful as its popularity amongst its attentive followers.

Historically speaking, then, the current power of the attention industries relates to an older phenomenon, the measuring of the value of a life under capitalism (see Chapter 6). This has seen, Rey Chow notes, the religious emphasis of the nineteenth-century's Protestant work ethic (make the world a better place through your actions whilst alive) shift towards a more secular capitalist ethos in the twentieth century (make as much profit as possible) (Chow 2002: 42–44). More recently, with the prominence of the attention industries in the twenty-first century, we can argue that the emphasis shifts again towards cultivating visibility (obtain maximum attention to increase your self-worth). Thus in the contemporary era, for Beller: 'the industrialisation of vision has *shifted gears* [emphasis added]. With the rise of the internet grows the recognition of the value-productive dimensions of sensual labour in the visual register. Perception is increasingly bound to production' (2006: 3). As the world's exploitable resources gradually become exhausted, global capital turns with greater focus to the appropriation of attention itself (Beller 2006: 8–12). What the contrast between 'Identity Crisis' and 'Columbo Cries Wolf' indicates, then, is the coincidence of the lifespan of *Columbo*'s run with this *shifting of gears*. This is particularly clear in *Columbo* precisely because it is a television show. As Citton observes, Crary's work on how late nineteenth- and early twentieth-century society shaped attention exemplifies how an exploration of *aesthetics* (for Crary it is art, and we can add that for Beller it is cinema) can illuminate the longer-term processes involved in the recent reshapings of attention with the introduction of new information technologies (Citton 2017: 14–15).[9] In this instance, of course, it is television which provides the aesthetic frame through which the late twentieth-century's shifting gears become evident: *Columbo* illuminates our contemporary world's coming-into-existence at that time.

Accordingly, following Crary, Beller and Citton, this book illuminates not just that *Columbo* enables us to visualise the emergence of what might be understood to be an attention economy, but, as importantly, the way in which the societal shaping of attention has 'shifted gears' in the period during which *Columbo* was originally on our television screens. This is not a milieu from which we are necessarily able to detach ourselves and view objectively when we are a part of it. Just as the massification of attention which could be paid to newspapers helped shape the construction of national identity in the nineteenth century (and in the mid–late twentieth century the oligopoly of the three US television networks, prior to the industry's move towards narrowcasting), so too, now, we exist as part of a larger, global, 'mediasphere' which works to shape how and to what we pay attention (Citton 2017: 28–31). Yet re-viewing *Columbo* as historical artefact can provide us with the necessary hindsight to detach it momentarily from its own position as an attention-channelling television show, allowing it to illuminate the changes to how attention is shaped that occurred during the period from the late 1960s until the early 2000s.

---

[9] Citton refocuses our analysis of attention away from economics to aesthetics by analysing data mined from Google Books to observe that the use of the term 'economy of attention' has had significant peaks in the late 1890s (noticeably, around the time of the invention of cinema), and again in the 1910s (when cinema became a mainstream theatrical practice) (2017: 13). What is key for Citton is that this term emerges in writings which do not typically explore economics per se, but, rather, from around 1850–1950, works which 'situated their reflections in an aesthetic order of questioning, which was more interested in the quality of the sensible and intellectual experience than in its quantification in productivist terms' (p. 13). This term seems to have been of interest between around 1890 until the Second World War, roughly coinciding with industrial manufacturing reaching full swing in Europe and North America as a result of the Industrial Revolution (pp. 13–15).

This shifting of gears coincides with the seeming triumph of neoliberalism as economic doctrine from the 1970s onwards (with the start of *Columbo*'s run with NBC in fact), and especially once the end of the Cold War suggested there was no apparent alternative to capitalism. This is the so-called 'end of history' thesis (Fukuyama 1989) which came to prominence in the 1990s, coinciding with *Columbo*'s return to the screen with ABC. *Columbo*, then, negotiates the contradictoriness of a situation – as Claudio Celis Bueno considers it after Deleuze and Guattari's critique of capitalism in *Anti-Oedipus* (1972) – designed to at once enslave people (or rather, their attention) to machines, and yet, paradoxically, to produce (isolated) social subjects in precisely this way. A pertinent example of this paradox is television, which at once 'addresses the spectator . . . as a subject (of communication) and as a cog in a larger machine (of ratings and audiences)' (Bueno 2017: 186; see also Lazzarato 2014: 23–94). Thus *Columbo*, analysed in light of not only theories of attention like those of Crary, Beller and Citton, but also existing work on the topic in Television Studies, provides an opening onto this operation.

Columbo illuminates what the shaping of attention means for contemporary life in four key ways. These overlapping dimensions enable us to consider: firstly, how the ubiquitous nature of surveillance (coupled with the extension of work into all aspects of life), determines how our identities are performed every day; secondly, the need for constant updating of our technological skillset to keep pace with work; thirdly, the importance of protecting the veracity of history against the anti-democratic manoeuvres of (often oligarchical) capital which has the power to 'edit' how the past is remembered; and, fourthly, our relationship to life in urban locations (LA in this case) which should be understood anew in a globalised world.

All four elements can be found, in miniature, in 'Identity Crisis' and 'Columbo Cries Wolf', the different emphases across the two episodes (fifteen years apart) indicating what happened when the gears regulating attention shifted. Whilst in both episodes the generic features of the show remain the same (Columbo and indeed *Columbo* are as we expect of a detective show) what happens in the 'background' has changed due to the changing historical context. This is not, though, to suggest that the two things (Columbo and his background) are separate. Rather, as Citton argues:

> *attention is an interaction*. It represents the essential mediator charged with assuring my relationship with the environment that nourishes my survival . . . *Paying attention* is a genuine activity – preceding any form of subsequent action: it implies weaving together observations and gestures while respecting the correct level of tension for maintaining tenable relations with our milieu. (2017: 22)

Thus, whilst the way in which Columbo pays attention (his 'weaving together' of 'observations and gestures' to 'interact' with his milieu) does not change much across the show's long run (he begins and ends, the ideal attentive labourer of neoliberalism), what he is ultimately paying attention to, and what is at stake in this process, changes considerably because his 'environment' changes once the 'gears shift'.

Observing *Columbo* within its transforming historical moment, then, enables us to see the changing 'environment' with which he 'interacts' in stark relief. In this way we can observe the shifting gears of attention and their shaping of the late twentieth century. Let us begin to round off this chapter by recapping how this can be seen in the show.

Columbo Shifts Gears

Firstly, performance. 'Identity Crisis' contains numerous allusions to the ubiquity of surveillance. In The Pike (a Long Beach amusement park) where Brenner first meets Henderson, they are photographed by someone selling Polaroids as tourist souvenirs. This later becomes a clue for Columbo, placing Brenner at the scene of the crime. However, it is when Brenner reveals that he has bugged Columbo's house that 'Identity Crisis' shows how the management of attentive labour has shifted from modes established by late nineteenth-century modernity (the amusement park, which emerged along with cinema, the photograph), to newer modes (the mass commodified instant camera), concurrent with the increase in invasive surveillance technologies. 'Identity Crisis' thus shows how the increase in surveillance technologies of the Cold War are monitoring the general populace of the USA (and not just its international neighbours), eradicating the separation between private and public life.[10]

'Identity Crisis' thus emphasises that, because we are always under surveillance, whether in the public or private sphere our identities are to some degree always performed for those paying attention. This is most evident in the episode's focus on two CIA operatives whose lives are performed as false fronts. Columbo's investigation of Henderson's murder uncovers that his identity is, in fact, a constructed façade. Both Henderson and Brenner are, in effect, 'undercover' when performing their everyday lives. Indeed,

---

[10] The ubiquitous spread of paranoia-inducing Orwellian state surveillance was revealed by the Edward Snowden leak of 2013, which indicated the extent to which the population of the USA is now monitored by its own National Security Agency, and indeed, that this is part of a wider, global surveillance operation.

in the performance of innocence of the duplicitous murderer, Brenner includes not only his everyday cover (his code name as a CIA operative is 'Colorado'), he also disguises himself to fake the supposed involvement of another (fictitious) person ('Steinmetz') in the murder. Identity, it would seem, is a complex performance of many layers (or disguises one might say) designed to present an innocent face, or 'cover' identity, to ubiquitous surveillance.

Secondly, learning. The importance of learning about the technologies which mediate our engagement with the world is also emphasised in the amusement park. Admittedly, in 'Identity Crisis' the technologies are not particularly new or sophisticated. Columbo learns about Polaroid instant photography and speechwriting/transcription via tape recording. However, these technologies are put into a historical lineage in an oft-discussed scene in which we are shown a point-of-view shot as Columbo examines an instant photograph through a magnifying glass.

This scene very pointedly foregrounds the coexistence of older and newer technologies for investigation and surveillance, indicating the embedded lineage underpinning the newer attention industries of late

Figure 2.1 Technological advances in enhanced looking, encapsulated in an image, in *Columbo* 'Identity Crisis' (1975).

capitalism as the gears shift. This juxtaposition is also created by the CIA Director's meeting with Columbo in a preserved steam train in the heritage tourism destination, the Travel Town Museum, to which he has flown in, by contrast, a helicopter. This is the scene in which this representative of national security advocates that Columbo pay strict attention.

This is a key moment in the lifetime of *Columbo*, as it provides the clearest instruction concerning the need for Columbo to constantly labour to ensure that he is able to pay attention adequately to his work, in an ever-evolving technoscape.

Thirdly, policing. It is not exactly the sophistication of the technology that is of key importance, but its use. Brenner's recorded speech provides his false alibi. As he records himself the morning after committing the murder, he sets a clock to chime 11 o'clock to suggest a late-night speech-writing session. However, Columbo polices this criminal use of technology to falsely align the past. He notices that a news story alluded to in the speech only broke after the supposed time of its writing. Columbo, then, pays 'strict attention' to the latest means of recording the past to ensure that those with the technical ability to falsify history are not able to get away with murder (literally or metaphorically).

Fourthly, LA The position of Los Angeles is described in a manner which situates its interconnected importance as much in relation to the USA (the nation) as with the wider world beyond. Whilst LA developed into its current shape due to the initial arrival of the railroad (Banham 1971: 75–94; Abu-Lughod 1999: 134–138), by the time of *Columbo* its transport infrastructure had developed significantly, facilitating ease of both national and global connectivity. This is evident in the episode's telling juxtaposition of the railroad with the greater border-crossing flexibility of the newer

Figures 2.2–2.3 Columbo is instructed to 'pay strict attention' by the CIA in *Columbo* 'Identity Crisis' (1975).

technology of the helicopter. Accordingly, as the CIA Director notes to Columbo, Brenner is a key figure for the entire US West Coast because he is a channel through which information flows (or, after Simon, we might say, is processed), from both the Pacific and South America. LA, then, is as much a hub for global information (we might nowadays say, data) transfer as it is a national urban centre.

In these ways, 'Identity Crisis' subtly indicates the manner in which Columbo's investigations – his individual acts of paying attention as attentive labourer – are embroiled in the channelling and shaping of attention during the tail end of the Cold War. Things are much less subtle in the immediate post-Cold War era in 'Columbo Cries Wolf'. Here the freer rein given to the global spread of capitalism after the fall of the Berlin Wall (or, perhaps more accurately, the collapse of the Soviet Union) directly enunciates the potential of the attention industries to monetise attention. The difference between the two episodes indicates, precisely, the shifting of gears which has been taking place in the interim.

A murder is faked by a fashion photographer, Sean Brantley (Ian Buchanan), the co-founder of a Beverly Hills *Playboy*-style magazine: *Bachelor's World*. Ultimately, it transpires that this was a publicity stunt designed by Brantley and his business partner Dian Hunter (Deidre Hall) to leverage the global media attention that Columbo's investigation creates to increase the magazine's circulation (after which, Brantley really does murder his majority shareholding business partner, Hunter). The initial ruse is so successful that the market value of the magazine doubles. Thus, this later episode of *Columbo* shows, it is now eminently possible to capitalise upon the attention you are paid to reap the financial rewards of another person's laborious looking in your direction.

The same four key indicators of engagement with attention are present. Firstly, performance. Brantley – who believes Columbo's 'naïve, bumbling' performance to be an act – repeatedly taunts Columbo to look for the body of Hunter, using bulldozers to dig up his Beverly Hills estate. We then enjoy the humorous spectacle of the LAPD fruitlessly searching the grounds, including Columbo in galoshes looking in the artificial lake, on a ladder looking down a chimney, and bashfully wandering – hopelessly lost – into the models' bedrooms.

When Columbo takes the bait, Brantley creates a media spectacle out of the investigation (performing the centrepiece himself by taking his models on a shopping spree) and prompting increased sales of his magazine. This is a literal evocation of the contemporary functioning of attention: the more people look at you performing, the more you are worth. Brantley's magazine, after all, trades in the display of women's scantily clad bodies for its circulation, as is reinforced by the episode's *Baywatch*-like lingering shots on the posing swim-suited bodies of the 'Chateau's' live-in models (the *Bachelor World* 'Nymphs'). In this way the attention industries, in magazines as on television, turn bodies into desirable objects from which to profit from the attention people pay them. Following the logic of surveillance capitalism, Hunter and Brantley are not only able to predict how consumers will react to the scandal, but even to influence their behaviour, as is shown by their success in increasing magazine sales through staged performances.

Here the cagey, 'undercover' performance of identity due to the ubiquity of state surveillance emphasised in 'Identity Crisis' gives way, fifteen years later, to a more 'stylish' performance for the ubiquitous cameras which create a duplication of quotidian reality (both the modelling world's photo shoots and the press coverage of events in the 'Chateau' being indicative of this everyday surveillance). As Columbo finds out when the press centre their attention on his investigation, everyday life is not only akin to being on television for the 'Chateau's' live-in-models, but for everyone: even everyman Columbo.

Secondly, learning. Columbo must learn to master new technology to solve the murder. This he eventually does after initially realising that the first trail of evidence left on CCTV footage (both private, at the 'Chateau', and public, at the airport) is false, and then by using an electronic pager to locate the body after Hunter's actual murder. The pager in particular is significant because this device, designed to enable immediate contact between professionals, is used by Columbo to rather literally link the murderer to the body of his deceased business partner. Columbo's dedicated attention to new gadgetry, his 'entrepreneurial' work updating his knowledge of technology, enables him to avoid obsolescence in his professional life. As the world shifts gears towards ever-more rapid electronic means of channelling attention (e.g. the instantaneous need for contact made manifest by the pager), Columbo labours accordingly, to keep his skillset up to date.

Thirdly, policing. Global surveillance culture is shown to be ubiquitous, occupying both private and public spheres. The ruse is perpetrated using CCTV footage, laying a false trail to make Columbo suspect that Hunter has been murdered and replaced by a similar-looking model. The 'Chateau' has internal CCTV (on which Hunter watches Brantley's infidelities with the nymphs and Columbo charts the arrival and departure of all cars) and Columbo examines forty tapes of CCTV footage at the security control centre for the airport. There he notes that visitors to airports are photographed 8–12 times. There is no longer any need for a cute

allegory involving Polaroids at an amusement park to indicate the historical development and contemporary ubiquity of surveillance. We are always
on camera, and Columbo's job is specifically to use surveillance technologies, in all spheres, to figure out the true history of events: to realise, in
effect, when events recorded by cameras have been faked so as to create a
false version of history.

Fourthly, LA. With the media interest in the investigation indicated
as global, Los Angeles is situated at the heart of the newly globalised
economy, a global gateway city providing access to the Pacific Rim and
beyond. The mayor is informed that along with US network and cable
and European news coverage, there is even Korean TV in LA working
the story. Similarly, Brantley watches news coverage on Japanese TV, and
newspapers are featured from around the world.

Columbo even questions an English media mogul who is in LA meeting with Japanese business associates. The mogul's appearance in the
episode is heralded by the arrival of a helicopter, this time the machine

Figure 2.4 The value of the attention Columbo pays to *Bachelor's
World* magazine is realised due to the global media spectacle it
prompts, in *Columbo* 'Columbo Cries Wolf' (1990).

being illustrative not of the mobility of the forces of national security (as in 'Identity Crisis', the CIA), but the private wealth of the international businessman. In the post-Cold War era, under globalisation, LA is now directly depicted as a global hub of international attention from which individual wealth can accrue.

Through these four key features *Columbo* engages its viewers with the question of how to live in a world where the 'industrialization of vision' is shifting gears along with the global diffusion of neoliberal economics. The next four chapters will explore each one of these features in depth: performing (paying attention to work 24/7, all the while knowing your performance is being attended to) in Chapter 3; learning (paying attention to new technology, ensuring a skillset of relevance rather than obsolescence) in Chapter 4; policing (paying attention to history, separating the innocent who are content to watch history unfold on television from the guilty who seek to tamper with the recorded past) in Chapter 5; and locating (paying attention to the rights of everyone under globalisation, realising the inequality-inducing border separating the haves from the have-nots) in Chapter 6. Together these four aspects indicate the awareness, and skillset, required of the attentive labourer. This *Columbo*, functioning as a complex memory game designed to attract and shape attention, seeks to hone, asking viewers to consider how they should perform, learn, police and locate themselves to be the most effective attentive labourers.

To conclude, *Columbo* can be understood to be a historical artefact indicative of the shifting gears which propelled a monetised form of attention to prominence in this epoch. This is more evident in *Columbo*'s return at the close of the Reagan era, after what might be considered a right-wing counter-revolution against the collective resistance to capitalism of the 1960s and early 1970s. This movement proliferated the worldwide spread of neoliberal doctrine, which was furthered in turn by the fall of trade barriers brought by the end of the Cold War (Crary 2013: 65–74). But this process had already begun as the Cold War continued apace in the 1970s when *Columbo* arrived. It is thus not a matter of noting neoliberalism per se, but rather its role in shifting the gears in terms of how attention is shaped in the 1980s and afterwards.

Two telling flashforwards indicate this clearly. Whilst the early twenty-first century show *Mad Men* (2007–2015) recreates the 1960s in retrospect to consider the growing importance of the attention industries with hindsight (the show introducing first television, and then the computer, and exploring their roles in revolutionising the advertising industry), *Columbo* negotiated their growth to economic prominence at the time of its production. *Columbo* also prefigured the representation of contemporary modes of paying attention in present-day detective shows like *Sherlock* (2010–2017). In *Sherlock*, Holmes's attentive labour (especially observing people) reveals the hidden secrets of their lives in the *mise-en-scène* as though it were surveilled data. It appears as writing superimposed over their bodies, interchangeable with the electronic data ('text messages, emails, and database searches' [Bull 2016: 326]) regularly integrated into the show's imagery. In *Columbo* the aesthetic sophistication was arguably more humble, but the emphasis on data surveillance was always integral to the investigation.

The remainder of this book, then, considers *Columbo* as a complex memory game which hones our attention via its very particular format, but in so doing supplementarily shapes how we pay attention in the four key ways introduced above. This provides an understanding of Columbo's actions as those of a character fully immersed in a world increasingly dominated by the attention industries. Yet, ultimately, he is also one who attempts to police the worst excesses of late capitalism by championing the rights of those which it would look to exclude from wealth, even from life itself. The 'game', as Sherlock Holmes would say, is afoot.

CHAPTER 3

Performing:
Falk Acts/Columbo Pays Attention

The most memorable thing about *Columbo* is Peter Falk's performance: his bedraggled appearance, his hair scratching and forehead rubbing, his dogged pursuit of the criminal, his 'Just one more thing . . .' catchphrase. From the second pilot, 'Ransom for a Dead Man' (1971) onwards, Falk performs Columbo as a paradoxical figure: a bumbling 'everyman' (introduced to the story searching for his dropped pen) with a wickedly sharp intelligence. As Falk summarises, Columbo is a 'regular Joe . . . with a mind like Einstein' (Falk 2008: 135). This makes the Lieutenant so loveable, his mannerisms and eccentric foibles so funny to watch. Yet, why such a performance for catching murderers exactly? Why not the more steely, trim and professional Columbo of the first pilot 'Prescription: Murder' (1968)? Put another way, the question motivating the research in this chapter is, why does Columbo – as much as Falk – 'act' like he does?

This chapter argues that the *how* of Falk's performance as Columbo (which is uncovered by considering the different influences on his acting style) determines to a great deal the *why* of his performance as the Lieutenant. Columbo personifies the need to pay attention 24/7. He performs the thinking process which typifies the attentive labour demanded by late capitalism. Falk's/Columbo's performance thus physically embodies attentive labour. This is evident in Falk's unique performance, mixing as it does aspects of the method, live television, US indie and early silent Hollywood comedy acting styles. Yet this *how* of his acting is really only important in that it is key to grasping the *why* of it. Columbo's investigative style proceeds through this performance, which enables a gently invasive unofficial intrusion into all aspects of a suspect's life. It facilitates a police surveillance of the everyday. This is *why* Columbo acts as he does.

This performance, by turns, casts doubt over whether the law assumes innocence or guilt, a confusion indicative of the always-on-trial (in public, in private) nature of life since the closing decades of the twentieth century. This confusion emphasises the ambiguity which surrounds *character* (real? performed?) in a life perpetually surveilled by cameras. Indeed, this ambiguity is a feature of Columbo's character. This chapter, then, shows how, whilst *Columbo*'s viewers are engaged in playing its complex memory game which hones attention, they are also encouraged to understand the supplementary matter of how the attentive labourer should 'act'. *Columbo*, in short, uses the crime-fighting success of Columbo to indicate how the attentive labourer of late capitalism can most effectively perform their duties.

Attentive 24/7

Scholars discussing Falk's performance often link it to the need to hold viewer attention, 'creating surprise and unpredictability in episodes where so much is already known, including the identity of the murderer' (Walters 2019: 71). Unpredictability aside, because after all Columbo's ticks are mostly trademarks and therefore actually quite predictable (e.g. as viewers we await the appearance of the catchphrase 'Just one more thing . . .'), this is as befits television's 'personality system'. Distinct from cinema's star system, television's personality system builds programmes around a personality marked by their everydayness (Langer 1981: 353). Columbo's recurring references to Mrs Columbo and his extended family, his appearance in the same bedraggled suit and raincoat over many decades, and his inability to locate a pencil when he needs one, are all good examples of his everyday personality. Viewing *Columbo* through the personality system, then, would seem to provide a good answer to the question of why Columbo acts like he does. Even so, something similar could be said for any number of TV detectives. For example, Lieutenant Theo Kojak (Telly Savalas) from *Kojak* (1973–1978) (CBS's response to *Columbo*, also made by Universal), with his perpetual oral activity (snacking, smoking, lollipop sucking), and his 'Who loves ya, baby?' catchphrase can be seen similarly. More nuance is thus required to fully grasp exactly why Columbo acts as he does.

   In fact, a close relationship exists between Columbo's bumbling persona and his investigative technique: what we might term the productive coexistence of his everyday inattentiveness along with the complete attention he dedicates to his professional life. As James Walters's brief analysis above partly indicates – illustrating how Falk's performance of Columbo is designed to wrong-foot his suspect – the more closely we pay attention to Falk's performance the more we realise the usefulness of Columbo's seemingly banal actions and observations of life in catching murderers. A much fuller way to answer the question of why Columbo acts like he does, then, is that Falk as Columbo performs the embodiment of late capitalism's channelling of attention, its emphasis on a certain kind of all-consuming attentive labour.

Columbo is so successful as a detective because of his incredible ability to pay attention to work 24/7. It is his willingness to allow work and life to overlap or conflate, rather than to balance these spheres, which makes him so successful. In *24/7*, Jonathan Crary outlines how all-consuming work now obliterates any separation between personal and professional spaces, even colonising sleep (2013: 1–28). Falk's performance as Columbo, then, is that of the twenty-first century's worker who labours by paying attention 24/7. As Columbo observes in 'Death Lends a Hand' (1971), the second episode of series one, his dedicated late-night case-file reading keeps Mrs Columbo awake due to the lamp being on beside the bed. This practice of taking work home with him is very effective. Not long afterwards, in 'Lady in Waiting' (1971), Columbo notes how a conversation with his wife unexpectedly provided the insight he needed to solve the case. Speaking to the fiancé of the murderer, Peter Hamilton (Leslie Nielsen), Columbo explains how the unusual sequence of events on the night of the murder indicates the inconsistency in the murderer's story. Hamilton heard shots fired, then an intruder alarm triggered, in that order. This contradicts the murderer's story, that an alarm awoke her, after which she killed someone who she thought was a burglar. Columbo explains to Hamilton:

> You know my wife, she's got a proverb for every situation [. . .] To be honest, she solved it for me. We're having an argument last night. She says to me 'you're putting the cart before the horse.' And I said . . . *right*. This case, the horse is before the cart.[1] And I had the answer.

This early example of what became a recurring feature of the show was not just intended to show that Columbo takes work home with him, as in the first example of late-night reading. Things are more involved than just that. Rather, Columbo effectively co-opts his time in the family sphere as extra time which he can dedicate to work. In 'Mind over Mayhem' (1974), Columbo even states that whenever a case gets 'tough', he goes home and speaks to his wife. Or rather, he tellingly clarifies, he talks about the case, but Mrs Columbo 'doesn't talk about the case, she talks about everything else'. This method, as expected, does enable Columbo to gain the insight

---

[1] Falk appears to mis-speak this line. In the very next scene Columbo does say 'cart before the horse' in the dramatic conclusion, when describing the events of that night to the murderer (that the sound of shots fired was followed by that of an intruder alarm, events in the incorrect order for the murderer's story).

he needs to crack the case. Work time, then, has become 24/7, Columbo's attention to his case all-consuming, his domestic life functioning as an integral part of his professional life.

Noticeably, the insights of Columbo's absent family members which help solve murders do not elaborate anything else about Columbo's character. This is the case whether they offer information directly (such as Columbo's nephew, a resident dermatologist at UCLA, who diagnoses Columbo's reaction to poison ivy in 'Lovely But Lethal' [1973]) or through an accidental nudge towards something important: these latter range from Mrs Columbo being perpetually mad at the timing of ice-cream truck routes tipping Columbo off to the murderer's ice-cream man disguise in 'The Most Crucial Game' (1972); to his mother-in-law's threatening of a slapstick frying pan blow for bending the spine of her cookbook making him super-sensitive to an incongruously bent first edition spine in 'Dagger of the Mind' (1972). As noted in Chapter 2, unlike the character development of a long-form television performance (Mittell 2015: 136), any grounding backstory which Columbo's familial anecdotes might provide is reset at the start of the following episode. Instead, the humorously shifting sands upon which these familial insights and accidental prompts position Columbo's thinking are ultimately what provide his character consistency: i.e. he can *consistently* be relied upon to find a link between a case and his family, or at any rate, to invent one if need be. The inconsistency which is then created – such as whether Mrs Columbo can really be the biggest fan of every celebrity murderer Columbo investigates – is, paradoxically, all that is consistent. Ultimately, Columbo's family chat thus indicates that his attentiveness is all-encompassing, his work 24/7, his investigative persona very self-consciously performed.

To dig a little deeper into the relationship between 24/7 attentive labour and Columbo's performance, let us consider his workaholism. This is behind the show's running gag that, although we rarely see Columbo drink, his arrival at crime scenes suggests he may be the worse for wear from alcohol. This is repeatedly intimated by his dishevelled appearance holding boiled eggs, as though an early hours call to a crime scene found him in a bar. For example, in 'A Stitch in Crime' (1973), Columbo appears hungover: unshaven and unkempt, he drops eggshell all over the crime scene, even cracking one open on the murder weapon, whilst asking for coffee. When a colleague enquires after his health, Columbo makes what seem to be vague excuses about his wife's stomach problems keeping him up all night. Such incidences recur numerous times. Noticeably in 'Forgotten Lady' (1975), Columbo arrives at the crime scene at 1:30 am, hunched, walking like a zombie, prominent posterior hair tuft at odds with the world, practically still dreaming, having forgotten to put on both jacket and watch (and as a result, without his badge). He sleepily remarks: 'lucky I didn't show up in my pyjamas'. This running gag culminates in Columbo's early morning arrival in 'It's All in the Game' (1993) including: trademark boiled eggs, request for coffee and, the final *coup de grâce*, a pyjama top visible under his jacket.

Yet, in spite of such indicators that Columbo may like to party (the repeated gesture of a hand to the forehead seemingly indicating a hang-over), in fact he is revealed to be an exhausted workaholic (the hand-to-forehead gesture being, in fact, that of the deep thinker). This is most evident in 'Any Old Port in a Storm' (1973) when Columbo receives a missing person's report, still in his office, at 2 am. Again, in 'An Exercise in Fatality' (1974), Columbo appears looking peaky, and even gags, whilst carrying a brown paper bag. Ultimately, though, the comedy 'reveal' is that the bag contains not liquor but a thermos of coffee. The gag is even rebooted when *Columbo* returns in the late 1980s. In 'Strange Bedfellows' (1995) a clearly nauseated Columbo complains of the supposed ill effects of clams, the brown paper bag this time containing Pepto-Bismol.

Even the one time when we are seemingly given a direct indication that Columbo has been called to a crime scene when the worse for wear for drink, whilst on a holiday cruise with Mrs Columbo in 'Troubled Waters' (1975) – during which he apologises for Mrs Columbo's getting carried away due to her love of a good time – he is revealed to actually be seasick rather than inebriated. Thus, Columbo's bedraggled appearance at early morning crime scenes ultimately expresses not the consequences of a wild night, but lack of sleep due to unsociable working hours.

Indicators of Columbo's workaholism proliferate. Most apparently, his identity is, literally, his job. Columbo's first name is never purpose-fully revealed in the show. When asked what it is, he replies: 'Lieutenant'. Whilst this might seem to indicate a desire to keep his private life private, it is also a truthful insight into the erasure of Columbo's private life by his working persona. His identity is, literally, his job. Whilst it is never clear if Columbo has children or not – in 'Any Old Port in a Storm' (1973) he dis-cusses whether he might arrange a babysitter – his bedraggled appearance might seem less that of a drunk than a sleep-deprived parent. But if so, his presence in the office at 2 am in this same episode indicates a terrible work-life imbalance for a father. In 'Suitable for Framing' (1971) Columbo falls asleep at his chief suspect's house late at night, whilst in 'A Deadly State of Mind' (1975) he sleeps in his car waiting to interview an unwitting accomplice as she arrives at work in the morning. Always on the job, for Columbo even sleep comes second to the case.

Columbo also repeatedly states that there is never a time when he is not working. As early as the second episode of the first series, 'Death Lends a Hand' (1971), Columbo describes himself saying: 'You know what my trouble is? I work too hard. Never out of the office.' The thinking process, specifically, continues perpetually. In 'A Matter of Honour' (1976) Columbo admits that even when he is 'supposed to be on vacation', he is 'thinking like a cop'. This he explains to a Mexican foreman as an 'occupational hazard', or 'when wherever you go you take your work with you'. Noticeably, the foreman responds by offering a different cultural perspective: 'we call it, loco'! Again, in 'The Bye-Bye Sky High IQ Murder Case' (1977) Columbo notes that he 'can't think of a time when I wasn't working'. Similarly in 'Try and Catch Me' (1977), that 'In my business the thinking never stops.' Topping all this off, in 'How to Dial a Murder' (1978), when evaluated by a 'life control' psychologist, Columbo declares the word 'murder' to be the one which dominates his mind. The point being, as Dr Eric Mason (Nicol Williamson) tells Columbo, that his work clearly overshadows his life and consumes his mind 24/7.

Added to this, the Lieutenant's home is never shown. We only know him from his workplace persona. The two occasions when we believe we see Columbo's home turn out to be traps set for suspects in rented or borrowed spaces. This reinforces our sense of Columbo's lack of domestic downtime: the only hints of home turn out also to be workspaces. This impression is furthered by Columbo's ravenous behaviour at crime scenes, where at times he eats everything in sight. His disregard for crime scene integrity indicates not only the obvious point – that he is missing home-cooked meals due to the time he spends working – but also that, as a result of this dedication to work, his professional life must provide that missing nourishment. Columbo's crime scene boiled eggs are in effect the equivalent of the busy office worker's sandwich at the computer. Finally, as noted previously, Columbo's references to how conversations with Mrs Columbo and other family members provide insights into cases again indicate that even when at home he never switches off. The two overlapping spheres of his life are, rather, mutually informing. It is a wonder then, that with work always on his mind, Mrs Columbo sticks with the Lieutenant like she does. Even their holiday cruise is interrupted by a murder case which he works to completion!

This willingness to dedicate to work 24/7 is what distinguishes Columbo from his peers in the NBC *Mystery Movie* wheel. Other, noticeably unmarried, investigators like Quincy (Jack Klugman) or Hec Ramsey (Richard Boone) find that the pressing nature of their work may thwart their amorous intentions. They are repeatedly pulled away from pleasurable female company by work (in Quincy's case this is a running gag), returning to the sphere of labour alone. McCloud (Dennis Weaver), for his part, seems to prefer to focus on the crime he is investigating rather than the many overtly interested women he encounters. Banacek (George Peppard), by contrast, has countless fleeting romantic liaisons, making work the only constant love in his life. Yet, for the married man Columbo, things are subtly different from all these peers. It is not quite that Columbo is pulled away from the familial by work, like Quincy or McCloud, nor that his private life has been backgrounded in favour of work as Banacek's has. It is the opposite for Columbo: work has invaded the family home and taken over his entire life.

Work bothers Columbo so much that it also stays with him on the odd occasions when he is neither at home nor on the case. Hence unexpected insights provide the inspiration for cases not only at home, but everywhere from the TV repair shop to the dog grooming parlour. In this way the erasure of any distinction between the public and the private spheres in *Columbo* indicates the 24/7 nature of the attention he is required to pay to work. The epitome of this work/life conflation, in fact, is given its fullest expression in the wheel's *McMillan & Wife* (1971–1977), in which Police Commissioner Stewart McMillan (Rock Hudson) and his wife Sally (Susan Saint James) solve murders together. The crimes they investigate occupy their attention in both public and private settings, creating a seamless unity between the two spheres.[2]

The 24/7 dedication to work in *Columbo* is easier to see in retrospect now that what was imminent to *Columbo* has fully actualised. What seemed a character foible in *Columbo* is increasingly the norm in contemporary television detective shows, as it is in life. If we flashforward to the present, in *Elementary* (2012–2019), a 24/7 workaholic, modern-day Sherlock Holmes (Johnny Lee Miller) inhabits a New York brownstone which doubles as his office/crime lab/firing range/gym. Holmes has even installed his own all-self-surveilling CCTV. Work and home life are now completely as one. Noticeably, this Holmes hardly ever sleeps, and as such, can almost literally work 24/7. In *Elementary*, a life of constant vigilance and endless work is thus portrayed as a middle-class lifestyle choice, the eradication

---

[2] The first episode, 'Murder by the Barrel' (1971), commences with the mistaken delivery of a body to their new home. In ''Til Death Do Us Part' (1972) they agree their preference for their new life, despite the Police Commissioner's public life invading his private, as opposed to their former life when McMillan was a lawyer. In the same episode, the 'Asylum Killer' targets them in their home, ultimately being apprehended by McMillan in this domestic space.

of any distinction between professional and private spheres having been willingly embraced. As the show concluded, this dynamic domestic work-space even includes Dr Joan Watson's (Lucy Liu) adopted son. Work and family, it seems, can seamlessly co-reside in the same 'private' space. Here, noticeably, the familial focus of such a work/life conflation already evident in *McMillan & Wife* at the time of *Columbo*'s release has been updated to emphasise the individualism of neoliberalism, and its attempted replace-ment of the traditional family with the so-called work family (Holmes and his associate Watson, plus adopted child). For lower middle-class Columbo, though, this is not a lifestyle choice, but the *only* available life choice (Crary 2013: 72).[3]

Columbo thus illustrates one way in which contemporary Western soci-ety responded to the issue which Herbert A. Simon pinpointed in the late 1960s (see Chapter 2) just as the show hit the screens, of how to maxi-mise the scarce resource of human attention in order to optimally pro-cess information. The ideal attentive labourer, Columbo, pays attention to work 24/7. *Columbo* emphasises this as an ideal by contrasting Columbo with less effective colleagues. In 'Negative Reaction' (1974), Sergeant Hoffman (Michael Strong) arrives at work fresh in the morning and, finding Columbo still at his desk, notes that he needs some sleep and a shave. Hoffman believes the case to be closed, hence he is well groomed and rested. Columbo, by contrast, is paying so much attention to the case that he has neglected himself physically. But he, of course, rather than Hoffman, will crack the case.

Columbo's physicality, indeed, brings the discussion closer to both Falk and Columbo's performance. It has been noted that Columbo embodies a work ethic often thought synonymous with the USA. Mark Dawidziak argues that 'Columbo is the American work ethic in practice. He gets to the conclusion through fierce dedication and Yankee ingenuity' ([1988] 2019: 5). Yet, with the above in mind there seems to be a very specific con-temporary emphasis to this depiction of an older, settler-colonist heritage. Falk's performance as Columbo is specifically that of the late twentieth and early twenty-first centuries' worker whose contribution is the labour of looking. Columbo's relentless pursuit of his suspects epitomises the

---

[3] The work/life conflation of the early twenty-first century in *Elementary* – 24/7 worka-holism as norm, the separation between home and work eradicated by choice – mirrors both the liberal ideal of private, entrepreneurial labour of the pre-twentieth-century West (the Victorian/Edwardian era of great social inequality of the original Sherlock Holmes literary stories), and the resurgence of such inequality under neoliberalism in the late twentieth and early twenty-first centuries when *Columbo* emerged.

attentive labour valued under late capitalism, and, indeed, the toll it takes on the body – in 'An Exercise in Fatality' (1974), it becomes apparent that the result of Columbo's absolute dedication to his profession is his entire lack of physical fitness.

Columbo's dishevelled physical appearance and sleep-deprived postures – one witness to a murder pointedly describes him as resembling 'an unmade bed' ('Dead Weight' [1971]) – illustrate his *embodiment* of perpetual attentiveness. In this the portrayal of Columbo is markedly different from, say, the *Mystery Movie* wheel's, Banacek, with his closely coiffured and cardiganed, classic car and Panatela-cigar-smoking cool and carefree confidence. This is in part a wealth and class distinction between the two investigators. In *Banacek* much is made of his Polish-American heritage. Even so, the show's prominent Italian-American character, sharing the same heritage as Columbo, is Banacek's faithful but none-too-bright chauffeur Jay Drury (Ralph Manza), the grandson of a Sicilian migrant. Despite both having immigrant heritages, then, Columbo is effectively Banacek's inferior in class terms. Furthermore, Columbo's slovenly dress and exhausted mornings indicate something which Banacek's super-silky smoothness elides: bedraggled Columbo's physical postures provide the bodily deterioration which accompanies an ever-alert mind. This is repeatedly apparent in Columbo's forward-inclined torso, arms folded, massaging of his temples. The price of paying attention 24/7 is Columbo's disintegrating physical appearance. Albeit, this performance of tiredness, as I explore later, is extremely effective for investigating murders.

Yet can we first do justice to Falk's performance? As John Caughie notes, analysing television acting is extremely difficult. It challenges existing critical discourse in particular by being 'a messily humanist component of the specific signifying practices of film and television, a kind of impressionistic marshland without shape or solidity' (2014: 144).[4] We can add to this the further problem of the longevity of Falk's performance of the role. In spite of the many consistencies of character and performance across the decades, different 'Columbos' appear across various episodes: some manifestations are tougher, some more gentile, some more comical. How best can we engage with Falk's performance as Columbo in a manner which can illuminate his process of paying attention?

As noted above, what has been argued of performance in episodic cop shows is only partially true for *Columbo*. *Columbo*, as discussed in previous chapters, is a remarkably inconsistent show with many discrepancies appearing across its episodes. In terms of Columbo the character these

---

[4] Discussion of the issue Caughie raises is ongoing (e.g. Fife Donaldson and Walters 2019).

include the extent to which what he says about his wife and extended family should be considered coherent to a 'Columboverse'. Yet it does not necessarily follow that character cannot develop depth under these circumstances, it is just that Columbo does not. Consider what Sarah Caldwell argues of the similarly episodic *Death in Paradise* (2011–):

> While the form is amnesiac in terms of plot, it need not be so in terms of character: a nuanced performance that is straightforwardly accessible to new viewers can simultaneously allow fresh insights into a character's disposition that will be detected and appreciated by the regular audience. (2019: 27)

Columbo is similarly 'amnesiac' in terms of much of its diegetic world. However, Falk's performance of Columbo does not provide new insights into his character across the decades. Rather, it tends to add layers of obfuscation regarding who Columbo might, or might not, coherently be. For example, should we believe that he speaks Italian well, as he does in several episodes in both the 1970s and 1990s, or that he never got the hang of it, as he seemingly disingenuously says in 'Strange Bedfellows' (1995)? As always, it is hard to tell whether *Columbo* is just unconcerned about such details or having fun with the viewer by multiplying inconsistencies. This is, after all, the same as *Columbo* has always done by refusing to reveal Mrs Columbo and solve fan curiosity as to whether she really exists or not. A different approach is needed, then, for the particularities of this show.

Accordingly, rather than looking solely at what appears on-screen, we should also consider where Falk's performance originates from and how it developed. Amongst the different influences on his acting style which Falk brings to bear on the part, the composite of Columbo can be brough to light along with, crucially, how Falk deploys his acting techniques to embody the thinking process of attentive labour.

Off Broadway via Brando, or from Keaton to Cassavetes?

Falk's performance as Columbo combines various stylistic characteristics from his acting background. Falk was a character actor whose early experiences include exposure to theatrical director Erwin Piscator (formerly a colleague of Bertolt Brecht) at The New School (Lertzman and Birnes 2017: 39–42). His early career initially off Broadway and then on Broadway, Falk had worked variously in television and the movies for nearly a decade before *Columbo* (Falk 2008: 21 and 133; Lertzman and Birnes 2017: 81–169). For Falk, the most important actor of his generation was the method actor Marlon Brando (Falk 2008: 233–236). Even if Falk's attempts to audition for The Actors Studio were unsuccessful (Lertzman and Birnes 2017: 71–72 and 83), Falk does resemble Brando stylistically on different occasions in *Columbo*. Most obviously he delivers a deliberately tongue-in-cheek homage to Brando's Don Corleone from *The Godfather* (1972) in 'Undercover' (1994). Accordingly, it would be logical to consider Falk's performance of Columbo as that of an aspiring method actor, especially considering *Columbo* included co-stars who were well-known method actors, such as The Actors Studio-trained Martin Landau playing identical twins with juxtaposed personalities in 'Double Shock' (1973).[5] Let us begin then, with the method.

Method acting, drawing on the practices developed by Russian theatre director Constantin Stanislavski (1863–1938), emphasises the need for an actor to control, and channel into performance, the otherwise unruly nature of emotions (Blum 1984: 3). The US variant of this, developed by The Actors Studio, emphasised in particular what Stanislavski's method offered in terms of the psychological dimension of character personification, drawing on the unconscious, personal experiences and affective memories (pp. 4–6 and 52). Method actors on US screens, then, are typically able to indicate something of the tensions which exist between inner turmoil and the outward-facing mask worn in everyday social life (p. 65). The oft-cited key examplar of this remains Dustin Hoffman's Benjamin Braddock in *The Graduate* (1967) (p. 65).

Whilst there are numerous method actors of note the most famous remains Brando, in part due to his hulking performance of Stanley Kowalski in the cinematic adaptation of Tennessee Williams's *A Streetcar Named Desire* (1951). This was under the direction of Elia Kazan, one of the original founders of The Actors Studio (Blum 1984: 51 and 63). In his movie work, Falk not only acts like Brando (e.g. as a Chief of Police in *The Balcony* [1963]), he also demonstrates a Brando-esque aptitude for gestures indicating submerged memories. Most terrifyingly, when playing a murderous gangster in *Murder Inc* (1960), Falk deploys the simple gesture of smoothing down his tie (combined with a distant gaze seemingly recalling the past) to communicate what we may presume to be the poverty, indignities and the personal sleights which formed the hideous character of Abe Reles (Reles runs a business committing murder to order and perpetrates violence against women for pleasure). It is perhaps unsurprising,

---

[5] This may be a nod to Landau's performance in the pilot of *Mission Impossible* (1966) as both a dictator of a fictional Latin American country, General Rio Dominguez of 'Santa Costa', and, also, US covert operative Rollin Hand impersonating him.

then, that there are clear moments in *Columbo* when Falk's acting seems attuned to the method, especially – as is explored below – in the first pilot 'Prescription: Murder' (1968).

Yet there is much more underpinning Falk's performance of Columbo than the method. This is evident especially if we keep in mind, as outlined in Chapter 1, that *Columbo* was an industrial product specific to its historical moment. What other influences, then, offer themselves to an eagle-eyed viewer?

Falk was one of a generation of actors who performed on live television during the 1950s, particularly in anthology shows producing a different television play each week. This was an era when the idea of purchasing a television for the home was sold to wealthier consumers as an 'enlightened investment' (Watson 2008: 22). The content which television provided access to was sophisticated live dramas more akin to New York theatrical works than Hollywood films – albeit along with advertisements for products like Kraft cheese. Falk's reputation was greatly enhanced, for example, by his performance in *Night Cry* (1958), which screened as part of the Kraft Television Theatre (Lertzman and Birnes 2017: 81–82).

Method acting was particularly well-suited to these television dramas, including live shows, due to their focus on 'tortured misfit' characters (as in a specific tradition of realist television exploring the 'everyday lives of the unglamorous'), and, indeed, because of the 'authenticity' valued of television from the 1940s onwards (Schneider 2016: 30–31). Live television was well suited to everyday psychological dramas played out in interior settings because of what the live event could not accommodate aesthetically. For example, it was not really possible to use shot/reverse shot camera setups, nor to create a montage in the editing process. Nor indeed, to incorporate much in terms of action sequences (Boddy 1990: 84). As a result, the aesthetic of live television becomes more 'frontal' because, as Caughie observes: 'the three-camera set-up of the "live" studio drama allows for mixing between a variety of views of the scene but makes it difficult to cut into the middle of it and identify the look of the spectator with the look of the character' (Caughie 2000: 122).

Live television had an impact on the style of method actors – such as James Dean or Rod Steiger – due to the intimacy demanded of the small screen when viewed up-close in the domestic setting. Whilst it is true that live television favoured method acting to get deeper into character psychology, nevertheless method acting became less internalised and more outwardly gestural than it would have been in, say, a Hollywood movie starring the same method actors. Such a movie could rely on editing techniques like facial close-ups to show interior emotion after all. Falk's performance of Columbo, then, also partly stems from this transformation of theatrical method acting to accommodate itself to industrial norms like live television.[6]

This is not to say that *Columbo* shares the frontal aesthetic of live television dramas of the 1950s. It is, however, to indicate how Falk's background in theatre and on live television *together* create a medium-specifically-nuanced form of method acting which blends into his performance of Columbo. For instance, in the first pilot, 'Prescription: Murder', when phrases are introduced which will later become character-identifying catchphrases (e.g. 'one more thing' and 'one detail that bothers me'), they are not as hammed up as they would later be in the series proper. Initially, they seem more like authentic character traits for Columbo. In his initial incarnation, Falk/Columbo is closely shaven, with neatly pressed clothes, standing straight, neat and tidy with raincoat over his arm. Minimal in terms of physical ticks, Falk ultimately uses his Brando-esque delivery – hand gestures suddenly included along with his lines – in a monologue seemingly designed to declare his character's psychology. He speaks, tellingly, about how his manner of investigation seems to 'bother people'. Here Columbo is, precisely, the 'everyday' and 'unglamorous' character of live television – the perfect foil to Gene Barry's suave, understated and unruffled delivery as wealthy psychiatrist and murderer, Dr Ray Flemming – yet, tellingly, Falk's physicality is a blend of the method's psychological depth and live television's necessary gestures.

As early as the second pilot, 'Ransom for a Dead Man' (1971), though, Falk's performance has changed and the Columbo of the series proper emerged. Now, when Columbo adopts a leaning posture (hand on forehead, deliberately foregrounding his idiosyncrasies to discuss the things that bother him), this is no longer the method combined with live television. These are seemingly spontaneous, or improvised idiosyncrasies coupled with humour as well. He has become a self-consciously performing everyman trading on his seemingly unthreatening demeanour. How can we understand this change?

It may be easier to answer this question by briefly considering, first of all, why this change? As noted in Chapter 1, Columbo's manner of investigating – his interruptions, his catchphrases followed by dramatic pauses, his tangential anecdotes, his departures and returns for 'Just one more thing . . .' – all serve to grab the attention of the easily distracted

---

[6] Falk's quirky physical mannerisms in his television performances were what got him noticed by Abe Lastfogel of the William Morris agency in 1957 (Lertzman and Birnes 2017: 77).

domestic viewer. Yet their dramatic purpose, as discombobulating aspects of the interrogation of the chief suspect, is equally important. As noted in Chapter 2, there is a big difference between Falk's use of pauses when delivering one of his catchphrases and when a detective like Quincy or McCloud says them as though in passing.[7] When Columbo interacts with lawyer Leslie Williams (Lee Grant), in the second pilot 'Ransom for a Dead Man' (1971), the intent to wrong-foot is clearly foregrounded. As Columbo repeatedly bumbles over the facts 'from all possible angles', even informally recreating the murder in Williams's law office, Williams is troubled by a disconcerting flashback to the event. Ultimately, she calls out Columbo on his mannered performance, deliberately revealing how disarming but also demanding of attention it is supposed to be:

> You know, Columbo, you're almost likeable in a shabby sort of way. Maybe it's the way you come slouching in here, with your shopworn bag of tricks . . . The humility, the seeming absent-mindedness, the homey anecdotes about the family, the wife . . . Lieutenant Columbo fumbling and stumbling along. But it's always the jugular that he's after. I imagine that more often than not he's successful.

This is a reworked version of a key speech from the first pilot, delivered by psychiatrist Flemming. Both speeches indicate how Columbo trades on the way in which people underestimate him, including by playing on their preconceived class-based prejudices.[8] The difference is that Williams's indication of how Columbo trades on the way in which people underestimate him is received by an entirely disingenuously-bashful Columbo. The revised scripting, then, is extremely accurate with respect to how Falk's performance of the Lieutenant's investigative style has been revamped to include these more idiosyncratic and comedically disarming elements.

---

[7] Various seemingly distinctive *Columbo* phrases appear unobtrusively in other shows, indicating how expressive Falk's performance is of such generic statements For example, McCloud says 'There's something that's been bothering me' in 'Encounter with Aries' (1971), the line delivered whilst musing with a fellow police officer, not an interrogative technique. Again, Banacek, during his revelatory round-up in 'To Steal a King' (1972), notes matter-of-factly that: 'Something bothered me there from the very beginning.'

[8] Williams's use of the term 'shabby' indicates that Columbo's performance now includes a stated element of class difference as part of this wrong-footing performance. This was less evident in the smart, upright Columbo of the first pilot. The 'shabby' Columbo of the series proper performs with exaggerated deference around the elite, especially the murderer, whereas with fellow workers he is courteous and respectful. These contrasting registers render apparent the performance of deference which Columbo directs towards the murderer, playing up to societal biases surrounding class to wrong-foot them (see also Chapter 5).

To return to performance, the how behind the why, how can we describe this kind of acting, and where does it come from in Falk's oeuvre? If neither method acting alone nor even method adapted to live television can explain the seemingly spontaneous and humorous, almost histrionic, performance of the fully developed Columbo character (Williams describes Columbo's investigative style as 'vaudeville'), where else does it come from? Two further influences can be identified to help answer this question.

Firstly, there is a close correlation between Falk's acting in US independent movies and his Columbo. This is especially evident if we consider Falk's work with close collaborators and friends John Cassavetes, the influential independent filmmaking pioneer, and Ben Gazzara. Both worked alongside Falk on *Columbo*: Cassavetes acted in one episode, and Gazzara directed two. *Columbo*'s creators Richard Levinson and William Link note that Falk 'returned to television reluctantly after a happy filmmaking experience' with Cassavetes and Gazzara on *Husbands* (1970) (1981b: 28). Falk's role in the burgeoning US independent movie scene is not often acknowledged as such, and *Columbo*, the programme, also played a largely forgotten role in this movement. Not only did the show provide work for Cassavetes, his wife and collaborator Gena Rowlands, Gazzara, and of course, Falk, but Cassavetes's *A Woman Under the Influence* (1974) (starring Rowlands and Falk) was part-funded to the tune of US$250,000 by Falk from his salary on *Columbo*. Without this television money the film may never have been made, as Cassavetes had to mortgage his house to put up his own share (Hastie 2017: 503; Carney 2001: 310).

Falk's indie work often ran parallel to *Columbo*. Falk ultimately starred in three of his friend's films, most famously alongside Rowlands in *A Woman Under the Influence*. Falk initially turned down Universal's offer of *Columbo* due to his previous experience making the unsuccessful *The Trials of O'Brien* (1965–1966) for television. It was the more limited commitment of *Columbo* (requiring fewer episodes as part of the *Mystery Movie* wheel) which enticed Falk back, *precisely because* it enabled him to continue pursuing movie and theatre work (Levinson and Link 1981a: 85, 1981b: 28). Perhaps unsurprisingly, then, considering that *Columbo* and Falk's independent career were concurrent, Falk's performance as Columbo shares characteristics with the acting style he developed working with Cassavetes. In particular, Falk's Columbo evidences Cassavetes's emphasis on what has been called 'the impression of improvisation' in his indie movies (Viera 2004: 153). For Cassavetes, improvisation meant using a script, but enabling an actor to adapt their part to character, creating 'characteristic spontaneity . . . which makes it appear not to have been planned' (Carney 2001: 217). Thus Cassavetes aimed for a type of rehearsed naturalism allowing for a degree of experimentation and authenticity of emotional response (p. 324). Cassavetes's challenging manner of direction, including, notoriously, surprising actors when they were in character, clearly rubbed off on Falk and *Columbo*.

Falk, seemingly drawing on his experiences working with Cassavetes, played pranks on his *Columbo* co-stars to the same effect. Whilst shooting key scenes, remaining in character Falk would surprise fellow actors with an unannounced prop (his packed lunch, a shopping list) or irrelevant aside (e.g. asking the price of the other character's shoes) (Falk 2008: 136–137). In-character spontaneity in *Columbo*, then, would seem to stem from US independent cinema. Cassavetes, after all, used exactly this technique to disrupt the actors' practised performance and create a less polished but fresher in-character response (Carney 2001: 324; Viera 2004: 161). Ironically, the joke was on Falk when co-star Landau in 'Double Shock' (1973) played exactly the same prank on him. Landau ad-libbed during a scene in which Columbo attends a televised cookery show. Landau's TV chef Dexter suddenly calls Columbo out of the audience, unrehearsed, and Falk has to stay in character and improvise a stage-struck Columbo appearing on live television (Dawidziak [1988] 2019: 136–137). Once again, *Columbo* evidences the impression of improvisation of US independent cinema.

The indie influence does not stop there. Much as Cassavetes's films illuminate how real lives are spent improvising through unscripted situations (Viera 2004: 154) – reality being so unpredictable it makes bad actors of us all – so too does Falk's acting out of possible scenarios via mime in *Columbo*. A good example of such amateur-ish crime-scene recreations occurs in 'Double Shock'. Here Columbo's 'mime scene investigation' (!) exteriorises his mental discernment of what must have been previous events in the bathroom he is inspecting. After first noticing an odd number of towels on the rail, Columbo wordlessly searches out the missing towel in the clothes hamper. Feeling the dampness of the towel he hypothesises that the bath had been used (which the murderers have tried to disguise). He realises this by *physically* thinking through the process – feeling the dried bath, the (still-slippery) soap – before *miming out* the act of drying himself after a bath. Columbo thus, precisely, improvises his way through a space to figure out how a crime (death by electrocution, in the bath) was committed there in the past.

This is not the only time this occurs. In 'A Deadly State of Mind' (1975), Columbo mentally goes over events as recently described by a murder victim's wife, Nadia Donner (Lesley Warren) to check her story. Donner was unwittingly involved in an unpremeditated crime of passion but has now

Figures 3.1–3.3
Mime scene
investigations:
Columbo physically
embodies the
thinking process in
Columbo 'Double
Shock' (1973).

turned accomplice to its cover-up. Columbo sits where Donner claimed to have been sitting when a home invasion supposedly occurred. He mentally recreates the past in miniature. We observe this mental recreation through Columbo's seemingly improvised mine. He makes non-verbal short grunts (to represent words), minimal hand and arm gestures (a raised hand for conversation, a knock on a table to indicate a knock at the door, hand movements to show people moving in the space, a horizontal sweeping arm gesture for the murderers' departure from the space) and finally a longer guttural sound (to indicate the departure of a car parked outside). At the close of this particular dumbshow Columbo speaks for the first time to state his verdict on the version of events described: 'Possible.' But then his continued inhabiting of this space begins to reveal the flaws in this recreated history: for example, that the headlights of an approaching car would have been visible in the room (even though Donner says they were not) which Columbo realises by sitting where she claims she was. Falk's/Columbo's use of mime, then, is a very literal example of Columbo's embodiment of the thinking process of the attentive labourer.

With all such mimes and physical crime scene interrogations, the 'improvisation' which seems to occur within these spaces is usually well *rehearsed*. This is unsurprising considering Falk's approach to his profession: Falk considered acting hard work and would sometimes wind up his fellow professionals with his attention to detail and repeated rehearsals (Lertzman and Birnes 2017: 366). What the rehearsals achieve, though, is the *impression* of an (apparently unrehearsed) naturalism.

Directly related to this, the visual emphasis on acting that Cassavetes championed in indie films, entailing a very deliberate use of framing and editing (Baron and Carnicke 2011: 41), also appears in *Columbo*. This was especially so when Gazzara directed. As *Husbands* was the film which brought Falk and Gazzara together as acting friends, just prior to *Columbo*'s commencement, again the influence of US independent filmmaking seems key. Gazzara's direction allowed Falk more takes than was usual in television to hone his performance, much to the chagrin of studio executives (Dawidziak [1988] 2019: 187–188). The result of this is that, as in indie film, the story at times takes second place to performance in the Gazzara-directed episodes. This has the effect of reinforcing Falk's exteriorising of Columbo's thinking process. Under Gazzara's direction Falk indulges his physical embodiment of thinking more than in many other episodes. In 'A Friend in Deed' (1974), for example, Falk performs significant head scratching, forehead rubbing, nose pinching, pointing, waving, and holding 'thinker' poses. This is especially so at the close of various scenes in which, the other person having departed, the camera lingers for a few seconds longer on Columbo. In these moments, he physically embodies the thinking process though his various characteristic hunched and head-rubbing postures.

Further foregrounding this emphasis on acting over story, Gazzara subtly uses the framing in ways unexpected of primetime television. A good example is a scene of dialogue in 'A Friend in Deed', which finds Columbo, again, examining an empty bath for signs of foul play (in this case, a suspected drowning). The conversation he has with his colleague, Lieutenant Duffy (John Finnegan), is shot with Duffy to the right of the image, looking off-screen at Columbo, and Columbo (standing up to his knees in the drained bath) off-screen, but framed in the centre of the image as a reflection in the four mirrored panels of a large closet, as though he were 'behind' the physical Duffy.

There is a degree of Brechtian[9] self-consciousness about this shot, due to its playful contravention of the most elementary rules of continuity editing. Most apparent in this respect, Duffy looks off-screen to the right, but Columbo (or rather, his reflection) responds to him from the centre of the image. Their eyelines are deliberately mismatched. Furthermore, Duffy appears 'twice' in the image. He is the only person physically in shot, but immediately behind Duffy his reflection also 'stands' with its back to us. Whilst this provides the necessary eyeline match between the reflections of the two men, the persistence of Duffy's physical presence in the foreground discombobulates the viewer with respect to continuity norms designed to help us forget the fourth wall. Against this comparatively static reflection, Falk's hand motions from within the confines of the bath – feeling for signs of dampness in nearby towels – are accentuated. Columbo's reflection seems as though at a 'distance' due to the way the

[9] In general, a seemingly Brechtian dimension emerges to Falk's/Columbo's interrogation of suspects and his crime scene mimes, creating something of the estrangement of actor from role thought which the actor, for Brecht, more 'quotes' than embodies their character (2014: 191). When improvisationally re-enacting the movements of the murderer in the past during a crime scene mime, it does seem as though Columbo is performing the walking through of another actor's blocking – one way in which Brecht describes how an estrangement effect can be observed in theatrical rehearsals – in the space where the murder was enacted (p. 191). Similarly, when interrogating suspects, it is as though Columbo is very deliberately performing the role of the policeman, all the while giving the impression of improvisation. This foregrounds that the policeman plays a role in society (the estrangement effect, for Brecht, is designed precisely to draw our attention to such ordinariness and make us see it anew [p. 192]), but equally that everyone is, to some extent, performing their innocent adherence to the law (see Chapter 4). I thank the anonymous reader for this prompt regarding Brecht.

mirrors reflect the bathroom. As a result of this, and the obstacles to our attention posed by Duffy's reflection, plus the frames around the mirrors interrupting the image composition, we are forced to look closely to realise what he is doing, to grasp, precisely, the import of his acting.

Compounding the self-consciousness of such framings, the long take is used by Gazzara to emphasise Falk's mannered acting out of the everydayness of situations. Again in 'A Friend in Deed', when Columbo's car won't start due to a flat battery, a long take indulges us in events of absolutely no consequence to the narrative. Columbo looks under the hood, an agonisingly slow process in itself because he struggles to open the catch, then has to flag down a ride to a gas station to source some jump leads. This he only manages on the third attempt. It is hard to know whether this entire scene was scripted or unscripted. Did the car really break down, or did Falk or Gazzara deliberately tamper with it so that it would, or was it all an elaborate set-up for the cameras to present a moment of rehearsed naturalism? The position of the camera when Columbo first realises that the car won't start suggests that this much, at least, was perhaps intended. Yet the difficulty Columbo has flagging down a car is either very well thought through for the appearance of naturalism (i.e. the first cars refuse Falk's/ Columbo's request and drive away, in a way which was scripted and presumably would have involved several extras and additional cars), or is the result of letting the cameras roll during a 'real' (improvised) moment when reality deviated from the script. Whether we know which, in fact, may not be as important as the effect on the viewer. All we can perhaps ever know for sure from watching is that Falk remains in character throughout: his performance of Columbo thus equating entirely with Columbo's performance of *his* role as Columbo.

Such a moment of dead time in which Columbo is not in the foreground of the diegetic world, but merely another part of a much bigger picture, also occurs in another long take at the start of the other episode that Gazzara directed. In 'Troubled Waters' (1975), Columbo's appears somewhat uncharacteristically at the very start of the episode, in a long take in which he gradually runs through a busy area of a port, dodging the crowds, even climbing over a barrier, to board a cruise ship. The joke being, of course, that we expect Columbo to be arriving at a crime scene, whereas in fact he is embarking on a holiday with Mrs Columbo. Throughout the drawn-out process Falk remains a diminutive figure often lost amongst the extras. He is not foregrounded via the cinematography as is typical of his introduction to an episode after a murder. Rather, as with the broken-down car, he is again rendered insignificant against a backdrop of everydayness through the use of a long take. Both moments, so normal in US independent cinema, stand out even to this day for being so uncharacteristic of primetime television.

Thus the close connectivity between the world of stage and large and small screen – which drew together such talents as Rowlands, Cassavetes and Falk to perform in a landmark US independent movie like *Woman under the Influence* one year, and *Columbo* the next (e.g. Falk was paired with friend and co-star Rowlands again in 'Playback' [1975])[10] – ensured that Falk's work on US independent movies rubbed off on *Columbo*. Although Falk's acting of Columbo was not improvised entirely in the sense that Cassavetes meant, Columbo's performance of himself as a police officer, his manner of questioning suspects – his attempts to catch suspects off guard as he probes their alibis for holes, interspersed with distracting mentions of his family – gives, precisely, the *impression* of spontaneous improvisation. As with the acting (Falk eliciting fresh in-character reactions from co-stars by catching them off guard with pranks when the cameras are rolling), so too the performance of the character (Columbo the policeman keeping the suspect forever on the back foot).

To Falk's theatrical background, method acting, live television and US indie experiments, we can finally add the Hollywood heritage evident in *Columbo*. Alongside the apparent influence of Hitchcock on the initial pilot (the plot is evocative of *Vertigo* [1958], the accomplice's difficulties with guilt reminiscent of *Rope* [1948], the colourful Rorschach title sequence hints at Saul Bass but with added pop culture) and the frequent references to film noir (see Chapter 6), key from the second pilot onwards are the gestures, and even stunts, evocative of early silent stars who migrated to film from the vaudeville stage. These include Charlie Chaplin and, especially, Buster Keaton.

Falk's aptitude for comedy is evident in numerous of his film roles, both before and after the first series of *Columbo*. Witness, for example, his exaggerated facial expressions as a comic book gangster in John Ford's *Pocketful of Miracles* (1961), not to mention his roles in slapstick comedy chase capers of the 1960s, such as *It's a Mad, Mad, Mad, Mad World* (1963) and *The Great Race* (1965). Then, in the mid- to late 1970s, as *Columbo*'s run on NBC drew to a close, came Falk's mimicry of Humphrey Bogart in

---

[10] Alongside Falk, Rowlands and Cassavetes, others who worked in both the independent arena and on *Columbo* included Fred Draper. Draper featured in several of Cassavetes's films, including *Woman Under the Influence*, plus six episodes of *Columbo* (Draper even played the murderer, Swanny Swanson, in 'Last Salute to the Commodore' [1976]). The link also extended the other way, with Universal producing Cassavetes's *Minnie and Moskowitz* (1971), starring Rowlands.

Murder by Death (1976) and *The Cheap Detective* (1978), before his iconic deadpan CIA agent in *The In-Laws* (1979). Even into the 1990s Falk was able to bag a comedy part in *Roommates* (1995). This aspect of Falk's acting aptitude, although perhaps not always remembered, provides a large degree of consistency to his star persona.

Unsurprisingly, then, from the second pilot on, *Columbo* is a funny show. Falk clowns around repeatedly, his choice of a beat-up Peugeot 403 cabriolet as Columbo's car – forever backfiring, breaking down, crashing or falling apart – rounding off the passing impression of a clown in his clown car. Indeed, when the show's running time was extended to enable the inclusion of more commercials, several of the added scenes were comedic set pieces. For example, in 'Candidate for Crime' (1973), Columbo is pulled over by the Californian Highway Patrol who check over his decrepit (clown) car to humorous effect. In this comedic respect, *Columbo* almost rivals its *Mystery Movie* companion, *McMillan & Wife*, which coupled screwball dialogue with frequent, and often hilarious, verbal and visual innuendos.

Compounding *Columbo*'s comedic effect, examples of early silent cinema-style comedy litter *Columbo*. Most obvious are Falk's various wordless indications of Columbo's physical discomfort due to seasickness and aviophobia, but there are several other, more pointed references. For example, the sight of Columbo's top-down Peugeot crammed full of cops careening haphazardly out of a driveway, with Columbo standing and gesticulating directions in 'Last Salute to the Commodore' (1976), is reminiscent of *Keystone Cops* movies. Laurel and Hardy, for their part, are evoked directly in 'How to Dial a Murder' (1978) – they are the names of the Dobermans that the murderer employs to kill his former wife's lover – and more obliquely in the spectacle of two cars trying to get into the same parking space (Columbo's repeatedly backfiring car accompanied by music reminiscent of vaudeville or the circus) in 'Caution: Murder can be Hazardous for your Health' (1991). These allusions also include a brief impersonation of comedian W. C. Fields ('How to Dial a Murder' [1978]), and numerous Chaplin-esque funny facial expressions: when unable to eat due to the presence of pathologist's photos of a dead body ('Dagger of the Mind'[(1972]); when puffed out from beach running to keep up with a suspect and emptying sand out of his shoes ('An Exercise in Fatality' [1974]); and when Columbo stays at a military academy and is surprised awake by a sudden slapstick smack on his buttocks ('By Dawn's Early Light' [1974]).

Columbo also self-consciously references the melodramatic traditions of early silent cinema in 'Columbo Goes to the Guillotine' (1989) when, in a psychic isolation chamber, Falk/Columbo enacts a beautifully histrionic

but soundless performance in imitation of a famous psychic: handker-
chief to forehead, feeling for the tightness of his collar, eyes closed, hands
clasped, running hands through his hair. Moreover, just as the story goes
regarding how Chaplin developed the character of the Little Tramp via the
choice of costume, so too does Falk credit much of Columbo's character to
the costume, especially his personal addition of the old raincoat and a dyed
suit (Levinson and Link 1981b: 66; Falk 2008: 87–88 and 138).

The most repeatedly foregrounded influence, however, is Keaton. Most
apparently, in 'Murder, Smoke and Shadows' (1989), *Columbo* recreates
the famous dream sequence from Keaton's *Sherlock Jr* (1924), in which a
sleeping projectionist dreams he enters a film, only for the backgrounds
to change unexpectedly, transporting him from desert to railway to snow-
drift. In homage, Columbo visits a film studio and wanders into the middle of a visual effects production. As he stands in front of the screen, the
backgrounds behind him change from desert to sci-fi space battle, to a
boat on an ocean. Each time Columbo reacts as though to his new environment, his acting style evoking early silent cinema as he ducks one way
to avoid laser blasts, another to avoid ocean spray. More physically, in 'The
Greenhouse Jungle' (1972) Falk executes an incredibly comic stunt: running too fast down a steep canyon incline, overtaking his more-balanced
colleague, limbs wheeling, falling dramatically and hilariously, but ending up precisely mid-shot. His facial expression at the moment during
the stunt when he realises he has lost control of his movements is a pure
Keaton deadpan.

Such visual gags, acrobatic stunts and pratfalls were the stock in trade
of silent cinema comedians like Keaton (Robinson 1969: 16), as was the
silent mime that Columbo employs in crime scene recreations. Keaton,
importantly for this discussion, observed that using the body to slowly
visualise the thought process could be extremely funny. From the success
with audiences of a delayed pause before reaction – which he inserted into
a routine involving a kick up the butt – Keaton observed that: 'Audiences
love the Slow Thinker' (Robinson 1969: 16). This use of *the body as the
conduit through which thinking can be visualised* is precisely the effect of
Columbo's (seemingly improvisational) crime scene mimes, in which he
physically figures out how things transpired in the past. Here, a cinematic
mode of acting, its heritage in vaudeville (an aspect of Columbo's performance identified by Williams in the second pilot), indicates that *attentiveness is a thinking process which is both embodied and performed.*

Thus, together all these influences on Falk's acting create the char-
acterisation of Columbo. What is important about realising this is that
it is the combination of the elements which enables what this persona

does: improvising through the everyday in a manner that embodies (thus, the influences of method acting, live television and the US independent tradition), effectively as mime, the thought process of Columbo's attentiveness (the influence of early silent Hollywood comedy).

The complexities behind the performed nature of Columbo's investigative technique crystalise in 'It's All in the Game' (1993). This episode was scripted by Falk, and in it Columbo cynically responds to the flirtation of an attractive murder suspect, Lauren Staton (Faye Dunaway), with a two-faced bashfulness. After accepting gifts of clothing, and going on dates with Staton, Columbo confronts his reflection in a mirror. He is drunk, seemingly intoxicated with the flirtation, and wiping Staton's lipstick off his lips. Momentarily the façade crumbles, and Columbo looks like a tired, ageing actor, reminiscent of an unhappy clown. As he removes the lipstick and the tie which Staton has bought him, Columbo's expression indicates his disgust with his own performance.

Here Falk self-consciously and honestly reveals his own part in this cynical performance. Falk is only credited with having penned this one episode of *Columbo* (albeit he was involved in the writing of many more). Evidently Falk has self-indulgently imagined a case in which he dates

Figure 3.4 Columbo the unhappy clown, in *Columbo* 'It's All in the Game' (1993).

and is flirted with and repeatedly kissed by the stunning movie star Faye Dunaway. But, perhaps to his credit, Falk also chooses in this episode to reveal the most cynical depth of Columbo's performance, with this scene of Columbo facing his own disingenuousness in the mirror with a look of tired disgust.

The episode's ending compounds this sense of Falk revealing Columbo's cynicism. Ultimately, Columbo shows no shame at his behaviour after allowing Staton, the woman he has flirted with whilst investigating her, to be imprisoned on a false confession. This she undertakes, nobly, to protect her daughter. And this is in spite of the mitigating factors surrounding the murder that the mother and daughter committed together (the maternal duo kill, but in retaliation for an abusive and manipulative gold-digging man two-timing them). When Columbo is asked by the bartender, Barney (John Finnegan), how he could behave in this way, Columbo callously responds: 'Who says I felt anything about her?' Barney observes that, in fact, he, Columbo, had said as much. Columbo responds: 'Listen, if you believe everything a cop tells you, you're a damn fool.' He then casually declares his return to his wife to take her bowling as a matter of weekly routine. At this point the credits roll with an upbeat musical flourish commencing the orchestral 'This Old Man . . .' theme tune, that which came, over the years, to define the Columbo character.

The close of 'It's All in the Game', then, most clearly indicates that Grant's lawyer Williams's assessment of Columbo in the second pilot was entirely accurate. Columbo is performing his detective role, entirely cynically. This is unsurprising. In the first pilot, 'Prescription: Murder', the key interrogation scene in which Columbo uncharacteristically leans on a young woman who is an accessory to murder, to get to the murderer, takes place on a deserted film studio set. The presence of the costumed extras walking the studio lot, the lights and camera equipment which crowd the *mise-en-scène* on the set where the interrogation takes place (including a mirror with lights as is typically used for make-up), all very effectively frame Columbo's aggressive interrogation of a woman who makes her living as a movie extra. She is even still in costume. This metacinematic foregrounding of the *act of staging* surrounding the interrogation foregrounds very clearly the theatrical nature of Columbo's performance as a detective.

Ultimately, Columbo's manner of interrogation, and considering how his work pervades his life, perhaps his whole being, is a well-prepared act enabling of 'characteristic spontaneity' from within the role. In fact, this very deliberate performing of *faux-naivety*, whilst effectively harassing suspects in a manner invasive of every aspect of their private and public lives, is entirely scripted. Very literal evidence of this can be found in the

directions given to Falk in a draft of the script for 'Fade in to Murder'
(1976). This is an investigation in which Columbo verbally spars with a
fictional version of himself, Ward Fowler, an actor who plays the television
detective Lieutenant Lucerne (William Shatner).

Television's Lieutenant Lucerne is deliberately introduced in a way
which equates his phenomenally high-salary, Emmy-award-winning
detective show, and disputes with the studio, with Falk's own real-life
experiences on *Columbo*. In the midst of this self-conscious playfulness,
the following revealing exchange (aspects of which remain in the episode
as it was finally filmed) was planned:

>   WARD
> Lieutenant, why don't you just
> ask me what you want to know.
>
>   COLUMBO
>   (bright-eyed, getting
>   the inside dope)
> <u>Where</u> did Mrs. Daley discover you,
> sir? That's something even my
> wife doesn't know.
>
>   WARD
>   (looking at him)
> But <u>you</u> know. Don't you?
>
>   COLUMBO
> Oh. Yes . . . as a matter of fact, I
> think I do. On a tour of some
> kind. Wasn't she? . . .
>
>   (Shaw and Feibleman 1976: 61–62)[11]

Even from this draft of the script it is apparent that Columbo's emotions
are intended to be performed ones. He may initially appear 'bright-eyed,
getting the inside dope', but this is scripted as a deliberate act to catch
Fowler off guard. This Fowler was also scripted to reveal by confronting
Columbo for appearing to know less than he does: 'But <u>you</u> know, don't
you?' Thus this revision of the script, although ultimately distinct from
the finished episode, illuminates how Columbo is supposed to perform his
role as detective. Indeed, in the finished episode, Fowler, himself an actor

---

[11] Script consulted at the British Film Institute, Special Collection.

who plays a television detective, calls out Columbo early on for his 'stumbling around, asking silly fake-innocent questions'.

Columbo, then, performs his thinking process for us to see in a variety of physical guises: from crime-scene-recreating mimes, to the unhappy clown momentarily disgusted with his own cynicism. But all are underpinned by the 'bright-eyed' faux-innocent Columbo persona which emerged in the second pilot, with direct acknowledgement by Grant's murderous lawyer, Williams. This performance of Columbo draws on the diverse influences evident in Falk's repertoire. The method, whilst it is in this mix, is not enough on its own to explain how Falk acts the role that Columbo performs. What is important about this amalgamated style is that, whilst Falk's acting with its myriad influences personifies Columbo (the *how* of his performance), the Lieutenant performs his characteristic interrogation of suspects for a specific purpose (the *why*): to uncover their guilt. Let us now explore this latter dimension in more depth.

Innocent until Proven Guilty?

Outside of the confines of a television show in which the viewer knows from the start who the murderer is, Columbo's manner of pursuing suspects would be, as they themselves often point out, harassment. This is a result of the performative nature of Columbo's hounding of suspects. For example, Columbo's purposefully unnerving interjection of 'just one more thing' at the end of an interview, even on one occasion after seemingly having departed a suspect's house, slamming the door behind him ('Lovely but Lethal' [1973]), is not forgetfulness on the Lieutenant's part. Instead, it is an unorthodox interrogation technique designed to unnerve the suspect as to the sanctity that their private home offers from the invasive law.

Admittedly, Columbo is not *as* invasive as retired, raincoated police commissioner Alfred Fichet in *Les Diaboliques/The Fiends* (1955), who critic Roger Ebert considers a cinematic precursor to Columbo (in terms of both his cigar and manner of questioning). Fichet even intrudes into the bedroom of his suspect at night, and – creepily – sits smoking, watching her, until she awakes. Nevertheless, the slightly more respectful invasiveness of Columbo's investigation has a similar effect, destroying the boundary between the private and the public spheres in a manner indicating the ubiquity of police surveillance.

In this respect, Columbo's harassment also stretches beyond the performative. Columbo involves the murderer in all aspects of the case.

Especially, he requires them to explain every anomaly in the history of events (as they have falsely constructed this history [see Chapters 4 and 5]) whilst he unravels the carefully constructed façade of their alibi.

This might seem, on the one hand, good policing: testing a suspect's story repeatedly until the cracks appear. Perhaps the pleasure of watching *Columbo* is thus in observing a courtroom trial without the stuffy procedures and the static location. This is the effect when Columbo pursues Grant's lawyer Williams in the second pilot and they chew over how his case might go in court. The same experience is recreated when Columbo investigates other high-powered lawyers – Oscar Finch (Patrick McGoohan) in 'Agenda for Murder' (1990) and Hugh Creighton (Dabney Coleman) in 'Columbo and the Murder of a Rock Star' (1991).

On the other hand, what Columbo's relentless pursuit of the killer shows is that we are always on trial, whether at home, at work or going about our everyday lives. Columbo's investigation involves an unofficial dry running of a proper trial *in public*. Its legality, then, is highly questionable. After all, this occurs without the suspect having the benefit of legal counsel or having been made aware of the charges and evidence against them, or being given the chance to formulate a counter-argument or call their own witnesses, and without the police officer being under oath. This last is key, as Columbo often bends or breaks the law to secure a confession (see further in Chapter 4). In 'Lady in Waiting' (1971), for example, Columbo is accurately accused of 'cross-examining' the suspect, and of being 'devious' in his 'hounding' of her. What life under late capitalism requires, *Columbo* shows, is for innocence to remain perpetually precarious, under surveillance 24/7.

With our performance forever under review, it follows, we are all guilty until proven innocent. To understand why this is, it is worth digging deeper into the literary origins of *Columbo* which illuminate – contrary to Ebert's view – the real roots of Columbo's investigative performance. As noted in Chapter 1, Levinson's and Link's inspiration for Columbo lies in literary characters like G. K. Chesterton's Father Brown, and Porfiry Petrovich the examining magistrate from Fyodor Dostoevsky's *Crime and Punishment* (1866) (1981b: 66). Father Brown is a diminutive Catholic priest who solves puzzling crimes amongst the well-to-do. He upholds the moral order wearing a 'commonplace overcoat' (Chesterton 2006: 64), he is shabby (pp. 51, 84), unassuming, forgetful, obsessively observes unusual behaviour, holds his temples (p. 45), enjoys cigars (p. 112) and uses recreations or entrapment (pp. 145, 31) to ensure confession (pp. 48, 55). These are all traits which Columbo inherits. *Columbo* retains this sense of the detective seeking confession more than conviction.[12] Yet, whilst Father Brown looks to uncover a *sin* to *absolve*, the everyman LAPD Lieutenant seeks (usually in vain) for a more secular sense of *guilt*, or preferably (although it is rarely offered), *remorse*.

Columbo works more in the manner in which, after Gilles Deleuze and Félix Guattari (1972: 107–113 and 332; 1980: 154–155), a psychoanalyst can be considered to work – performing the societal role of a secular priest (taking 'confession' and offering a way to move on through analysis). In the first pilot, 'Prescription: Murder', Columbo specifically equates his role as a detective to that of a psychiatrist, due to both professions involving the observation of people's behaviour (whether rational or irrational). There follow numerous occasions where such a process is again heavily alluded to. In 'Murder by the Book' (1971), the first episode of series one, Columbo asks the wife of the murder victim to just talk about her deceased husband's relationship to his murderous writing partner (whilst Columbo sits patiently, listening, rather like an analyst), so he can locate the piece of concrete evidence he needs for the conviction. She agrees to help, describing the situation, precisely, as: 'Kind of like analysis, but without the couch.' That this is a more secular form of working through, as opposed to a confession of a spiritual nature, explains why, with the noticeable exception of Johnny Cash's gospel star, Tommy Brown in 'Swan Song' (1974) (whose conscience is pricked seemingly due to his religious beliefs), typically the murderers are not contrite. Wealthy wine connoisseur Adrian Carsini (Donald Pleasence), in 'Any Old Port in a Storm' (1973), even declares that there is 'no remorse attached' to murdering his younger brother over control of his family's business.

This secular emphasis might be traced to Porfiry's persona and manner of questioning of the murderer Raskolnikov one century earlier. Like Father Brown, Porfiry's influence on Columbo's character is also evident. He initially dissembles that he is formally questioning his chief suspect, but then attempts to entrap him with an unexpected question when the informal interrogation seems over (Dostoevsky [1866] 1994: 201). When caught out in his ruse, Porfiry plays dumb, and 'tapping his forehead' claims he confused the dates (p. 202). Later, his manner of questioning includes appearing out of the blue and claiming to be just passing (p. 355), disarming discussions of off-topic trivia, questioning accompanied by

---

[12] Not coincidentally, 1970s' network thinking held that an unobjectionable 'little morality tale' would attract viewers choosing between the three major networks (MacDonald 1990: 196).

erratic movements to and from the suspect interrupted by requests to smoke (p. 258), and rushing after the suspect when an examination has concluded, breathlessly shouting 'Just one word. . .', only to impart the news that more questions will follow later (p. 276). Raskolnikov soon realises, as do all Columbo's suspects, that Porfiry 'is not such a fool as he may look' (p. 205).

The secular approach to guilt (or lack of guilt) emerges from Raskolnikov's belief in *Crime and Punishment* that he is 'exceptional' or 'extraordinary' in relation to his peers (Dostoevsky [1866] 1994: 193–194). Thus he experiments, tragically, with the idea that he might be a Nietzschean superman, and murders, before finally realising the value of life (p. 364). Columbo, similarly, often observes to murderers that what marks them out from others is their belief in their own exceptional abilities. It is seemingly this which makes them believe that it is their right to murder, and which fools them into thinking that no one will discover their guilt. The (elusive) quest for guilt which Columbo seeks in vain in his suspects appears somehow vitalist in approach. Columbo pursues the (secular) realisation that their crime has taken life from another, for which there must be at least an acknowledgement, even if there is not atonement.

Dostoyevsky's emphasis on the tension between guilt and the belief of the Nietzschean murderer in their exceptionality has influenced crime drama ever since. To briefly flashforward, the same morality tale is played out in the serial killer-focused television show, *The Fall* (2013–2016), which even has the murderer quote Nietzsche to illustrate his detachment from contemporary morality. What is revealing about this literary root to *Columbo*, specifically, is that the discussions between Porfiry and Raskolnikov also play out what is effectively a trial amidst the everyday life of the suspect. Porfiry, unlike the more clue-oriented Columbo, has little evidence against Raskolnikov. Rather, he has figured out by psychologically profiling Raskolnikov that the young man believes himself to be exceptional, above the law. The modus operandi of Porfiry in conducting an informal (everyday) trial is exactly that of Columbo: informal questioning to back the suspect into a corner – engaging them in considering how a likely prosecution/defence argument would play out in court (Dostoevsky [1866] 1994: 271), even discussing likely sentencing (p. 364) – until the suspect realises their case is hopeless and is offered a chance to confess (p. 362).

Both Porfiry and Columbo, then, are as interested in reading the reactions of the suspect as they are in the facts surrounding the murder; albeit for Columbo this is a way of building upon clues so as to convince the suspect that they have no choice but to confess. As early as episode one, 'Murder by the Book' (1971), Columbo questions the murderer as to why, when phoning in the discovery of the dead body of his writing partner on his lawn, he also absent-mindedly opened his mail. Amongst many more such examples, great emphasis is placed on reading characters in 'Candidate for Crime' (1973). In this episode Columbo deduces from watching a sad-looking secretary that she is romantically involved with her (married) employer, a politician running for senate, Nelson Hayward (Jackie Cooper). Columbo also correctly reads Hayward's lack of relief over a detail which he has cleared up as a sign of the politician's unease that Columbo is creeping closer to uncovering his guilt. 'I thought you'd be relieved', Columbo incredulously tells the irate murderer, indicating his critical evaluation of the senator's lack of conviction to the realism of his performance of innocence.

Columbo, the ultimate performer, thus interprets the actions of others rather like a theatre critic might, assessing how 'in character' an actor is. Specifically, he is looking for behaviour indicating something other than a genuinely innocent reaction. To return to 'Murder by the Book' (1971), Columbo ultimately tells the murderer that one of the things which tipped him off to his guilt was that he never showed any 'genuine emotion' for his deceased writing partner of ten years. Although perhaps the most playful example of Columbo behaving like a theatre critic occurs in 'Dagger of the Mind' (1972), in which he ironically compliments a murderous thespian couple on how well-rehearsed and in-sync their performance of their alibi is. His intimation being, of course, that it is so well-rehearsed and synchronised that it ultimately seems unrealistically *staged*.

This emphasis on evaluating performance is doubtless unsurprising to fans of crime fiction. For instance, Arthur Conan Doyle's Sherlock Holmes, when not himself perfecting disguises for his undercover work (investigation as performance, not entirely dissimilar to Columbo's mannered snooping), often looks to unmask the performances of others. Raymond Chandler's Philip Marlowe, alternatively, is ever watchful for the duplicitous charade of a *femme fatale*. Accordingly, in 'Fade in to Murder', Lieutenants Columbo and Lucerne spend a lot of time analysing and complementing each other's performance, both as detectives and as actors. Thus, investigating in the manner of a suspicious theatre critic, Columbo's role is to remove the mask from these guilty performers. As with the tricks Falk played on his co-stars, demanding in-character improvisation on camera, so too then Columbo's investigative style.

Yet despite these similarities with such literary predecessors, especially Father Brown and Porfiry Petrovich, what distinguishes *Columbo* is that the Lieutenant is not interested in sin, a chance at contrition, or the spiritual or mental well-being of the suspect – but *only* in uncovering guilt. Hence, a different literary precursor can illuminate how the ubiquitous attention paid to the criminal by the law (their effectively being on trial amidst their everyday life), indicates how lives become self-consciously performed when under surveillance. It is in Franz Kafka's *The Trial* (1925), the most famous work of an author known to Levinson and Link, that Columbo's relationship to guilt becomes much clearer (Levinson and Link 1981a: 10).

In Kafka's *The Trial* the law is everywhere, erasing any distinction between everyday life and an ongoing trial (and as a result, between public and private spheres of life).[13] In *The Trial*, the anti-hero, K, is arrested at home by low-ranking functionaries of the law who unquestioningly assume his guilt. His hearing is in a court which is also someone's home, or someone's workplace (the point being, the boundary is unclear). K meets his lawyer in their bedroom. K's workplace becomes the site of punitive floggings for functionaries of the law. K inhabits a world where the suspect has the right to a defence lawyer but does not have one and is unaware of what the prosecution knows. The most K ever learns about his arrest is that the law is attracted to his guilt, and in this sense he is the victim of his own downfall.

If reading *The Trial* is like entering *Crime and Punishment* just after the opening murder (the reader never knowing if any such event happened), then watching *Columbo* is a little like entering *The Trial* in the belief that because the suspect is under suspicion they are probably guilty. Like the law's functionaries in Kafka's novel, but unlike its readers, as viewers of *Columbo* of course we do actually *know* that the suspect is guilty. We have seen the murder. Even so, it is worth pausing momentarily to wonder whether this justifies what follows. The suspect's every waking move from then on – at work, at home (in public, in private) – is haunted by the ever-annoying presence of this low-ranking functionary of the law. Columbo seems attracted to the murderer as though to their guilt itself. Forever on trial, always receiving the attention of the ubiquitous law, the murderer (without a defence lawyer due to their apparently free status and lack of formal charges) is ultimately entrapped by the system. In *Columbo*, as in *The Trial*, suspects become guilty before the law, their trial ongoing even of their most everyday actions.

This always-on-trial nature of Columbo's investigative method is fore-grounded on several occasions. In 'The Most Dangerous Match' (1973), Columbo presents his proof to a murderous chess master in front of a

---

[13] Deleuze discusses *The Trial* when describing the functioning of the control society, which I discussed in Chapter 2 (1992: 5).

crowd that has assembled to watch him play consecutive chess matches. In 'Publish or Perish' (1974), the concluding scene is staged as though playing out a dry run of an actual trial (the suspect attempting to put the case for the defence), in which a suddenly revealed new witness – a manuscript delivery man who the suspect was bribing – dramatically proves the flaws in the suspect's defence. Indeed, Columbo's complete disregard for due process or a suspect's rights is humorously foregrounded in 'Columbo and the Murder of a Rock Star' (1991) when he struggles to read a suspect his rights without having them written down in front of him, presumably never having done it before. As a low-ranking functionary of the Kafka-esque law, Columbo regards his suspects as always on trial, even to the point of invasively photographing a suspect at his wife's funeral, like an insensitive paparazzi or indiscrete private eye ('Negative Reaction' [1974]).

The close connection between perpetual guilt, contemporary society's emphasis on surveillance and how our lives are performed, is clearest after the show's revival with ABC. For example, in 'Agenda for Murder' (1990), which focuses on a murder close to the Congressman Paul Mackey (Denis Arndt), Mackey metaphorically describes Columbo's case as a house floating on thin air. Columbo replies that it is a house made of glass, and that Mackey is inside it. Thus, the greater emphasis on celebrity and fame in the revival era episodes, coinciding with the shifting gears of the industrialisation of vision (including the network television coverage enjoyed by Mackey), more directly indicate the all-surveilled nature of contemporary life. There are now no secrets due to the transparent nature of a life lived perpetually on camera, and the corresponding capacity for the media, police and state security apparatuses to scrutinise all aspects of a person's life. We all now inhabit a transparent 'house', our lives entirely under scrutiny. As Richard A. Lanham observes, due to the all-surveilled nature of contemporary life it 'is irremediably and self-consciously dramatic. It brings with it heightened dramatic self-consciousness' (2006: 10). This is very evident, for example, in how the media is manipulated by the performance of a (fake) murder, to raise the value of a magazine in 'Columbo Cries Wolf' (1990) (see Chapter 2).

Revealing both this performative self-consciousness and its potential to reap financial reward, many of Columbo's suspects are attention industry performers by trade: musicians, magicians, celebrity chefs, theatre actors, chess masters, and, especially, stars of the large and small screen. All are in the business of being looked at, of attracting the attentive labour of audiences. But as a result of this, their guilt becomes transparent under Columbo's attentive gaze. As a low-level functionary of the law, Columbo's chief weapons are attentive methods of surveillance. He describes his job as: 'listen and look, look and listen' ('Make Me a Perfect Murder' [1978]), and again, 'looking and thinking, thinking and looking' ('How to Dial a Murder' [1978]). Paying attention, then, can be enough to reveal guilt. For example, in 'The Conspirators' (1978), the murderer, Joe Devlin (Clive Revill), is an Irish poet fundraising for Sinn Féin to purchase arms to smuggle to Ireland for the IRA. Devlin is a well-practised entertainer, attending book signings, talking on the radio, playing banjo and singing. Devlin's worth as a fundraiser, then, depends on his remaining in the spotlight. The more attention he can gather the more he is worth to Sinn Féin's cause. As a result, all Columbo finally has to do is pay attention and eventually Devlin's guilt is revealed. In the closing scene, Columbo races along the shore as a ship soon to contain the smuggled arms sets out to sea. The ship has been searched before sailing, and no guns found. Columbo continues looking, even though he is not sure what for, until, through a touristic viewfinder set into the dock, his attention is rewarded by the sight of the guns being loaded onto the boat from a tug. If ubiquitous surveillance is 24/7, all crime will ultimately be uncovered by the vigilant police.

Ultimately, Falk's performance as Columbo draws attention to three things. Most obviously his investigation – attracting the attention of the easily distracted viewer with his 'just one more thing' catchphrase, to maintain focus on the unfolding story. Also, as this chapter has uncovered, the necessity of paying attention 24/7. Finally, the importance of exteriorising the process of attentive labour as though to an invisible audience: attending to the cameras which are perpetually watching an all-surveilled society for out-of-character slips revealing guilt.

In Chapter 4 I will consider how *Columbo* justifies the need for such invasive investigative practice by emphasising the technological advancements that render history uncertain. This, by turns, raises questions over how this can be, reassuringly, policed (the subject of Chapter 5). We will find that Columbo embodies the paradox which emerges at the boundary of the law under neoliberalism (Chapter 6 and the Conclusion). At once dedicated to the protection of the right to life of all citizens, ironically Columbo's exhausting, all-consuming professional life threatens to reduce him to the dog-tired 24/7-working status of those he seeks to protect.

CHAPTER 4

Learning:
Columbo vs Modernity

The key question addressed in this chapter is: Why are there so many machines in *Columbo*? For anyone watching *Columbo* with any degree of regularity the presence of technology is hard to miss. Technology is often integral to the crime itself, and knowledge of how it works is vital to Columbo's ability to solve the murder. Yet why do so many *Columbo* murders involve technology, and why is this technology so often explained to the viewer in detail, as though in a tech class? Extensive probing of this question over many episodes and re-viewings of *Columbo* indicates that the answer is as follows: Columbo's proactive engagement with the rapid technological advances of modernity – his learning about new machinery – indicates the perpetual labour needed to avoid obsolescence in an increasingly hi-tech world.

Columbo is constantly 'upgrading' his technological knowledge to ensure he can pay attention productively. He is, then, an archetypal 'entrepreneur of the self' (Lazzarato 2014: 52), a mode of work-engaged subjectivity which neoliberal ideology advocates for all in the absence of a supportive state. Alongside the complex memory game which *Columbo* provides to hone viewer attention, then, this supplementary concern (like that explored in the previous chapter, of how to *perform*), is one of realising how best an individual can *learn* such that they maximise their attentive labour.

Columbo's engagement with modernity reassures viewers that if lower middle-class 'everyman' Columbo can master new machinery, anyone can. Screen media in particular are key here. Those busily engaged in watching – paying attention, especially to film and television as act of labour – are typically innocent figures. Contrariwise, those who misuse technology to give the impression of such 'innocent' adherence to attentive labour (in fact, using technology to cover up that they are engaged in criminality), attempt to 'get away with murder'. To catch these criminals requires that Columbo stays up to date technologically. Yet in a world where technology enables near-constant surveillance, it is debateable just how reassuring this techno-savvy police presence really is.

Tech Class on TV

A feature of most *Columbo* episodes is the need for him to learn about another profession, so as to understand how the murderer has both committed the crime and created their alibi. Over sixty-nine *Columbo*'s this includes everything from chef to bullfighter. For this reason, and perhaps curiously for a detective show, Columbo is often pictured reading or carrying around an armful of books. This learning process is foregrounded to the point where murderers compliment Columbo on his learning, which he seems to genuinely appreciate. But the learning does not stop at a new profession. Very often it involves new technological know-how.

In the first episode, 'Murder by the Book' (1971), it is immediately established that Columbo is a man engaged with technological modernity. His introduction sees him comment on a building's water fountains, coffee machines and – with some marvel – heat-sensitive elevator call buttons. From then on, Columbo is repeatedly depicted learning about the latest technologies as part of the investigation. Whilst it might not be unusual for a locked room mystery to use a fiendishly clever technological solution to explain an otherwise puzzling murder, *Columbo*'s engagement with modernity has a more integral purpose than this. It is a foregrounded feature of the show which relates specifically to its context, setting it apart from both the other programmes in the NBC *Mystery Movie* wheel and crime dramas of the era more broadly.

For example, although the hi-tech nature of modern business is conspicuous in another Richard Levinson and William Link creation, *Mannix* (1967–1975), here an impressive roomful of whirring computer banks will typically provide a scenic backdrop to the action. The machines rarely help solve the crime directly. Rather, their static presence accentuates the foregrounded physical prowess of the detective whose actions do catch the criminal. Moreover, *Columbo* is not only fascinated with the latest techniques for policing, an aspect of other shows in the *Mystery Movie* wheel. The western *Hec Ramsey* (1972–1974) sees Deputy Police Chief Ramsey (Richard Boone) and Doctor Coogan (Harry Morgan) undertake ballistic and forensic tests. They use a magnifying contraption to compare the markings on fired bullets, a microscope to identify intoxicating substances (like a cocaine-infused snuff), and, repeatedly, Ramsey undertakes his trademark dusting for fingerprints (e.g. in 'A Hard Road to Vengeance' [1973]). For its part, *Quincy, M.E.* (1976–1983) foregrounds scientific processes for their ability to provide forensic evidence to solve murder investigations. Typically, *Quincy, M.E.* includes close-ups of microscope slides, even projected displays of them, to illustrate the scientific conundrum puzzling the eponymous coroner (e.g. in 'Who's Who in Neverland' [1976]). The difference is that *Columbo* does not worry itself much with such scientific methods for detection, or at least, when Columbo does so it is part of a broader, foregrounded engagement with *all* the new everyday technologies of the late twentieth century.

The list of gizmos which Columbo encounters which were 'new' at the time offers a rapid-fire rundown of the highlights of the last fifty years of technological development. A brief list is useful to register the scale of *Columbo*'s engagement with technology. In addition to the aforementioned water fountains, coffee machines and heat-operated elevator buttons, Columbo encounters: remotely triggered tape recordings; pacemakers; metal detectors; wiretapping bugs; hearing aids; pagers; automatic shut-off features on trash compactors; phone systems with call lights; burglar alarms; subliminal advertising images inserted into films; World War III computer simulations; robots working computers; aeroplane crash site forensic techniques; edited tape-recorded phone calls; office computers; photographic negatives; CCTV; sound-operated doors; digital watches; hidden microphones; golf ball typewriters; LED clocks; record players with internal computers; multi-reel cinema projection; live TV; a Titan movie crane; fax machines; home computers; ghetto blasters; last number redial functions on push-button phones; programmed speed-dial phone functions; miniature television screens; floppy disks; VHS; radar ticketing; date/time features on home video cameras; satellite TV; cellular phones; email, and the *coup de grâce* in the final episode, ground-penetrating radar.

This rapid retrospective review on the show's engagement with the late twentieth-century's transforming technoscape indicates the extent of Columbo's labour in keeping up with the latest gadgetry advances. Columbo's constant updating of his knowledge of technology is directly related to how attention is shaped under modernity. As Jonathan Crary notes:

> It is possible to see one crucial aspect of modernity as an ongoing crisis of attentiveness, in which the changing configurations of capitalism continually push attention and distraction to new limits and thresholds, with an endless sequence of new products, sources of stimulation, and streams of information, and then respond with new methods of managing and regulating perception. (1999: 13–14)

Crary succinctly describes the never-ending, Sisyphusian nature of endeavouring to keep up with modern technology which Columbo undertakes.

The growth of the attention industries, especially, requires post-Fordist workers to stay up to date with advances in information technology for their labour (paying attention to machines) to remain productive (Crary 1999: 81–84; Bueno 2017: 39–77). Indeed, this goes for Columbo and the viewers of *Columbo*, both of whom inhabit the rapidly advancing world so famously described by Alvin Toffler in *Future Shock* (1970). Toffler, like Herbert A. Simon notes the 'information overload' of the 'fast and irregularly changing' modern world, which requires that people rapidly 'scoop up and process far more information than before . . . at extremely high rates of speed' (1970: 318–319). (*Columbo*'s mention of Toffler is discussed in Chapter 2.) *Columbo* reassures viewers that such an anxiogenic context can be mastered though constant vigilance and autodidactic upskilling as we see Columbo do. In this way, *Columbo* equally assists in the spread of knowledge about the late twentieth-century's fast-shifting technological aspect, also keeping the audience 'up to speed' with ever-emerging new technologies. Let us consider the two dimensions of this process in turn: Columbo's perpetual upgrading first; then the viewer's schooling.

Columbo often undergoes what can only be described as on-the-job-training in the latest technologies. In 'Make me the Perfect Murder' (1978) we watch as Columbo is taught about multi-reel cinema projection, including the flashes in the top right-hand corner of the screen which indicate an imminent reel change (crucial to the solving of the crime). We then see him give the process a try, rather like a bumbling junior apprentice might. In the same episode he is taught about the controls used for monitoring live TV. In both instances, Columbo has hands-on experience under the guidance of an experienced mentor (as though undergoing work experience), and although he humorously fails to develop an adept mastery, he learns enough to realise how the technology can be manipulated to cover up murderous deeds. If Columbo is an 'old model' – as his love of Sinatra over Rock 'n' Roll and his dilapidated 1950s Peugeot remind us – nevertheless his knowledge of technology is constantly being upgraded. The perpetual labour of engaging with a transforming environment is thus of great import for Columbo, and this functions as a reassurance in the face of rapid technological and, indeed, accompanying social change.

That this is a form of reassurance should not be underestimated. For commentators ranging from Toffler and Simon to Franco 'Bifo' Berardi (2009b: 107–108), the point is made that the pace of change, and resulting information overload, has become impossible to keep up with. Attention is stretched thin. Yet for Columbo, albeit he may have to work 24/7 to manage it, he *can* keep pace with modernity. This is quite a reassurance considering that the opposite may well be the reality for many people. Consider, for example, the following from Berardi, discussing the difference between the manual labour typical of industrial manufacturing, and the new 'mental labour' typical of the industries that have come to dominate in the developed world since the 1970s (2009b: 75).

> Labour has become part of a mental process, an elaboration of signs rich with knowledge. It has become much more specific, much more specialized: attorneys and architects, computer technicians and mall vendors all sit in front of the same screen and type on the same keyboards: still, they could never trade places. The content of their elaborating activities is completely different and cannot be easily transmitted. On the other hand, also from a physical point of view, chemical, metal and mechanical workers do completely different jobs, but it takes only a few days for a metal or mechanical worker to acquire the operative knowledge necessary to do the job of a worker in the chemical industry and vice versa. The more industrial labour is simplified, the more it becomes interchangeable. (2009b: 76)

The repeated spectacle of Columbo rapidly learning about all the latest technologies, in fact, gives the *opposite* impression to this reality. *Columbo* goes out of its way to offer repeated reassurances that it is entirely possible to quickly become familiar with very specialised forms of mental labour. Moreover, Columbo's perpetual learning also reassures those of a class which one might typically expect to associate with manual labour that they can also make this transference to mental labour with relative ease.

Columbo, then, purposefully flattens the distinction between new kinds of mental labour and older kinds of manual labour. It reassures that the situation in which there was relative ease of movement between simplified manual jobs continues, even if the kinds of jobs (and associated technologies) have transformed. If unschooled Columbo can keep up with all the newest technological wizardry needed for these jobs with just some reading and on-the-job training, the viewer is reassured, then surely anyone can. Or rather, as Columbo is an everyman, *everyone* can.

This idea of necessary self-improvement to stay competitive as a labourer is a feature of neoliberalism. With the withdrawal of the state as a social support mechanism, responsibility for the improvement of the citizen is left to the individual to organise. As Maurizio Lazzarato observes:

> the promise that 'work on the self' was supposed to offer 'labor' in terms of emancipation (pleasure, a sense of accomplishment, recognition, experimentation with new forms of life, upward mobility, etc.) has been transformed into the imperative to take upon oneself the risks and costs for which neither business nor the State are willing to pay. (2014: 53)

For those already wealthy, the cost of being an 'entrepreneur of the self' is bearable. The *Mystery Movie* wheel's *Banacek* (1972–1974) features an extremely well-to-do eponymous protagonist whose expertise – which is crucial to both his professional and social status – is taken for granted as being his privileged, personal prerogative. For those less well-healed, like Columbo, of course things are different. Even so, *Columbo* also smooths over the potentially prohibitive costs of self-enterprise. It does so by fig- uring this as a process of engaging exploration without the attendant per- sonal debt and risk: whilst the lower middle-class everyman encounters a new trade that he can master in every episode, even so all the time he remains gainfully employed as a cop. Thus, alongside the reassurances which Columbo's rapid mastery of technology offers to viewers (you can do it too), there is also a degree of incentivising (to avoid obsolescence, this is what you should also do), and, finally, of a kind of celebration which is at odds with many people's financial reality (look at the world of opportuni- ties for jobs you could potentially do, well, that is if you have the money). The cherry on the cake is that Columbo never pursues any such learning beyond what he needs from it for each case, because being a cop, whilst a 24/7 job, is still a secure profession.

Here the comparison with *Mannix* is again helpful. *Mannix* reassures viewers that computers are no substitute for the (often violent) *actions* of the detective. Hence there seems little point in Joe Mannix (Mike Connors) learning about or from them. Indeed, this was also true of other late 1960s' shows in which, for all the foregrounded hi-tech wizardry (the functioning of which was taken as read), it was the actions of humans, rather than the technology per se, which was ultimately championed (e.g. *Star Trek* [1966–1969], *Mission Impossible* [1966–1973]). In *Columbo*, by contrast, *learning* about emerging technologies is shown to be vital if the attentive labourer is to keep pace with the modern world.

Compounding this sense of a tech class for Columbo, as he conducts the work on the self required of late capitalism, is the amount of screen time *Columbo* gives to technology. This renders information technology something of a spectacle, or subject, in its own right. For example, in 'A Deadly State of Mind' (1975), when Columbo visits a scientific institute, the *mise-en-scène* is dominated by banks of computers, whirring away in the background, their lights flashing in intricate patterns. As the computers are operating without human input, they seem to indicate an intelligence of their own. Encompassing much of the room, information technology literally provides the backdrop to Columbo's life. Or, more precisely, to the world which coexists with Columbo's everyday experience, and which he engages with on occasion. This coexisting world seemingly surrounds

Columbo much as an alien artificial intelligence might as it slowly takes over the human world.

In addition to its position in the *mise-en-scène*, information technology is also featured via the editing for longer than is necessary for the narrative. This aesthetic feature of the show brings into focus the didactic function of *Columbo*, its provision of a tech class for the viewer. A key example of this occurs in 'An Exercise in Fatality' (1974). Here an office computer, the Tricon Delta 2-14, is introduced to Columbo when he seeks information about a Tricon company employee. As the Tricon Delta 2-14 searches for the data, the scene is drawn out and Columbo's patience tested as he waits for it to be retrieved.

The editing cuts repeatedly back and forth between Columbo waiting, frustrated by the delay, the administrator who is dealing with his request via the computer (as well as fielding Columbo's questions), and – most importantly – repeated close-ups of the computer itself. In some respects, this feels like dead time. Certainly, the waiting does not advance the narrative of Columbo's investigation. As a result, both Mark Dawidziak ([1988] 2019: 200) and Sheldon Catz (2016: 38 and 137) consider the scene to be padded out so that the show can include more commercials. At first glance this seems a reasonable conclusion. After all, the Tricon Delta 2-14 is depicted in a way which seems almost commercial-like, in the middle of a programme which – as noted in Chapter 1 – was part of a televisual flow that included advertisements for the latest modern machines: cars, washing machines, typewriters, etc. However, there is another way to consider the scene, in terms of the rather direct address to the viewer which concerns the computer.

The noticeable screen time devoted to the computer, when considered in the light of *Columbo*'s overall emphasis on Columbo's perpetual learning about new technology, seems devoted to raising audience awareness of: firstly, the importance and the role of new technology in processing information, and, secondly, of the need to get used to the tempo of interaction with new technologies. What the editing *showcases* for the viewer in *real time*, with accompanying explanation from within the diegetic world, is how quickly this new machine can sift through the masses of available information. Noticeably, the administrator dealing with Columbo's request ignores him and performs other duties, even stating that a phone call would be 'much too complicated' in comparison. Columbo's irritated lingering, punctuated by his impertinent questions and the cutting back and forth with the computer (as it first searches and then prints) may indeed seem redundant in terms of narrative exposition. Yet its real purpose seems to be to offer a dedicated sequence of close-ups *of the computer*,

Figures 4.1–4.3
The viewer, like
Columbo, learns
to pay attention to
technology at its
nonhuman pace, in
Columbo 'An Exercise
in Fatality' (1974).

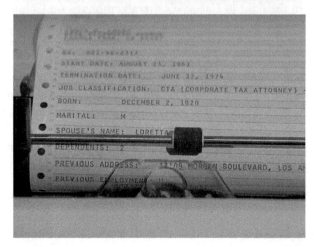

a spectacle in its own right, as it processes information. What the viewer learns from experiencing this montage is the amount of time they will need to wait for a computer to do its work.

The Tricon Delta 2-14 section, then, directly answers the question asked by Simon at this precise historical moment of how this task of paying attention could possibly be achieved when there is so much information to process. Especially considering that 24/7 attentive labour on the part of humans like Columbo will not be enough in itself. *Columbo*, like the every-man Columbo himself, pays attention to new technology on behalf of the viewer, providing the Tricon Delta 2-14 sequence with sufficient screen time for the answer to Simon's question to sink in: computers.

Such sequences celebrating computers were not uncommon in other detective shows of the era, but in *Columbo* it is this real-time engagement with them which stands out. For example, in the episode 'This Case is Closed' (1974) of *The Rockford Files* (1974–1980), from the same year as 'An Exercise in Fatality', a telling contrast is found. Jim Rockford attempts to get information under false pretences; specifically, the name of the owner of a car which is tailing him. Rockford makes a phone call to the Department of Motor Vehicles and cons the operative into searching for the name. The operative punches the licence plate number into the computer. There follows several seconds of fluid montage, showing: two reels of tape whirring, then a computer panel with lights flashing, followed by cards moving along an automated track, back to the two whirring reels of tape, and then to the operative once more. This sequence, effectively dramatising a machine seeking information as a spectacle in its own right, ends with the name and address Rockford seeks appearing on the operative's screen.

In both examples the intent is the same – to celebrate the ability of computing technology in processing data for the detective. The key difference is that the experience of waiting for the machine is a much shorter one for Rockford – and viewers of *The Rockford Files* – than it is for Columbo and *Columbo* viewers. Rockford waits an acceptable amount of time for a viewer of an action-packed detective show, whereas Columbo has an experience of waiting that is closer to the reality of the tempo of the human-computer interface. In both instances the process of information retrieval is the same, only staged and edited differently. Crucially, *Columbo* does not show us the 'backstage' workings of the machinery, just the portal through which the data will eventually flow. This is, tellingly, much more like the average person's experience of their interface with computing technology. As such, it is precisely this tempo which the *Columbo* viewer is taught to get used to in this scene.

Noticeably, once Columbo has the results from the computer he makes a phone call. On the other end of the line he encounters a recorded voice on an answering machine. Initially Columbo does not realise this and begins to try to engage in conversation. This is a humorous moment, in which the already nonplussed-with-computers detective encounters more evidence of the increasingly automated nature of everyday life. He is so effected by this, in fact, that when prompted to leave a message he even speaks in the slow and stilted manner of an automated voice. Thus the way in which the already protracted scene with the Tricon Delta 2-14 closes with the auto-mated phone message gestures towards the increasingly machinic nature of the organisation of our world. This scene compounds the sense, noted above in relation to the presence of computers in *Columbo*'s *mise-en-scène*, of information technology as a ubiquitous alien artificial intelligence which is increasingly shaping the human world. This is now a world in which, for many, something as fundamental to being human as the learning of a lan-guage may proceed as much (or more) through the interface with machines (including television) as it may with humans (Berardi 2009a: 37). The role of the human in this context, as Lazzarato elucidates, has become one of outsourced labour in the service of someone else's profit:

> If I have a problem with unemployment or my welfare check, I contact a call centre which each time asks me to press 1, 2, or 3. The same thing happens when making an appointment with the electric company, subscribing to an Internet service, obtaining information about my bank account, and so on. I have to figure things out for myself even if I lose time doing it, since it is impossible to find a human being within these networks. Moreover, the time that I lose is gained by the company or institution, time that I have graciously made available to them. (2014: 92)

What Columbo learns from his experiences with machines in this scene is entirely in line with Lazzarato's observations: under late capitalism the human is an insignificant cog in an increasingly machinic world of data processing, one whose labour may be drawn into the process due to the limitations of the technology. In addition, a human's time may have to be spent deferring to the pace of the technology. In short, attentive labour will involve attending to machines.

What is being learned, then, both by Columbo and the viewers of *Columbo*, is how to interface patiently with an increasingly inhuman, almost alien, technologically dominated world of late capitalism. In this sense, the Tricon Delta 2-14 scene provides an updating of a film like *Modern Times* (1936). Charlie Chaplin's iconic physical entanglement with the modern machinery of industrial capital now gives way to the figure of Columbo equally powerless-before-the-vastness-of-the-machinery which surrounds him. This time, however, rather than being swept into the machinery as the manual labourer Chaplin was due to its rapid speed, Columbo's interface with the computers of his era is one of attentiveness to their equally nonhuman but this time seemingly slower machinic pace (or rather, of the need to learn that that is what is required of him) (Lazzarato 2014: 93).[1]

Columbo's Tricon Delta 2-14 sequence is drawn out, then, to indicate that humans must now take their pace from technology, and not vice versa. This may mean, as Columbo's speech changes to a more machine-like speed and register when he leaves a message on the answering machine, that the humans become more like a machine in the process. Coming as it does in an episode in which Columbo is shown to be completely out of shape physically – in comparison to the health and fitness obsessed minor celebrity Milo Janus (Robert Conrad) – this scene raises the question of what humanity's fate will be now that machine time increasingly demands a relentless 24/7 attentiveness from the everyman labourer.

In addition to this expanded screen time, to reinforce *Columbo*'s didactic showcasing of the increasing integration of human and machine Columbo, or a colleague or other professional expert, may act as intermediary for the viewer. Their role is to explain how new technologies work in an everyday way. In 'Blueprint for Murder' (1972), when a doctor explains how a pacemaker runs on miniature energy cells, Columbo summarises: 'Oh, it's sort of like an electric watch.' Again, in 'The Greenhouse Jungle' (1972), the overly-earnest Detective Sargent Frederick Wilson (Bob Dishy) – who Columbo believes is sent to expose him to 'modern techniques' – explains about policing using a 'camera-mounted starlight scope' and the replacement of footprint plaster casts with 3D photographs. Perhaps the most evidently and humorously didactic in retrospect is the minute-long lesson in exactly what a FAX machine is and does, and even the reason for its name, in 'Agenda for Murder' (1990). All these various explanations which Columbo receives about new technologies over the years (and his ability to understand them with only preliminary research) are intended as introductions, instructions and reassurances regarding such machines. They function, in conjunction with the visual focus on the technology itself, to teach the show's viewers about the latest modern machines, gadgets and gizmos.

---

[1] A contemporary filmic comparison which reaffirms the difference would be *Three Days of the Condor* (1975), the opening of which overtly emphasises the inhumanly relentless speed of computers as they process the data that relates to humanity's – by comparison – chaotically rapid life and death 'stories'.

A standout moment in which *Columbo*'s pedagogic element is fore-grounded in both respects – screen time and expert explanation – takes place in 'Swan Song' (1974). At the site of a plane crash, Mr Rowland Pangborn (John Dehner) of Air Safety Division, National Transportation Safety Board, explains to a film crew about the usual causes of private plane crashes (such as mechanical failures) and the forensics they will per-form (including X-ray, chemical analysis, microscopic and metallurgical analysis). As the viewer watches Columbo searching the wreckage, we hear the anchor who is interviewing Pangborn state: 'I think the public is very interested in these aircraft accident investigative techniques.' Columbo does indeed look very interested in what he is learning, and as the anchor's voiceover indicates, he is clearly intended as a stand-in for the general public watching the show. Thus *Columbo*'s role as Joe Public's informal tech class is acknowledged every time Columbo states: 'you learn some-thing new every day'.

That everyman Columbo is a police officer, however, has a bearing on the type of reassurance viewers are offered. *Columbo*'s viewers are also reassured that, like Columbo himself, *the law* is quick to master technolog-ical development. New machines can be rapidly understood and deployed by our guardians and Columbo will ensure that their use will remain on the right side of the law. This is nowhere clearer than in 'Mind over Mayhem' (1974), in which Columbo figures out that a futuristic robot (in fact, Robby the Robot from *Forbidden Planet*[2] [1956]) has worked the com-puters in a nuclear war simulation to provide the (fake) alibi for the absent murderer. In this respect, the importance of the time Columbo spends paying attention to technology – looking in particular – relates directly to police surveillance and, as the rest of the chapter will explore, to the ques-tion of whether surveillance is adequately policed by the police themselves.

The Innocent Watch

In terms of police surveillance as legitimate attentive labour, Columbo cracks several cases by spending hours going over recorded footage (some-times security footage, sometimes television footage) which has been used to supply a false alibi. In each instance he pays attention until an error reveals itself. As an attentive labourer, Columbo is able to solve murders

---

[2] Robby the Robot also cameos in shows like *The Twilight Zone* (1959–1964), *The Addams Family* (1964–1966), *Lost in Space* (1965–1968), *Wonder Woman* (1975–1979) and *The Love Boat* (1977–1987).

just via the labour of looking: noticing the flaw in the alibi which the technology was supposed to conceal by exhaustively reviewing footage of the past. For example, Columbo notices: a pink carnation absent during a Hollywood Bowl concert which miraculously appears in a lapel after the murderer retrieves it from the crime scene ('Étude in Black' [1972]); an invitation letter which could not have been in a room at the supposed time of the footage being shot ('Playback' [1975]); the impossible regrowth of a trimmed hedge on edited footage ('Caution: Murder can be Hazardous to your Health' [1991]); a blown-up still from a film taken by a police radar gun revealing a mask worn by an accomplice ('Columbo and the Murder of a Rock Star' [1991]); a bomber caught on tape flinching prior to an explosion which only they can have known would happen ('A Bird in the Hand' [1992]). Thus not only does *Columbo* reassure that the pace of technology will not outstrip the ability of the general public to keep up with it (*Columbo* as tech class), but so too is the role of the police legitimised in ensuring that new technologies will be put to lawful usage; or at least, any attempt to use them to nefarious ends will be spotted by the vigilant police. They will use this technology, CCTV in particular, to correctly perform their roles as society's watchmen.

Yet there is an assumption of innocence surrounding this surveillance which bears closer investigation. In *Columbo*, watching is what the innocent do. As early as episode two of series one, 'Death Lends a Hand' (1971), when a married woman is murdered, her lover is not even suspected by Columbo even though his only alibi is that he was home alone watching television. This unquestioned innocence makes sense, however, if we remember that for attentive labourers, to look is to labour. The lover is innocent because he was, effectively, at work. In *Columbo* this innocence is seemingly as true for the general populace as it is for the police. Hence, the idea that the police's labour of looking will keep us safe is integral to the distinction *Columbo* draws between the innocent and the guilty. But which side are the police really on?

In 'The Most Crucial Game' (1972), Paul Hanlon (Robert Culp), General Manager of American Football team the LA Rockets, murders its playboy owner, Eric Wagner (Dean Stockwell). Hanlon uses technology to construct a false alibi, giving the impression that he was watching the game in his box at the Los Angeles Memorial Coliseum. Instead, Hanlon dresses as a rather grim-faced ice-cream vendor to leave the stadium unnoticed. Stopping on the way to Wagner's house he makes a phone call and uses a transistor radio playing coverage of the game, placed next to the phone, to suggest he is calling from his box at the stadium. However, his ruse is undone when a wire-tapped recording of this phone message (which he knew about and was relying on to provide his alibi) does not contain the expected half-hourly chime of the box's ornate clock.

What stands out in the opening scene is the cross-cutting between the crowds enjoying the game at the stadium and Hanlon's murderous adventure. There is a clear juxtaposition between those who are innocently watching the game (those labouring by looking) and Hanlon, who only pretends to be looking. This deception covers up an act of deviance not only with respect to the legal prohibition against murder but also from what is expected of the attentive labour. Hanlon's attempt to use technology to profit from an unsanctioned break in his allotted role is depicted as a desire to 'get away with murder'. Those who watch, those who pay attention, like the crowd at the stadium, are innocent. The guilty only *pretend* to watch, manipulating technology to cover for their refusal of honest attentive labour. Indeed, whilst *Columbo* contains many examples of large sporting events, classical or gospel musical performances, magic shows, or plays, frequently it is the more technological presence of film or television which most firmly establishes this distinction between those who innocently watch and those who only pretend to.

In 'Double Shock' (1973), Dexter Paris (Martin Landau), a television chef by profession (one who directly profits from the attentive labour paid to him by others), enters into cahoots with his twin brother to kill their wealthy uncle, Clifford. The clue to the unravelling of the murder is the interruption of the television viewing of housekeeper Mrs Peck (Jeanette Nolan). The murder is committed by Dexter, who throws an electric food mixer into Clifford's bath. The resulting power cut, however, interrupts Mrs Peck's viewing. Murder, we are thus shown, subverts the innocent labour of looking. Indeed, this interruption of Mrs Peck's attentive labour provides Columbo with the clue he needs to uncover the crime: the time of electrocution, and the need for both a murderer and accomplice to pull it off (by quickly replacing a fuse elsewhere in the house).

Columbo's everyman status is vital in maintaining this distinction between innocence and guilt. In spite of Mrs Peck's initial dislike of Columbo's slovenly-ness – she calls him a 'bum' who belongs in a 'pigsty' and throws him out – the house-proud and outspoken housekeeper warms to him because she recognises how hard he works. Peck, a working-class character identified by her fearsome work ethic, also comes to appreciate Columbo because of his dedication to the investigation (his paying attention to the case). In cracking the case it is their halting friendship which ultimately provides Columbo with the revelation that there was a murder, rather than an accidental death. Thus, in a 'below stairs' act of begrudging bonding between Peck and Columbo there is a conflation between labour, looking (watching television) and innocence (indeed, of the innocent being manipulated by those criminals who commit murder instead of being attentive to their labour). Importantly, watching television is considered an innocent activity not because it is a *respite* from productive labour (leisure time effectively), but because it is in itself attentive labour, and – as is shown in more than one *Columbo* – one enjoyed by the working classes in particular.[3]

This distinction between leisure and labour helps illuminate how Columbo uses attention to entrap those only pretending to innocently watch, by deploying what he has learned about technology. In 'Double Exposure' (1973), Columbo investigates a murder committed by Dr Bart Kepple (Robert Culp), who makes motivational sales packages. Kepple uses a recording of his own voice to suggest that he is on stage, watching a film screening for clients and providing the voiceover live, when the killing happens. Yet Kepple lures his victim out of the screening by inserting a single frame – containing an image of a soda on ice – into the film during a section about the desert. Kepple then shoots his suddenly thirsty victim dead at the water fountain and returns to the screening room without anyone noticing.

Columbo sets a trap for Kepple after learning about the editing technique Kepple developed: the subliminal cut. He learns this from Kepple's own book, along with a conversation he has with another projectionist. The subliminal cut is, supposedly, the insertion of single images into a film to influence audience purchasing choices. These single frames cannot be discerned in the passing moment but can register subconsciously. In terms of advertising, such cuts can spark the desire for commercial products. Or so the idea goes. Columbo, for his part, then inserts images of himself, in Kepple's office, into a film Kepple watches. These subliminal edits lure Kepple back to his office, where he inadvertently reveals to Columbo the hiding place of his incriminating pistol calibration converter. The images Columbo inserts into the film are of himself in Kepple's office, looking

---

[3] In 'Forgotten Lady' (1975) something similar occurs, with the murder intercut with scenes of the butler and housekeeper (a couple) watching Johnny Carson on television. There is little distinction between this activity and their continued work for their employer. The butler's television viewing is twice interrupted as he goes to change the reels of a film for the former movie star Grace Wheeler Willis (Janet Leigh), who is watching a rerun of one of her own old movies. Wheeler Willis's fake alibi is that she is (seemingly) innocently watching a movie whilst her husband is being murdered.

around, even though he does not know what is hidden, or where. They are simply images of Columbo *looking*.

That this is an innocent act of looking Columbo observes to reassure the photographer, acknowledging by using this word ('looking'), specifically, that he is not illegally 'searching' the office. The photographer is understandably jumpy, after all, because they do not have a warrant.

As in other instances when Columbo reveals the truth by examining recorded footage without knowing what he is looking for – looking and looking until the false alibi is revealed – here again Columbo has nothing to go on except the attention he can pay to the investigation (the act of looking as labour) and the autodidactic knowledge he has developed about new technologies. This is enough, though, to entrap the criminal. The innocent watching the same screening do not react as Kepple does to the subliminal cut. They have no reason to because they are innocent. By virtue of his actions, then, Kepple reveals that he is not an innocent watcher, but, by definition, is guilty of faking his attentive labour.

On the surface, Columbo's apprehension of Kepple echoes a concern prevalent since the late 1950s surrounding unscrupulous advertisers

Figure 4.4 Columbo catches criminals through the labour of looking, in *Columbo* 'Double Exposure' (1973).

manipulating consumers (Acland 2012: 91–110). Yet historically the subliminal cut is actually an unproven phenomenon, relating back to nineteenth-century ideas concerning our ability to attend to modernity (2012: 19–20 and 43–64), which resonates once again with the information overload associated with new technologies of the late twentieth century (p. 42). As importantly, then, this particular case indicates something else altogether: a wider application of technological manipulation, by the elite in particular, to reconstruct history in order to conceal that they are not paying attention where and when they should (see further on class in Chapter 5). What, then, does Columbo's ingenious act of police entrapment signify in this world of ever-updating technology for recording, where to contribute to the attention industries by watching is both to labour and to be innocent?

If the World is Television, then Society Polices Itself

Columbo, whilst extremely charming, is a very bad Lieutenant. Along with entrapment, Columbo often tampers with evidence at crime scenes (eating food in particular), picks locks ('Ransom for a Dead Man' [1971]), commits theft ('Any Old Port in a Storm' [1973]), deliberately produces a fake witness ('A Deadly State of Mind' [1975]), knowingly frames and arrests an innocent man (a murderer's son) to force a confession from his father ('Mind over Mayhem' [1974]), falsifies official police records ('A Friend in Deed' [1974]), pre-prepares a confession for a suspect to sign ('A Case of Immunity' [1975]), fakes seemingly scientific evidence to solicit an admission of guilt ('Uneasy Lies the Crown' [1990]), sanctions physical violence against a suspect to trick him into a confession ('Strange Bedfellows' [1995]), deliberately plays off murderer and accomplice against each other (e.g. 'Prescription: Murder' [1968], 'A Trace of Murder' [1997]), and even plants evidence ('Dagger of the Mind' [1972]). Such unorthodox and often unlawful, 'everyday' methods can be understood in light of the show's endorsement of a surveillance culture that ensures the daily policing of society by society itself. That is, to recap the idea introduced in Chapter 3, a society of amateur sleuths in constant surveillance mode as per the Deleuzian control society.

Such an interpretation also explains *Columbo*'s various self-conscious references to film and television. They indicate the attention industries' replication – albeit in dramatic form – of everyday life. As Sebastian Lefait observes regarding surveillance culture, we are experiencing the 'televisualization of everyday life': a world always surveilled has effectively become televised (Lefait 2013: v–xxvi and 93–96). This at the same time that our work paying attention to screen media often becomes equivalent to watching television (Beller 2006: 8). It follows, then, that the attentive labour of looking extends into society (those who are innocent, after all, watch), which must learn to use technology to police itself via constant vigilance: paying attention, looking as (perpetual) labour, as the extension of everyman Columbo's job to us all.

Columbo's life is forever being equated with television. In numerous episodes Columbo visits film or television sets, getting in the way of shooting to comical effect: a sword and sandal movie ('Prescription: Murder' [1968]); a television murder mystery ('Requiem for a Falling Star' [1973]); a detective show ('Fade in to Murder' [1976]); a Hollywood blockbuster ('Murder, Smoke and Shadows' [1989]); a television crime watch show ('Caution: Murder can be Hazardous to your Health' [1991]); a soap opera ('Butterfly in Shades of Grey' [1994]); and a movie soundtrack recording ('Murder with Too Many Notes' [2000]). The Universal Studio lot alone features four times. Murders are committed by film and television stars (actors, celebrity chefs, fitness instructors, art critics, etc.), or other industry personnel like writers, producers or musicians. In 'Fade in to Murder' (1976) the murder is committed using a costume and a weapon usually used as props in television shows. In 'Murder, Smoke and Shadows' (1989) the murder weapon is – literally – a film set on the Universal lot, and in 'Murder with Too Many Notes' (2001) it is part of a disused film set. In 'Columbo Likes the Nightlife' (2003), the first (accidental) death is caused by a television actress. In 'Columbo Goes to College' (1990), the murder is committed using a gun rigged to a television camera, the murder being inadvertently broadcast as live television by the inept murderers. Thus, Columbo's amateurish presence on film and television sets foregrounds the role of paying attention in the lives of viewers, who are themselves daily walking around being recorded, rather like actors improvising their way through life on a giant reality television set.

Understanding *Columbo*'s exploration of the everydayness of surveillance culture in this way makes sense of the otherwise gratuitous cameo by famous Hollywood designer Edith Head (who joined Universal in the late 1960s [Chierichetti 2003: 168–169]), her costumes and numerous Oscars on display in 'Requiem for a Falling Star' (1973). And, indeed, of an equally unlikely scene in which Columbo interrupts an investigation to guess who the real-life television stars are at a card game – including cameos by Nancy Walker and Dick Sargent, alongside the Los Angeles Dodgers baseball star, Ron Cey ('Uneasy Lies the Crown' [1990]). In these scenes, *Columbo* dramatises that we, its viewers, are increasingly like Columbo, exploring life as though it were a film or television set – not only paying attention to new technologies and labouring to ensure that the version of reality that they record is accurate, but, also, realising that those around us are equivalent to *co-stars* appearing in our televisualised lives. As Andrew Crisell observes: 'One could almost say that by prompting people to behave in theatrical ways, television has had the effect of turning reality into an artefact or fiction' (2006: 157).

To further emphasise that reality is increasingly becoming like television due to the pervasiveness of surveillance culture, Columbo's world references cinematic and televisual versions of itself. The most obvious such knowing wink is the first appearance of William Shatner of *Star Trek* (1966–1969), playing Ward Fowler, a shorter-than-average television detective, just like Columbo, in 'Fade in to Murder' (1976). Not only is the scenario used to lampoon the famous disputes between studio and Falk over *Columbo*, but so too is the plot of the mystery being filmed extremely similar to that of 'Now You See Him' (1976), from the previous (fifth) series of *Columbo*. Watching Columbo interact with such TV stars is to observe the melding of his character's 'reality' with television. Hence Columbo repeatedly finds himself *on television*. In numerous episodes he bumbles onto sets uninvited, disrupting shooting, whilst in 'Double Shock' (1973) he is invited to participate in a cookery show as himself, Lieutenant Columbo. Most illuminating of all, though, in 'Double Exposure', Columbo realises that he has been caught on CCTV whilst in a supermarket. Whilst doing his everyday job of policing, Columbo wanders 'backstage' in the store to locate his suspect, only to spot himself on-screen (Dr Kepple has set up monitors to illicitly observe customer shopping habits). When Columbo spots himself, tellingly, he performs his usual impressed befuddlement at having wondered onto a television set during shooting. This repetition of his usual act in the supermarket setting conflates, precisely, the everyday nature of our performance on CCTV with the act of performing on television: reality and television are now one.

'Fade in to Murder' in particular rewards further investigation in this respect. Columbo is filmed by Fowler who is demonstrating his new home video system. As viewers, however, we do not at first realise that this is what is happening. The filming occurs at the start of a scene and initially Fowler (holding this home movie camera) is out of shot. Instead, we see Columbo overacting in the role of a television detective, a charade he cannot keep up for long without corpsing. Only when Fowler comes into shot do we realise that we are watching Columbo being filmed. We then get to re-watch the scene on home video on Fowler's television. With this in mind, Falk's very mannered physical performance of Columbo, as noted in Chapter 3 in part indicating the influence of live television, also evokes the everyday theatricality that emerges in a life lived for the cameras. The shooting script (discussed previously in Chapter 3) calls for an overdone performance, directing Falk to play Columbo as 'stilted, acting':

> Columbo is slowly taking off his raincoat . . . but there is something artificial and self-conscious about his actions. In fact, he is acting like crazy. Camera pulls back and we see Ward video-taping Columbo with the hand-held camera that comes with the unit. (Shaw and Feibleman 1976: 67)

Falk's mannered performance, then, illustrates the theatricality which an all-surveilled life brings to our actions. This recurring conflation of Columbo's reality with film and television thus drives home the normality of both the ubiquitous surveillance of life in a constantly recorded world, and the resulting sense that one is performing (overacting even), for those watching – whether live, or for later on when the past becomes video footage.

There are many such instances in which *Columbo* reveals, or more accurately, unmasks, that the performance of the self is faked for the cameras that observe our everyday world. Not least of these is 'Columbo and the Murder of a Rock Star' (1991), in which Columbo uncovers a false alibi by realising that the image of a suspect caught on camera speeding is in fact an accomplice wearing a mask. In this way, *Columbo* justifies the ubiquitous nature of surveillance cameras as a necessity. This normalises the spread of surveillance, prefiguring today's use of facial recognition software to monitor mass transit hubs and urban areas (Murgia 2019), and even, in some contexts, how well students are attending in educational settings (Connor 2018). To have any chance of escaping such all-encompassing surveillance, which *Columbo* repeatedly reassures is not possible even for the most fiendishly clever murderer, it is necessary to pretend to be someone else (much as an actor does performing a role or wearing a mask). This Columbo matter-of-factly indicates in 'Suitable for Framing' (1971) whilst bracing his chief suspect, high-profile art critic Dale Kingston (Ross Martin) in a television studio. Kingston has just finished recording and is preparing to have his make-up removed. They briefly discuss how unglamorous the television studio seems backstage. In this setting, where the performance of the professional self for a recorded image is the norm, Columbo, who is there specifically to cast doubt on the murderer's alibi, pointedly, notes: 'Things aren't really what they seem to be, are they?'

Yet, the epitome of *Columbo*'s exploration of what living within a recorded reality does to society is 'Caution: Murder can be Hazardous to your Health' (1991). Security expert Wade Anders (George Hamilton) hosts the television show 'Crime Alert'. Anders is a key part of the attention industries, a television host with his mind ever on the ratings and due to appear on the cover of *Celebrity Profile* magazine. He murders a rival presenter who is blackmailing him over a pornographic movie he appeared in when younger with an under-age co-star. Anders murders to save his reputation, as the scandal would surely cause the sudden withdrawal of attention from his celebrity, and, as a result, his worth would plummet.

This is the same motive for murder which drives several of the men who murder in *Columbo*. For example, Dr Flemming (Gene Barry) in the first pilot, 'Prescription: Murder' (1968), murders his wife because she has threatened him with divorce. The scandal created by the exposure of his adultery would ruin the lucrative psychiatric practice he has built. Other murderers also fear that their privileged position in the attention economy will be overturned due to crimes hidden in their pasts: army desertion, embezzlement, sexual transgressions, destroying evidence, corpse robbing and, most unexpected of all, having been a sergeant in the Nazi *Schutzstaffel* (S.S.).[4] Their anxieties indicate in a dramatic manner the more mundane precarity of the attention industries, and contemporary life more broadly, in which your personal brand is your worth (see Chapter 2).

In 'Caution: Murder can be Hazardous to your Health', this concern with reputation is intimated as being directly due to the all-surveilled nature of society. Everyone is being watched at all times, and not only by security cameras but also by everyone else: as Anders tells his 'Crime Alert' viewers, their phone operators are available, twenty-four hours a day.

Consider, for instance, how Columbo is figured in the episode, watching Anders. Columbo appears numerous times at the television studio to question Anders. His suspicious gaze fixes Anders (who is in front of the cameras), Columbo's investigative attention being thereby aligned with the viewpoint of the crime show's viewers at home (viewers who are encouraged to call in and provide information concerning the re-enactments). Hence, what the crime show as 'set' for the episode indicates, by aligning its vigilant viewers with the Lieutenant's eagle eye, is that everyone is always being watched. Even the watchmen like Anders are under surveillance by everyman Columbo and *Columbo* viewers. Innocence is thus not only attached to attentive labour; so too should this act of looking extend in everyday life to the (self-)observation of all of society. Attentive labour,

---

[4] The hidden Nazi past featured in 'Now You See Him' (1976), written by Michael Sloan (Sloan 2019: 1–5).

then, equated with both innocence and surveillance, seemingly fosters a culture akin to that of a police state.

This all-surveilling gaze is located at the core of *Columbo*, because viewers are always put in the position of witness to the opening murder (see Chapter 2). This omniscient knowledge which the viewer has indicates the ubiquity of societal surveillance, with the all-knowing audience playing the role of the innocent who watch. In this sense, the police become, effectively, secondary to the ubiquity of societal self-surveillance. Just as in 'Caution: Murder can be Hazardous to your Health', which aligns us with Columbo as he watches the watchmen, in *Columbo* more broadly the everyman Lieutenant is always the viewer's representative. By virtue of the fact that we initially witness the murder before the police arrive, we are then aligned with the innocent in the show, those who watch. Columbo, the one acting on behalf of the deceased by deploying his attention to discover (as in, to dis-cover, unveil, or *see through*) the murderer, is thus seemingly the most innocent of all.

This is clearest in the live arrest, filmed by the 'Crime Alert' cameras, of two suspects previously featured on the show. Their whereabouts, Anders tells viewers, have been provided by a tip-off from a viewer. The episode started with a rather noir-ish recreation of their murder, initially fooling us into thinking this might be the killing that Columbo will investigate, before revealing it to be a salacious 'Crime Alert' restaging of events. A murder, after all, is the first thing we see in a *Columbo* episode. The usual initial position of the *Columbo* viewer, of witness, is then later aligned with that of Anders's viewers when the couple are arrested after the 'Crime Alert' audience tip-off. Thus the *Columbo* viewer learns the significance of their role in societal self-surveillance, something which the show always intrinsically indicates anyway by showing us the opening murder.

Yet there is still a final twist in this tale. Curiously, this particular episode also renders ambiguous such police-state-like vigilance. Although aligning viewers with Columbo in policing Anders, the very particular depiction of Anders in 'Caution: Murder can be Hazardous to your Health' may also solicit viewer empathy. It is Anders's attempts to manipulate the surveillance tapes at his office (to suggest his presence there when he is away committing murder) which convict him. The false alibi created by Anders is a video of himself apparently innocently arriving and departing his office, smartly dressed, briefcase in hand. Anders walks self-consciously, aware of the security camera but trying to act normally. His overacting is not apparent as such, like Columbo's when caught on a home movie camera in 'Fade in to Murder', but even so it appears stilted and he looks aware of its artificiality. Anders, in fact, appears rather like the last remaining humans in *Invasion of the Body Snatchers* (1978), trying to act as though they are one of the extra-terrestrial colonisers by impersonating their uniform, drone-like movements. In science-fiction films from *Dawn of the Dead* (1978) to *They Live!* (1988), such body snatchers act as a loose allegory for late twentieth-century USA's mass conformity to consumer capitalism. Once again, then, the idea obliquely emerges in *Columbo* that the ubiquity of technology may feel like the alien presence of an artificial intelligence that is controlling humans. This unsettles any-too-easy a celebration of surveillance culture, perhaps inviting a degree of empathy with Anders in spite of his criminal actions.

As discussed in Chapter 2, after Jonathan Crary there is a very real downside to the idea that to labour attentively is to be innocent. The emergence of the widespread practice of attending to screens in the mid-twentieth century also indicates a shift in the perception of what it means to be a citizen. Those who watch are actively involved in growing the economy, but their citizenship has taken on a passive manifestation. If, for Jonathan Beller, the average consumer attentively labouring at their computer is like the imprisoned humans in *The Matrix* (1999), paying attention to a simulation of life, then Anders, like the protagonist Neo (Keanu Reeves) in *The Matrix*, is similarly attempting to break out of the conformism which attunes all citizens to monitor others for deviant behaviour (to spot anyone not paying attention where they should be). Anders's impersonation of normality, after all, is borne out of his desire to continue to profit from the attention industries. For this he must ensure that no one discover his secret past, of participating in a more illicit form of attention seeking, pornography. The empathy we are perhaps invited to feel, then, is for the attentive labourer's precariousness.

If we briefly flashforward, much the same ambiguous terrain is explored in the *Black Mirror* (2011–) episode 'Crocodile' (2017), indicating that little has changed in the interim. Here once again, even though the murders (including of a blind child) are abhorrent, the viewer may yet feel empathy for the mother who kills for fear of losing everything due to the invasive presence of surveillance into our private lives (in this dystopian future even memories can be accessed and replayed by third parties, as though recorded footage).

There is a connection between this precarity and the passivity required of the neoliberal citizen. Anders is guilty of the crimes which he attempts to 'edit' out of existence, and Columbo's correcting of the timeline of events therefore seems entirely appropriate. Yet, paradoxically considering Anders's job, in his murderous action he rejects the 'immobilization' of society created by television (Crary 2013: 80). The transformation of

citizen participants into passive viewers is akin, this episode obliquely suggests, to the activities of the once-human pod people in *Invasion of the
Body Snatchers*. Anders's attempts to control his destiny thus indicate his
resistance to the paranoia that accompanies ubiquitous surveillance.

In post-war US society, paranoia was widespread concerning the potential for the loss of individual agency to unscrupulous shadowy 'secret
agents, hidden persuaders, and malevolent organisations' (Melley 2000: 6;
see also Knight 2002).[5] Columbo's policing of the technological advancements which could be used to manipulate people's perceptions of the truth
thus seems to counter such paranoia: the reassuring everyman ensures that
individuals retain their agency. However, Anders's depiction, as at once
the arch manipulator of the truth and yet simultaneously the last human
treading warily amongst the brainwashed, suggests something more complex. As Timothy Melley notes, post-war 'conspiracy, theory, paranoia,
and anxiety about human agency . . . are all part of the paradox in which a
supposedly individualist culture conserves its individualism by continually
imagining it to be in imminent peril' (2000: 6). The ambiguity around how
we interpret Anders's actions dramatises this paradox. Whilst Columbo
seems to be an innocent who watches (the power of the individual), he
also seemingly represents the malevolent organisations that threaten the
individual's agency (the paranoia surrounding the forces that may threaten
the individual). In terms of the latter, leaving aside the salacious and illegal nature of the pornographic movie which Anders would rather forget,
the police are shown to be so accomplished at surveillance that seemingly
they can even delve into people's pasts and dredge up a recording of it
that can shatter their lives. Albeit in this case it is just Columbo snooping
around in a sex shop for an old pornographic video, by the time of *Black
Mirror*'s 'Crocodile', twenty-six years later, the capacity for surveillance
culture to discover the secrets buried in our pasts against out will is terrifyingly imagined as the ability of third parties to access our memories. The
precarity of the attentive labourer, then, depends upon the way reality is
recorded, stored as history, and policed.

Nowadays, in the internet era which Columbo prefigured, with recordings of people's lives proliferating via social media, legislation has been created to address who has legal access to an individual's data (for example, the
European General Data Protection Regulation). It is increasingly understood that attention (brand, identity) and history are connected. Being visible is imperative in the attention economy, as attention determines worth.

[5] My thanks to Laurence Kent for prompting this insight, and subsequent research into
    paranoia.

In any case it is unavoidable because of ubiquitous surveillance. What is memorable, though, what is stored historically, is the amount of attention which accrues to your particular identity/brand.[6] In 'Caution: Murder can be Hazardous to your Health', the murderous Anders thus attempts to *distract* attention from how he *should* be remembered (as a criminal) by recreating a false history of his seeming compliance with the surveilled norm of the everyday. Anders's requires his brand to be continuously 'remembered' for his law-abiding aspect. For this to happen, he must ensure that any 'alternative' view on his past, which would see his brand tainted, is forgotten. Under the circumstances, Anders's only recourse is to try to falsify the (similarly video-recorded) record of the present, by imitating innocence, much as a human walking amongst body snatchers imitates the aliens in order to hide their true identity. Once this present is recorded, it becomes the acceptable version of the past which Anders needs to cover over his actions. As the next chapter will explore, what is at stake in *Columbo*, then, is the veracity of history.

To round off this chapter, what have we learned? *Columbo* illustrates the perpetual learning about technology required of the neoliberal entrepreneur of the self. Keeping pace with technology is key to this learning. Not just keeping up with the latest advances but learning to move at the *pace* of the technology itself. This is represented on-screen through Columbo's dedication to his own education, reassuring the viewer that they too can keep up with modernity. Moreover, the viewer is given explanations of how new gadgets work, and even an opportunity to experience in real time what is required of the attentive labourer now that their primary interaction is increasingly with machines. Hence information technology is at times figured as though it is an alien artificial intelligence surrounding and shaping the human world.

The role of the individual in this technologically surveilled society, if they are to be understood to be innocent, is that of one perpetually on the lookout. That is the contribution to surveillance culture required of all neoliberal citizens. The labour of looking which propagates a more passive form of citizenship is represented as crucial to everyone's safety. Yet a conundrum arises from this, over whether we consider the channelling of attention into societal self-policing to be a case of the everyman watching

---

[6] This was made apparent by a tweet sent by movie star Arnold Schwarzenegger in 2017 as a rebuttal to a Twitter troll who questioned the need for the Special Olympics. Schwarzenegger tweeted: 'I know that all you really want is attention, so let me be clear. If you choose to keep going this way, no one will ever remember you' (Pearson-Jones and O'Connor 2017).

the watchmen, or, alternatively, an Orwellian police state turning its citizens against each other. Related to this is whether in such a paranoia-inducing context some murderers are rendered so as to solicit a degree of viewer empathy over the precarity of the attentive labourer. This last point takes us into Chapter 5 and Columbo's policing of history.

Policing:
Not Class, History

What exactly does Columbo police? It is often thought that *Columbo* offers a critique of class inequality. To a certain extent it does. However, Columbo does not *police* class per se. *Columbo* indicates much about changing attitudes towards class, gender and race in late twentieth-century USA. However, Columbo is not just, or not solely, a lower middle-class detective policing the upper classes. There is a degree of such critique involved, but ultimately Columbo's key role is to *police history*. Columbo seeks to recreate the veracity of history, in contrast to faked versions of the past used as alibis by murderers. This is crucial in an all-surveilled, technologically mediated world (as discussed in Chapter 4), in which reality is doubled by its recording. To ensure the truth of history against its fiendish manipulation by technology, Columbo uses older, theatrical devices to trap killers. Specifically: staged entrapments and recreations of the past. Columbo is thus akin to the idea of 'revenge' from the theatrical tradition of the revenge tragedy. Acting on behalf of the murdered victim he seeks justice for an unjustly taken life, or rather, on behalf of *life itself*.

Whilst enjoying *Columbo*'s complex memory game which hones our attentive faculties, another of the subsidiary processes we are involved in is that of discerning the attentive labourer's proper position within late capitalist society. This is not a matter of learning about what it legal, per se, but about what is accepted about society. Namely, that whilst social inequality may seem unjust, it is not 'criminal'. Class differences are simply a fact of life: some have more than others. Murder, however, marks the limit of the extent to which one person may benefit at the expense of another. This is, specifically, because it threatens the status quo which retains the existing social inequality. It is this which the viewer learns with respect to their role in the policing of society. It is partly discerned from Columbo's pointed indications of class inequality and his different interactions with the elite, but also from a broader investigative process which polices the veracity of history against those (typically from the elite class, but typically only a rogue few) who would fool us into believing that the past was otherwise than it really was so as to 'get away with murder'.

The Class (et al.) Conundrum

One of the most-asked questions of *Columbo* is whether a lower middle-class New York cop pestering the Californian elite provides a class commentary on US society. Some are decided: Mareike Jenner argues that *Columbo* depicts 'relatively open class warfare' (2016: 64). Others are less so: Hal Himmelstein observes that the seeming 'celebration of the working cop' provides a pretext for 'a skilful voyeuristic journey into the land of the rich and infamous' (1994: 221). *Columbo*, on this latter view, seems equal parts critique and celebration of the wealth potential of the American Dream. For their part, *Columbo*'s creators, Richard Levinson and William Link always denied any political intent, noting the 'dramatic' rather than 'political' nature of the show's class contrasts. (1981b: 27) We do not have to look far to find other such examples. NBC *Mystery Movie McCloud* (1970–1977), initially from a script rewritten by Levinson and Link, uses McCloud's rurality much as *Columbo* uses class. McCloud's policing by 'country hunches' ensures that he provides a telling dramatic (rather than political) contrast to the urban folk he encounters.[1] Yet, as it is normal for creative personnel to dissemble around politics, for fear of putting off potential viewers, we should not take Levinson and Link entirely at face value. The question requires more nuanced investigation, commencing with the socio-historical context of the show's initial run.

Like the hard-boiled, raincoated detectives of authors like Raymond Chandler, Columbo is positioned as a class outsider amongst LA's elite. But outsider status alone does not explain *Columbo*'s popularity in the 1970s, or why Columbo seems more akin to Elliot Gould's scruffy incarnation of Chandler's Marlowe in *The Long Goodbye* (1973) than Humphrey Bogart's

---

[1] In *Columbo* an urban/rural divide appears in 'Blueprint for Murder' (1972), to recode class distinctions as cultural differences. The murderer and his victim are pointedly contrasted. Elliot Markham (Patrick O'Neal) is urbane and sophisticated, an architect by profession and a classical music lover. His victim, Beau Williamson (Forrest Tucker), is brash and outspoken, a rancher and lover of country music. Markham, using Williamson's car, ignores the country and western tapes and tunes the radio to a classical station. This clue sets Columbo in his pursuit because: 'Carnegie Hall and Nashville. They don't mix.' Thus what might be understood as a class distinction is recoded as a contrast which transcends class (both murderer and victim are wealthy), suggestive more of a cultural clash internal to the USA's historical divisions – town and country, North and South, Carnegie Hall and Nashville.

spick-and-span Marlowe from *The Big Sleep* (1946). Rather, Columbo's outsider status suits a more general anti-establishment mood of the time. Coinciding with the arrival of *Columbo* on television screens across the USA, the general public 'began to "warm" to the issue of white collar, especially corporate, crime' on the box (Stephenson-Burton 1995: 135; see also Taylor 1991: 50–51). Hence for Mary Ann Watson, *Columbo* reflects the early 1970s perception, which arose as post-war prosperity ceased to be a given for most Americans, that businessmen are effectively criminals profiting off the struggling workers (2008: 139–140). As is observed of US literary crime fiction, prior to the 1970s there was a degree of 'silence' surrounding class, due to the unquestioned status of the myth of a class-less US society (Diehl 2014: 49–52). By the time of *Columbo* in the 1970s, by contrast, with this myth now bust, primetime crime drama can wear class distinction on its sleeve. In *Columbo*, the social stratification of class seems permanent, giving the lie to the myth that hard work can enable a rise through the ranks. Not only does the Lieutenant's rank never change over many decades of service to the LAPD, neither does Columbo – for all his hard work – raise himself beyond his original class status. For all that Columbo is able to learn about the lives of others in order to help him solve crimes, demonstrating with every conviction that he can cut it with his 'betters', Columbo never becomes any more 'classy' than he already is.

Furthermore, the television cops which emerged in the wake of the social turmoil of the mid–late 1960s/early 1970s – the civil rights movement, the Watts riots, the hippy movement, anti-Vietnam protests, women's liberation, indigenous rights – were depicted as 'unorthodox' loners to appeal to the increasing non-conformist, anti-establishment 'youth culture' of the time (Buxton 1990: 122). Hence Columbo is similar to many 1970s television detectives, such as a McCloud or Kojak, with respect to his non-conformist look and eccentricities (Moore et al. 2006: 199). This is very evident if we think of a telling contemporary contrast also featuring the LAPD. That is, Columbo's bumbling manner of investigation is completely at odds with the 1960s revival of the right-wing procedural *Dragnet* (1967–1970) which was also made for NBC by Universal at the same time.[2] Columbo's unorthodox investigative style contrasts sharply with the super-strait-laced *Dragnet* detectives, with their earnest and ever-righteous policing of the counter-culture.[3] The overly-bureaucratic

---

[2] My thanks to John Trafton for suggesting this productive comparison.

[3] Jack Webb considered the revival of *Dragnet* a response to a breakdown in moral values in society, and the need to reaffirm respect for police authority (Ousborne 2016: 32). For Christopher Sharret, *Dragnet* sought to 'define "American values" and to separate the

attention to detail of repeatedly cited police reports in *Dragnet* are openly resisted by *Columbo*'s scatty and dishevelled Lieutenant. *Columbo* captures a different understanding of what constitutes righteousness, emerging in an era of increasing suspicion of the establishment amidst the social turmoil of the 1960s and the early 1970s realisation of corporate greed. It is hard to imagine, for instance, *Dragnet*'s Sargent Joe Friday (Jack Webb) trying out transcendental meditation, as Columbo does in order to interact with the younger generation ('Last Salute to the Commodore' [1976]).

Admittedly, this does not *necessarily* make *Columbo*'s depiction of the LAPD less conservative. The unorthodox television cops of the era, whilst often loners, granted, nevertheless often worked *within* the system. Even when Columbo polices his own boss, the Deputy Commissioner in 'A Friend in Deed' (1974), he still remains a cog in the same machine. Nevertheless, the apparent contrast with *Dragnet* tellingly reveals *Columbo*'s ability to tap into the anti-establishment mood of the period. *Columbo*'s indication of a shift in public thinking regarding the establishment has historical roots in his inspirational predecessor G. K. Chesterton's Father Brown. Brown emerged in early twentieth-century England at a time of growing social unrest over increasing wealth inequality, during the years preceding the First World War (Kestner 2000: 222–229). Brown was, specifically, a reaction to his famous peer, Sherlock Holmes (Hynes, in Kestner 2000: 229). Hence Brown was the antithesis of Holmes's detached scientific rationalism. Where Holmes appears every bit the genius he is, Brown is, as his name suggests, a disarmingly ordinary 'everyman': Holmes is skinny and sharp, Brown dumpy and dull. Where the hyper-rational Holmes is practically amoral, Brown is highly moral. Whilst Holmes is scientific, Brown is spiritual (Kestner 2000: 229–257). *Columbo* is a product of a markedly different era, but these similarities in terms of growing social unease with the status quo resonate. The workers' strikes, trade union militancy, anarchism, the suffragettes and whispers of revolution of Edwardian/Georgian England are reflected in the hippy and civil rights movements, indigenous rights occupations, race riots, revolutionary movements (e.g. the Black Panthers) and second-wave feminism of 1960s/1970s USA. Equally, then, Columbo can be seen as the antithesis of his predecessor, Jack Webb's Sergeant Joe Friday in *Dragnet*. Scruffy not smart, bothersome minor details not facts, unorthodox not procedural, sympathetic not sententiousness. These differences make Columbo, like Father Brown before him, a character in tune with the social tensions of the time.

---

righteous not just from criminals but from all the misfits, oddities, and malcontents who pollute the American landscape' (2012: 165).

How does such an anti-establishment *Columbo* relate to class? Initially, Columbo's investigations are predominantly family affairs, frequently entangled with business, as befits the country house drama. At *Columbo*'s origin, then, is a concern with policing the oligarchical elite, albeit in the later series murders are more typically just business affairs. The murderers Columbo polices are often 'exceptional' people, brilliant professionally and intellectually: psychiatrist, chess master, surgeon, famous actors, a film director, composer, gospel star, CIA operative, political campaign manager, even the Deputy Commissioner of police. This is, as per Fyodor Dostoevsky's Raskolnikov (see Chapter 3), an understanding of the murderer as an exceptional – as opposed to ordinary – person, which has been historically coded as such since the nineteenth century (Downing 2013: 1–15).

From the very first pilot, 'Prescription: Murder' (1968), it is clear that the exceptional person does not believe that society's norms apply to them. As murdering psychiatrist, Dr Ray Flemming (Gene Barry) states: 'Morals are conditioned, Lieutenant, they are relative, like everything else is today.' Accordingly, everyman Columbo's role is seemingly to reassure that a more 'authentic' belief in right and wrong, unsullied by the corrupting power of wealth, remains in the lower middle and working classes, reinforcing thereby 'the moral superiority of the common viewer' (Himmelstein 1994: 221).

Columbo writer Steven Bochco interprets its social function precisely in this way: 'the show exploited people's basic mistrust of the rich. The villain was always enormously rich, successful and arrogant. The cat-and-mouse game that ensued was incredibly satisfying for the audience' (Bochco, quoted in Dawidziak [1988] 2019: 6). In fact, Columbo performs his class status differently depending on who he is interacting with. He behaves with studied deference when engaging with the elite, with mutual respect when questioning fellow workers, and with relaxed familiarity when off duty.[4] As part of this 'tiered' performance, class contrasts are pointedly foregrounded by Columbo to highlight social inequality. When meeting a maestro conductor Columbo notes that he could not afford piano lessons when a kid ('Étude in Black' [1972]); whilst playing at a suspect's pool table,

---

[4] When Columbo questions those in the services and manual trades – housekeepers, butlers, maids, gardeners and workmen – he is professional and courteous. He does not deploy the quasi-ironic register he often uses with the elite, a disingenuous performance which often winds up those he is questioning. That his different registers are performed is evident by contrast when Columbo is jawing with the chefs, waitresses and bartenders of diners and restaurants. Here off-duty Columbo's deferential 'sirs' and 'ma'ams' are replaced by the easy familiarity of first names, especially in memorable scenes with Bert (Timothy Carey), Gracie (LaRue Stanley) and Barney (John Finnegan).

that he cannot fit one in his basement ('The Greenhouse Jungle' [1972]); of a wealthy attorney with US$60 shoes, Columbo enquires whether he might buy similar shoes for around US$16 ('The Most Crucial Game' [1972]); and when it's a wine connoisseur, Columbo jokes that during prohibition his father was a tail gunner on a beer truck ('Any Old Port in a Storm' [1973]). These references to Columbo's extended Italian-American family – with its connotations of working-class origins – juxtapose his background with that of the wealthy suspect. The contrast highlights the murderer's abuse of their privilege due to unpoliced personal greed. The reason for this seemingly straightforward class-based critique is summed up in 'Suitable for Framing' (1971) in which an art critic murders and robs a collector. The victim was his uncle, who had bequeathed his art to the people (schools, museums, etc.) as opposed to his wealthy relatives. Thus Columbo restrains the greed of the elite because all such attempts to 'get away with murder' mean there is less for everyone else.

Yet, despite this highlighted critique of structural inequality, *Columbo* never questions the elite class's position per se. Bochco's view, accordingly, is not wholly illuminating. Most apparently, high-profile events indicative of the structural inequality of the USA, such as the LA riots of 1992, never feature, even though they do in a comparable show, *The Rockford Files*.[5] In addition, Falk plays Columbo as without class hatred. He is rarely happy when concluding a case, as though disappointed by the murderer's waste of the benefits of a privileged background (Falk in Dawidziak [1988] 2019: 7). Moreover, Columbo often amicably discusses cases with other members of the murderer's social class. He even proclaims in a public speech that he may sometimes like or respect a murderer for their human qualities: that they might be 'intelligent, or funny, or just nice' ('Try and Catch Me' [1977]). Thus, if Columbo does not 'dislike' the elite *on principle*, there seems little in terms of critique of US society's class stratification.

To bring in another flashforward to the present, *Columbo* is somewhat akin to *Game of Thrones* (2011–2019), in that the viewer is not offered a position from which to critique the structural inequality fostered by oligarchy, but only one from which they must distinguish between 'good' and 'bad' representatives of the elite. In *Columbo*, whilst the wealthy murderer is clearly bad, their class compatriots are not essentially so. Despite the well-documented links between oligarchy, big business and the curbing of democracy (MacLean 2017), in *Columbo* the elite, it seems, are generally good, with a few bad elements.

---

[5] In 'I Still Love L.A.' (1994), the LA riots provide the motivating backdrop to the action.

Columbo, on this view, only polices the few rotten apples, reassuring viewers that the barrel itself (which maintains the elite's hierarchical privilege) is not itself rotten. This is perhaps unsurprising considering the roots of *Columbo* in the country house drama. As Gill Plain observes in *Twentieth-Century Crime Fiction* (2001: 4), the 'classical' detective,

> enters an enclosed environment that has been invaded by the 'cancer' of crime. With surgical precision the detective identifies the criminal and exonerates the community from any imputation of responsibility or guilt. Order is restored and stability is returned to what is depicted as a homogenous society.

Columbo, then, polices murder as the absolute limit of the extent to which crime can be tolerated within late twentieth-century society. Any number of other 'crimes' can be permitted, or just accepted as usual (the barrel can be pretty rotten in places due to wealth inequality), but not murder. Society is not equal, but, even so, this cannot be changed through deadly force. This clarifies why, in 'The Conspirators' (1978), Columbo will not turn a blind eye to assist the Irish Republican Army (IRA) in a conflict that some might consider to have parallels with the USA's historical struggle for independence from the British. Here Columbo's position on where the line of the law is drawn is evident: he literally scratches a line with his thumbnail on a bottle of whisky, stating 'this far, and no further'. Columbo, then, is not a revolutionary. Whilst he will not allow for murder, neither will he advance the bringing down of the existing social order. Unchecked murder, in fact, is what most threatens the status quo. This, whether it is the insurrectionary violence of a revolution, or, as more typically concerns Columbo, the elite extending its standing such that it even wields power over life and death. The class boundaries as they currently exist and the inequality they foster will remain. Whilst such inequality may seem unjust, it is entirely legal and everyone has the right to advance themselves at the expense of others, but only up to – and not including – the point of taking another's life: 'this far, and no further'. In such a situation, what *Columbo* teaches its viewers is what is accepted and allowed about society (inequality), and yet where the line is ultimately drawn for everyone, including the elite, in a democracy (murder) (see Chapter 6 and the Conclusion).[6]

---

[6] In this there is some resonance between *Columbo*'s policing of murder and what Michel Foucault describes as the new era of security's 'bandwidth of the acceptable that must not be exceeded' (2007: 21), for which insight I thank the anonymous reader. However, Foucault's notion of the *dispositif* is far more complex and sophisticated than the argument made here about *Columbo*, as is illustrated by its admirable deployment in full to expertly analyse *Spooks* (2002–2011) by Colin Gardner (2018).

If Columbo did police the elite per se, then it would be possible to consider him an example of 'sousveillance' (Mann et al. 2003: 333; Ganascia 2009), of surveillance from below. We might consider lower middle-class Columbo akin to the return of the gaze of surveillance society by ordinary people, such as when protestors film protests in which the police intervene physically. An oft-cited example of sousveillance is George Holliday's videotaping of the Rodney King beating by four LAPD officers in 1992 (Mann et al. 2003: 333; Lefait 2013: 148), which led to the class revolt of the LA riots. On this view, when watching *Columbo* we would be reassured that, in class terms, there is someone – an ordinary someone like us – watching the watchmen.

However, as Columbo only polices the few rotten apples amidst the elite, he is more accurately considered as state surveillance (see Chapter 4). Obviously Columbo is not George Holliday (sousveillance), he is, literally, the LAPD (state surveillance). Hence any view of *Columbo* as, after Bochco, 'satisfying', erroneously emphasises the *false* reassurance that it offers – that the benevolent police ensure society's proper functioning. For example, in 'A Friend in Deed' (1974), Columbo protects the innocence of an ex-con burglar from the machinations of the murderous Deputy Commissioner of police from Bel Air. In this instance Columbo seems to be an everyman policeman going out to bat for the little guy (literally watching the watchmen). But ultimately this offers a falsely reassuring image of LAPD do-gooding which obfuscates reality. Law enforcement in LA in the last fifty years, after all, has protected the spaces of the wealthy from incursion by the poor (see Chapter 6). In terms of a class reading, then, *Columbo* creates a conundrum: is Columbo really involved in class warfare, or, if only in policing a few rotten apples amongst the elite, simply maintaining the status quo? The evidence thus far suggests the latter, albeit this is something to return to anew later on in the chapter.

A further conundrum emerges around gender in *Columbo*'s treatment of women murderers. There are women murderers in only fourteen of the sixty-nine episodes, and sometimes they are joined by a man. Several of these women murderers conform to negative gender stereotypes: killing out of jealousy because of an unfaithful husband ('Sex and the Married Detective' [1989]); on the spur of the moment or by accident ('Dagger of the Mind' [1972], 'Lovely but Lethal' [1973], 'Columbo Likes the Nightlife' [2003]); to protect a threatened child ('It's All in the Game' [1993]); or because their mental health is compromised ('Forgotten Lady' [1975]; 'Rest in Peace, Mrs Columbo' [1990]). This emphasis on 'emotional' causes, rather than 'rational' motives, contrasts with the majority of mentally brilliant and calmly calculating male murderers. Such a distinction propagates the (Western) stereotype of masculinity being equated with the mind, femininity with the body (a physicality which often unfortunately exceeds the control of the woman's rationality). It also reinforces the related idea, that the 'exceptional' status of the murderer relates to their being a man, because only men have the potential to transcend the ordinary – whether as geniuses, artists or, indeed, murderers (Downing 2013: 1–2). This stereotypical representation of women is not surprising considering that *Columbo* had no women directors (and only two women producers, both in the 1990s) whilst its half-dozen women writers accounted for only four episodes overall.

Yet things can appear more positive. And by this I mean in more ways 'positive' than just that there are fewer women murderers than men in *Columbo* (itself a reflection of reality [Downing 2013: 27]), or that many of the women murderers are just as calculating and ingenious as the men. The differences lie in motive. On several occasions women murder due to their inability to progress through the glass ceiling. This exposes the gender inequality of even the socially elite. For instance, Beth Chadwick (Susan Clark) is unable to rise within the family business due to the controlling influence of her brother in 'Lady in Waiting' (1971). Or again, Kay Freestone (Trish Van Devere) is passed over for promotion by her lover/boss, in 'Make Me a Perfect Murder' (1978). In such instances, *Columbo*'s women murderers resort to crime where a man in their position would not have to. On other occasions, murder is committed by successful businesswomen whose position is threatened by men. Viveca Scott's (Vera Miles) younger, male employee/lover, Karl Lessing (Martin Sheen), has stolen her cosmetics formula and is threatening to sell it in 'Lovely but Lethal' (1973). Again, Ruth Lytton (Joyce van Patten) murders her brother, Edward (Tom O'Connor), to stop him from selling the family business she runs in 'Old Fashioned Murder' (1976).

Thus women murder to obtain the positions they are unfairly denied by men, or to retain the position they may unfairly lose due to men. In either case, their actions – as per women criminal antiheroines in television generally (Buonanno 2017: 10–13) – disrupt the structural inequality of the patriarchal status quo. Accordingly, although it is possible to consider the murdering men arrested by Columbo as a few bad apples that prove – by contrast – the seeming healthiness of the rest of the barrel, something is different with respect to women murderers. That women resort to murder to breach the glass ceiling, or to remain above it against the criminal machinations of men, illustrates instead *the rottenness of the entire barrel*. If, as noted in Chapter 4, certain men who murder are figured in ways that may evoke empathy (not for their deeds, but because they fear losing everything due to the precariousness that accompanies value accrued from attention), women who murder do so for reasons that may similarly solicit empathy, or even sympathy, due to their precariousness within society more broadly. This critique of patriarchy is worth further exploration, as it indicates a similar conundrum to that of *Columbo*'s treatment of class.

In 'It's All in the Game' (1993), Lauren Staton (Faye Dunaway) murders a violent, manipulative, philandering, gold-digger, Nick Franco (Armando Pucci). In an oblique nod to Dunaway's role in *Chinatown* (1974), Staton kills to free her daughter from an abusive relationship with Franco. Thus, Staton's ultimate imprisonment, taking the fall so that her daughter (an accessory to the murder) may go free, again indicates that the system which Columbo polices is rotten to the core. This is reinforced by the Lieutenant's dubious actions in allowing Staton to take the fall, after first using the façade of romance to obtain her confession. Noticeably, Staton has been deploying the same seduction tactics on Columbo as her former, manipulative lover, Franco, reinforcing that what is permissible for a man is not for a woman. In *Columbo*, the whole patriarchal barrel is, indeed, rotten.

The conundrum around gender which emerges is whether such a con-servative conclusion 'outweighs' the preceding description of women's agency in combating inequality. This is an old one for television, with various genres historically offering women viewers both an affirmation of patriarchy and a fantasy space within which to explore the (utopian) possibility of escaping its constraints (Geraghty 1991: 107–130). Thus, in 'Lady in Waiting' (1971), is it more important that a wealthy woman who murders her brother to take control of the family business is arrested by Columbo, as though proving that she was never legitimately entitled to this managerial role (that patriarchal norms are restored in the *narrative*), or, rather, will viewers enjoy the escapist *spectacle* of a liberated woman break-ing free of her brother's (financial) control – re-imagining herself with a makeover, taking over the family business's boardroom, and announcing her engagement to her fiancé – all of which indicate that she *could* indeed play that role if given the chance? Again, at the close of 'Make me a Perfect Murder' (1978), when television executive Kay Freestone is arrested by Columbo, her words, whilst rooted in her character's rags-to-riches back-story, also speak to the centuries-old struggle of women to escape the yoke of patriarchy: 'They say there's a great sense of relief that comes when something like this is over. I don't feel that at all. Quite the opposite . . . I think I know what will happen. I'll fight, I'll survive, I might even win.' As equality is not guaranteed by the system, the desire and drive for wom-en's liberation persists. So too, accordingly, does the conundrum.

When race is included things are no clearer. *Columbo* implicitly equates Italian-American Columbo with various marginalised demographics (those excluded from society's riches), such that his representative every-man status might embrace more than solely a white European heritage. Most obviously, Columbo's love of chilli aligns him with Latin American culture (in LA, often linked to Mexico). This is never stated explicitly, but the only time Columbo walks out on a bowl of chilli, in 'Rest in Peace Mrs Columbo' (1990), is when the waitress tells him that the former chef, Rama, has returned to Mazatlán (Mexico) and the new chef's name is Heinrich. On hearing this, Columbo departs, saying: 'You got a guy named Heinrich to make chilli?' Hence, whilst of European heritage, Columbo is aligned with a Latin American heritage (specifically a heritage from Central or South America, as might be expected of California) in his love of an 'authentic' chilli. Columbo is also aligned with other heritages. He is mistaken for 'the help' (actually an African American butler, Charles, who is on his day off) by a wealthy white woman in 'Lady in Waiting' (1971). This temporarily aligns Columbo with an African American history of enslavement and servitude. In 'Caution: Murder can be Hazardous to your Health' (1991), Columbo talks about how his cheap US$29.95 shirt is Korean, in contrast to the US$300 shirt of his wealthy white suspect. This suggests a financial affinity with the West Coast Korean immigration wave into LA in the 1970s (Soja 1989: 217). Most apparently, in 'Swan Song' (1974), Johnny Cash's gospel singer, Tommy Brown, *likes* Columbo.[7] This illustrates how much of a man of the people the Lieutenant is, through association with the singer of 'The Man in Black' (1971) (a song about the downtrodden and forgotten American underclasses). Finally, in 'Negative Reaction' (1974) and 'Butterfly in Shades of Grey' (1993), Columbo is mistaken for a homeless person, aligning him with the most marginalised of all in society, including those from racially diverse backgrounds (see further in Chapter 6).

However, such attempts to conflate Columbo with the USA's demo-graphic diversity also elide the societal differences they evoke, especially in Los Angeles. By the 1970s the population of Los Angeles was nearly 10 million. After thirty years of African American migration, Los Angeles came to 'rival Chicago as the most racially segregated' of the USA's cities (Soja and Scott 1996: 10). Furthermore, in the twenty years from 1969–1989, around two million new residents entered LA from the developing

---

[7] This even if Columbo is ambivalent about Brown, seemingly admiring his songs, but, equally, suspicious about Brown's close attention to impressionable teenaged band members.

world (Soja 1989: 215). In such a context, Columbo remains the most 'acceptable' of all such demographics, due to the racial hierarchising attendant upon whiteness.

As Richard Dyer elucidates, there is a hierarchy within the (imagined) racial category of whiteness (1997: 19–20). The placement of Italians in this hierarchy relates to early to mid-twentieth-century fascist ideas conflating Italian-ness and whiteness (p. 51). Italian-Americans, then, are not the 'purest' of (imagined) white categories – as the Anglo-Saxons became considered during the historical development of the USA (p. 19) – but they are still included towards the lower echelons of whiteness's assumed hierarchy. Italian-American-ness thus connotes whiteness by virtue of being 'higher' in terms of social standing than, say, African, Asian or indigenous Americans. This is the difference which aligning everyman Columbo with different heritages (i.e. through his love of chilli) elides. In fact, Columbo is, at best, a, paradoxically, *privileged representative* character of US society. This is doubly ironic considering that Falk is of Russian Jewish heritage (Lertzman and Birnes 2017: 2–9), exposing just how performed such an imaginary hierarchy of whiteness really is.

Over the course of *Columbo*'s lifespan it did gradually become more racially representative. Admittedly there are no indigenous, African or Asian Americans actors amongst the stars who played murderers. These were practically all white (seemingly of European or European American heritage) with two or three Latin American actors providing an occasional 'foreign' otherness.[8] Yet the supporting actors do demonstrate a gradually changing culture.

Initially there were few non-white supporting characters, mostly in background roles or portraying service industry workers subservient to the white elite: series one sees an African American secretary, make-up artists, butler, maid, hairdresser, chauffeur/minder, construction workers, cops, and an occasional plain-clothes detective. Then, gradually, diversity became more foregrounded. By series two, along with the surprise appearance of African American Los Angeles Lakers' players, an African American reporter appears (the only reporter with a speaking role amongst a predominantly white crowd), as does an African American crime scene investigator, both indicating professional status. An increasing number of

---

[8] In 'A Case if Immunity' (1975) the murderer is from a fictional West Asian/North African country but is played by (US) Latin American Hector Elizondo. In 'A Matter of Honour' (1977) the murderer is a Mexican bullfighter player by the Mexican star, Ricardo Montalbán. Previously, in 'Mind over Mayhem' (1974), José Ferrer (Puerto Rican by birth) played the murderer, albeit his identity and heritage are not foregrounded.

African American detectives with speaking parts follow, along with other supporting roles (as well as more reporters, chefs, undertakers, cabbies, security guards and administrators). Most noticeably, James McEachin, who had previously helmed the *Mystery Movie* wheel's *Tenafly* (1973–1974), plays the projectionist Walter in 'Make Me a Perfect Murder' (1978). By series nine there is an African American psychoanalyst (Roscoe Lee Brown in 'Rest in Peace, Mrs Columbo' [1990]), before African American women play: a television producer (Penny Johnson Jerald in 'Caution: Murder can be Hazardous to your Health' [1991]), judge (Ann Weldon in 'Columbo and the Murder of a Rock Star' [1991]) and District Attorney (Kymberly Newberry in 'A Trace of Murder' [1997]). Whilst neither the Latin American nor the Asian American presence crescendos in the same way,[9] the decades illustrate a gradual recognition of diversity in terms of professional roles, especially for African Americans. This, even if few outrank the privileged whiteness of lower middle-class Italian-American Lieutenant Columbo.

By contrast, Columbo's superiors at work, not to mention his social 'betters', remain predominantly white. Considering the turmoil created by the Rodney King trial, Columbo also provides a very homely image of the LAPD, contrasting starkly with the critical cinematic depictions of the city's police force in movies like *Boyz n the Hood* (1991), *Strange Days* (1995), and *L.A. Confidential* (1997) (Klein 1997: 263–291; Martin-Jones 2011: 182–184). It is as if *Columbo* reassures viewers that racial profiling by the police is not an issue as long as Columbo is around. In 'A Friend in Deed' (1974), for example, an African American man inadvertently appears at a crime scene, and, noting the police presence, pointedly remarks: 'the way things look around here I'd like to get out of here'. Columbo rapidly eliminates the man from his enquiries. Yet this decision is pointedly shown to be entirely unlike that of his colleague Doyle (Victor Campos) who is lazily suspicious towards the man, immediately asking him his whereabouts at the time of death. The reassurance, then, is that the LAPD's finest (everyman Columbo, that is) will ultimately pursue the truth based on evidence and the innocent will be believed regardless of their heritage.

---

[9] Whilst providing occasional murderers, the Latin American presence is mostly limited to uniform cops, with rare sightings of Latin American plain-clothes detectives in series three and eight. Asian American actors typically play maids, butlers and gardeners (including Pat Morita, later Mr Miyagi in *The Karate Kid* [1984], in '*Étude in Black*' [1972]), before an Asian American crime scene investigator appears in the very final episode in 2003.

Ultimately there is much truth in Umberto Eco's summary of Columbo as 'a little man' in a 'struggle with the powers of evil, with the forces of capital, with an opulent and racist society dominated by WASPs' (1994: 100). In the final episode, 'Columbo Likes the Night Life' (2003), the closing revelation is that a murdered son of a mobster has been interred beneath the city's newest nightclub. Such an image suggests, historically, a settler-colonist view of US history familiar to films like *The Godfather* (1972): whatever had to be done in the past, that is now dead and buried, and the USA is 'legitimate'. Yet what is really buried beneath the USA's capitalist gains – as horror films like *The Amityville Horror* (1979) and *Wolfen* (1981) acknowledge – are the centuries-old graves of indigenous Americans and enslaved Africans. The murdered mafioso's son, by contrast, suggests that this history only began with the recent waves of European immigration, including Italian-Americans like Columbo. Thus, despite the occasional joke comparing Columbo to Columbus,[10] *Columbo* never seems to question the white supremacy ensured by the 'racial contract' which has privileged European settler-colonists since 1492 (Mills 1997: 20–22). Or, at least, when approached in terms of its depiction of race it does not. Things may look different once we turn to *Columbo*'s engagement with history.

To round off this discussion, then, with *Columbo*'s overall avoidance of sustained critical engagement with class, gender or race now in focus – the show also only very rarely engages with non-heteronormative sexualities[11] – the relationship between *Columbo* and the post-war US paranoia

[10] Levinson and Link claim not to remember the origin of Columbo's name, suggesting it: 'popped into mind', may have derived from Philadelphia restaurant Palumbo's, or from Columbus (Dawidziak [1988] 2019: 20), or was influenced by Allie Colombo (Rocky Marciano's trainer), or the fictional Spatz Colombo from Billy Wilder's *Some Like it Hot* (1959) (Catz 2016: 315). Other speculative punts which I would add, include: the 1920s/1930s Italian-American crooner and movie actor Russ Columbo, or Gene Kelly's character Giovanni 'Johnny' Columbo – another crime-fighting Italian-American – from *The Black Hand* (1950).

[11] Whilst sex or at least sexiness is everywhere in *Columbo*, the Columboverse remains almost totally straight. There is the vaguest of allusions to homosexual desire in 'A Matter of Honour' (1975), albeit it carefully treads the line between apparent friendship and the merest hint of an inference of a history of desire between an ageing murderous bullfighter and his victim. When *Columbo* returned there is a stronger inference of a relationship between two magicians/pseudo-psychics when previously incarcerated in a Ugandan prison in 'Columbo Goes to the Guillotine' (1989). Finally, in 'Butterfly in Shades of Grey' (1994) an openly gay character appears, Gerry Winters (Jack Laufer). Winters's sexuality is discussed during the investigation after his murder by his former employer, the muck-raking radio pontificator, Fielding Chase (William Shatner).

noted at the close of the previous chapter becomes far less ambiguous. For Robert Sklar, *Columbo* 'fulfils not modern urban paranoia but old-fashioned secularized Puritan paranoia: Nothing is as it seems; the devil lurks in unsuspected places; behind the apparent world of good there's a hidden world of evil' (1980: 14). This interpretation helpfully indicates the settler-colonist roots of the socio-historically determined sense of paranoia which *Columbo* reveals at the close of the twentieth century. Yet there is something slightly more particular about how *Columbo* evidences paranoia. For Peter Knight, post-war US paranoia indicates, specifically, a perceived threat to WASP identity in response to the increasing multiculturalism of the period, in particular due to globalisation towards the close of the century (2002: 5). This was the case especially in Los Angeles where *Columbo* is set. Columbo's policing of the rotten apples, then, is not sufficiently explained by Puritan paranoia. It is more like the 'modern urban paranoia' Sklar disregards. In line with Knight, we can say that Columbo's policing actually keeps intact the normative hierarchy of the white supremacist barrel against the 'threat' of increasing cultural difference.

Thus, examining *Columbo* in terms of class, gender and race really only uncovers the ambiguities typical of all popular genres. Even a show seemingly critiquing the system functions to maintain it. Another way is needed, then, to understand *Columbo* in a manner which escapes such interminable conundrums. Accordingly, I turn to *Columbo*'s relationship to the recording of the past. Columbo as policeman not of class, but of history. Or, rather, Columbo as policeman of history against its falsification in *ways designed to deepen precisely these historically determined inequalities* (around class, gender, race, and so on) which have propped up the settler-colonist status quo historically. Policing the rotten barrel, in other words, to ensure things do not get any worse for those at the bottom of the barrel.

Columbo the Historian

As discussed in Chapter 4, what often characterises the murderers is their attempt to manipulate how the past is recorded, technologically in particular, to establish a false alibi. In this way they create a duplicate version of reality to replace the actual facts of history: seeking to 'edit' their murderousness out of the past, much as one edits a film. Columbo's role, accordingly, is to recover the real history of events. This means paying close attention to the recorded version of the past (by looking and listening) until he finds a flaw. Columbo's job, then, is to police history – or rather, the veracity of history. Noticeably, in terms of the preceding class critique, those who think they can manipulate history are typically from the elite, but this is because they have greater access to the latest techno-logical means with which to manipulate how the past is recorded.

There are many examples emphasising the importance of money in enabling murderous means. When television star Ward Fowler (William Shatner) foolhardily shows Columbo the home video recording equipment which he used to create his false alibi in 'Fade in to Murder' (1976), noting that it cost upwards of US$3,000, Columbo replies that he could pur-chase a new car for that amount (should be need one, of course). Again, in 'Playback', (1975), Harold Van Wyck (Oskar Werner), the president of an electronics firm, has kitted out his luxury home with the latest in hi-tech surveillance gadgetry – everything from sound-operated doors to CCTV. This expensive system he deploys to cover up his guilt, using a cunning timer-delayed playback of footage of the murder of his mother-in-law (committed earlier that evening) to provide himself with an alibi. Here the elite's financially-privileged access to new technologies able to manipulate the historical record is shown to permeate the very fabric of their world.

To put this emphasis on history into perspective a flashforward is again helpful. This paying attention to the revision of history continues today with a more scientific emphasis in detective shows like *CSI: Crime Scene Investigation* (2000–2015), which emerged to popularity just as *Columbo*'s run was ending. Like *Columbo*, a feature of *CSI* is that it is equally circum-spect, if not ambivalent, about science's potential misuse for falsifying the past (Cohan 2008: 13–15). The difference is that *Columbo* reveals how the policing of history relates not only to the recent past (the murder itself) but also to the recognition of the *social inequality fostered by modern history more broadly*. The cover-up of a murder, in this sense, alludes to the bigger historical cover-ups upon which contemporary US society's inequalities are predicated.

This is clearest in 'Old Fashioned Murder' (1976), in which engage-ment with history is the backdrop to the action. A museum, also a family business, is the location for a murder committed to shore up the business. The failing museum indicates the public's increasing lack of interest in this older way of recording the history of the USA's European heritage.[12] A tele-phone call recorded on an answer phone is set up by museum curator Ruth Lytton (Joyce van Patten) to suggest that the murder of her brother, Edward (Tim O'Connor), took place at 9 pm. Columbo, to counter this falsifying

---

[12] The museum's contents are Eurocentric in historical orientation, as opposed to, say, preserving the indigenous past of the Americas. The *mise-en-scène* is dominated by suits of armour and associated weaponry, the artefacts specifically mentioned range from a Bronze Age gold belt buckle to William the Conqueror's battle axe from 1066.

of history, has recourse to another technological record of the past. After more than seven hours of listening repeatedly to the audio tape-recording of a stock take that Edward was undertaking, Columbo realises that an item noted in the stock take – a Bronze Age belt buckle – was in place at the time of the murder. This foils Lytton's attempt to frame her niece for Edward's murder by planting the buckle in her room and suggesting it was stolen two weeks previously. The careful attention which Columbo pays to keeping the official story straight, by turns, uncovers a previous murder, also by Lytton, upon which the museum of European antiquities maintained its heritage. Thus, Columbo uses his attentive labour to police the correctness of history against the use of technology to falsify how the past can be recorded – both in the recent and the more distant, historical past.

Here the museum as a setting is very important as a context for two reasons. Firstly, because it indicates that what Columbo is looking for when he scours the recorded past is an *anachronism* – an item that is out of place or sequence in history, or, at least, in the false historical time-line the murderer has created. Alongside the buckle, on other occasions such anachronisms include an invitation letter ('Playback' [1975]) and a miraculously regrown hedge ('Caution: Murder can be Hazardous to your Health' [1991]) in edited security footage. These are, effectively, *continuity errors* spotted by Columbo which reveal the constructed nature of the recorded past. Secondly, the museum, which stands in for the USA's European settler-colonist heritage (a storehouse of this specific view of the past), is shown to be 'founded' upon a historical murder. Considering the foregrounded class inequalities of *Columbo*, in this episode it is hard to avoid seeing Columbo's (usual) attempt to uncover guilt by addressing the past as entwined with a broader interrogation of the conscience of US society regarding the historical 'murders' upon which its persistent structural inequality was founded.

Whilst in Chapter 3 an interpretation of Columbo emerged suggestive of his being akin to an invasive (Cold War) state security operative (harassing suspects, irrespective of their rights), and in Chapter 4 of *Columbo* as indicative of a paranoid self-policing society, now, with Columbo's policing of history in mind, we can equally see the show more 'positively': *Columbo* foregrounding the need for vigilance from the everyman (surveillance from below, sousveillance) to ensure that the socially privileged do not rewrite history however they see fit. This war may have always been lost in the past, it is true. As Charles W. Mills observes, for many, including indigenous and African Americans, US history may seem akin to science fiction which speculates on what the world might be like if the Axis powers had won the Second World War. Mills states: 'we live in an actual, nonalternative world where the victors of racial killing really did win and have reconstructed and falsified the record accordingly' (1997: 104–105). This, indeed, *Columbo* itself illustrates in its emphatic whiteness. Nevertheless, in the present, *Columbo* also reminds us, it is for everyone to be vigilant and police history. With the idea of sousveillance in mind, the conclusion reached in Chapter 4 – that society must police itself – seem less a vision of an authoritarian state turning its citizens against each other than of a citizenry adapting to new technologies to protect itself from the privileged few who would – now, as ever before – fake the recording of history to 'get away with murder'.

It is worth remembering that the period of late capitalism which *Columbo* negotiates saw the emergence of the idea of the so-called 'end of history' (Fukuyama 1989). For some, with the collapse of the Soviet Union, communism was thought to have 'lost' the Cold War, leaving no political alternative to capitalism (Fisher 2009). This discourse, however, obscures that the Cold War saw the deliberate eradication of communism as a political alternative via state-sanctioned massacres of left-wing political opposition movements across Africa, Asia and Latin America (Klein 2007; Kwon 2010). Neoliberalism, then, brings with it the increasing likelihood of authoritarian governments, as is obvious from its emergence in tandem with ubiquitous surveillance. The policing of history in such a context becomes crucial, to guard against government attempts to falsify the 'official story' of history in the 'post-truth' era: Orwellian doublethink (Martin-Jones 2018: 3–10). To flashforward once again, this is the point of *The Man in the High Castle* (2015–2019). This programme engages directly with the idea that in the post-Second World War era of the twentieth century, recording media like film became vital to the preservation of a history different to – perhaps even resistant to – that of the official story. Without such hindsight, *Columbo* explored this terrain during the moment when the late twentieth-century's shifting of gears surrounding the industrialisation of vision rendered vivid the importance of such media for the representation (true, or false) of history.

Let us add depth to this linkage between Columbo and the policing of history by considering the ways in which he *restores* the veracity of the past, and the link between this and the aforementioned critique of structural inequality.

Addressing the Past: The Play's the Thing . . .

Columbo's method of replaying the historical record technologically is part of the show's broader theme of addressing the past. As noted in

Chapter 3, whilst Columbo's interrogation of suspects is not quite that of a priest seeking confession (like Chesterton's Father Brown), it is a secular updating of this, akin to Gilles Deleuze and Félix Guattari's (1972; 1980) argument that a psychoanalyst performs as a secular priest. As such, whilst the aim is confession, there is a sense that the investigative process is helping 'patients' (murderers, admittedly) to recover and work through repressed memories.

In 'Requiem for a Falling Star', the mode of investigation clearly evokes a form of therapy. By working through the past with the murderer, Columbo uncovers both her guilt with respect to a recent murder and a previous murder which she has 'buried' in the past (the body of her husband which is buried in her garden). If we did not know she was guilty, the viewing experience would be like watching a psychoanalyst getting someone to face a dark secret in their past. In 'Forgotten Lady' (1975) this is precisely the case, as the murderer no longer remembers her actions (a medical condition is affecting her memory). Perhaps the most playful of all such examples, though, is 'Murder, a Self Portrait' (1989), which contains two scenes directly evocative of analysis. Columbo investigates the death of Mrs Louise Barsini (Fionnula Flanagan), who was murdered by her former husband, famous painter Max Barsini. Firstly, Columbo seeks out the murder victim's psychologist (and lover) and in a humorous role reversal ends up conducting a therapy session for the reclining doctor. There Columbo learns of the existence of audio tapes of Mrs Barsini's nightmares, which include a repressed memory of a haunting event from the past. Secondly, Columbo and the murderer listen to the tapes of the late Mrs Barsini's nightmares whilst Columbo sits for a portrait. The tapes reveal another murder buried in the couple's past, committed by Max Barsini. Columbo teases out this crime using Freudian interpretations, such as the association between the French for my uncle (*mon oncle*) and the word 'monocle'. As the tapes of Mrs Barsini's dreams play, the events unfold on-screen in black and white, but Columbo and Max Barsini incongruously appear within the dreams, still in their poses as artist and model. It is as though the past evoked by the dream temporarily returns to coexist with the present, portrayed on-screen in a self-conscious nod to the surrealist cinematic dream sequences of Luis Buñuel and Salvador Dalí from the 1920s. Columbo the shrink, then, is professionally skilled at interpreting 'distorted' versions of the past (technologically recorded for future replaying), from which he can ascertain the real truth of history.

Columbo's key strategy in returning the past to its correct state is deploying theatrical devices to prove guilt. That this is a much older media throws into relief the manipulation of history attempted by those adept at using new technology – film and television especially – to do so. Film, television and theatre, after all, all offer constructed *representations* of reality (including of the past). This theatricality is part of *Columbo*'s meditation on performance and attention which so often sees murders in the film, television or other spectacle-creating show business professions (e.g. the music business, advertising, theatre, magic). Two such theatrical methods recur: staged entrapment and re-enactment of the past.

Staged entrapment is repeatedly used to trick suspects into revealing guilt. In the first pilot, 'Prescription: Murder', Columbo fakes the suicide of the accessory to murder so as to reveal the callous disregard which her murderous accomplice and lover, psychiatrist Dr Flemming (Gene Barry), holds for her. This revelation then secures her statement confirming Flemming's guilt, without which Columbo does not have the evidence to convict. Often the staged entrapment is a sting staged by Columbo with police officers as witnesses. For example, in 'Negative Reaction' (1974) Columbo gives the impression that he has bungled the development of a photograph in a manner that will convict Paul Galesko (Dick van Dyke). To save himself from this seeming blunder – even though it is unjust that he should have to correct (even staged) police incompetence – Galesko incriminatingly reveals his knowledge of which camera originally took the photograph. Which camera it was, from amongst all those in the room, is something only the murderer could know. Over the years the stagey-ness of these events become more elaborate. 'Murder, Smoke and Shadows' (1989), for instance, reaches a Fellini-esque crescendo in its final scene. In a film studio, Columbo explains to the murderous film director Alex Brady (Fisher Stevens) how he has entrapped him in a previous, staged scene in a restaurant. As Columbo introduces the 'actors' who appeared in the scene, his fellow officers as witnesses, in the entrapped director's mind's eye Columbo fleetingly appears in the garb of a circus ringmaster. This emphasises, as Columbo bows, the theatricality of the sting.

It seems particularly ironic that these entrapments assume that Columbo and his fellow officers will be considered to be impeccable witnesses, in spite of their having staged the sting in the first place. After all, as discussed above, an innocent African American man who inadvertently arrives at a crime scene in Bel Air is justifiably paranoid that he will immediately fall under suspicion in 'A Friend in Deed' (1974). This is before we consider the perception of the LAPD in the wake of the Rodney King trial. Indeed, the at times illegal nature of Columbo's staged entrapments is somehow 'excused' by its very theatricality. It is as though the act of presenting a play is purely playful. In 'Mind over Mayhem' (1974), for example, Columbo falsely arrests the murderer's son to trick him into a confession, later apologising for framing an innocent man by having, he says, 'staged that scene'. Their questionable legality notwithstanding, Columbo's staged entrapments foreground that history is, as Hayden White famously revealed, a narrative that is constructed with an identifiable poetics (1973: 1–42), or, put another way, history can be considered a story that is told (and we might extrapolate further, a play that is performed, or a film or television show that is recorded). Indeed, it is a fiction in which, in the moment of its making, we are all performing roles.

Following on from this realisation, it is re-enactment of the past which is most revealing of Columbo's investigation of history. The recurrence of historical recreations or re-enactments in *Columbo* emphasises Columbo's awareness that history is a story, or, more precisely, *a story staged like a play, film, or television programme*. Columbo's interrogation of false alibis to reveal the truth of history which they attempt to obscure thus dovetails with Columbo's analysis of the performance of the murderer (like a suspicious theatre critic seeking flaws in the performance of innocence, as discussed in Chapter 3). History, *Columbo* stresses, is a story that should be checked and double-checked to reveal the faults in its dramatic reconstruction. The epitome of this is the scene in 'Dagger of the Mind' (1972) discussed in Chapter 3, in which two professional actors role-play their alibi for the night of the murder so flawlessly that it raises doubts in Columbo's mind precisely for this reason. Recalling the past, Columbo explains to them, is a much messier affair, involving disagreement between people due to the subjective nature of memory. History, then, is a story (a play, film or television show), but it is the role of the detective to police the *veracity of the manner of its telling*. This is both to catch murderers in the immediate present and to acknowledge, in so doing, the deaths upon which US history is founded. In this respect, *Columbo* looks to prick the national conscience: Columbo as secular priest or shrink once again.

Typically in *Columbo* re-enactments of the past function in a rather Shakespearean mode, as a play with which to catch out the murderer. In 'Dagger of the Mind', for instance, the two murderers are thespians playing the roles of Macbeth (Richard Basehart portraying the actor Nicholas Frame) and Lady Macbeth (Honor Blackman as Lillian Stanhope) on stage. At the end of the episode Frame/Macbeth embodies the role to the extent that he literally goes mad (as the fictional Macbeth did) when Columbo uncovers his guilt. The denouement of a murder mystery being like the enactment of a play, of course, is a common feature of the country house drama. In Agatha Christie's *Peril at End House* (1931), to take just one example, Hercule Poirot describes his staged revelation of the murderer as a 'little drama' which responds to the murderer's 'fine drama' (their own theatricality in falsely concealing their guilt) (pp. 220 and 216). What is at stake in such theatricality, for Columbo as for Poirot, is the uncovering of the falseness of the murderer's alibi and the correct realignment of history. Re-enactment, then, does not just recreate the crime, but also the veracity of history. For this reason, Christie's re-enactment alludes to an influential Shakespearean predecessor (one closer to what is being argued here than *Macbeth*), *Hamlet*. Noticeably, *Peril at End House* includes a ghost in the play, a haunting presence from the past, returning to set the story straight, which functions to disturb the killer (Christie 1931: 195–196; Shakespeare [c. 1599–1602] 1980). As Shakespeare's Hamlet has it, the eponymous hero using a theatrical re-enactment to expose his father's killer: 'The play's the thing wherein I'll catch the conscience of the King' ([c. 1599–1602] 1980: 121).

The re-enactment of history as play in *Columbo*, then, is designed to produce a psychological disturbance in the guilty party. Thus, examining theatrical re-enactments of the past in *Columbo* better assists understanding of the link between policing history and the pricking of the US conscience – by Columbo, the shrink, or secular priest – over its history of social inequality. This is particularly clear when Columbo's policing of history requires him to convict women murderers who seek an alternative to their allotted societal position: when they seek a different history that can inform their future, releasing them from subservience under patriarchy.

A detailed example can illuminate this in some depth. 'Sex and the Married Detective' (1989) humorously situates the old-fashioned and shy-around-sex-talk Columbo amidst a more open discourse on sex (as popularised at the time by the release of steamy mainstream movies like *Body Heat* [1981] and *Fatal Attraction* [1987]), to pose the question of whether two versions of history can coexist. This exploration of the very definition of Orwellian doublethink is conflated with the woman murderer's encroaching schizophrenia. Her split personality indicates, precisely, the two informing histories which underpin her fractured performance of the self.

Radio presenter Dr Joan Allenby (Lindsay Crouse), a psychologist and sex therapist, is the author of *The Courtesan Complex*, a book whose findings – including the identification of a courtesan fantasy amongst women – she performs as her personality splits. Allenby disguises herself as black-clad *femme fatale* Lisa, a courtesan character she embodies to murder her philandering husband, David Kincaid (Stephen Macht). Later, about to dispose of her courtesan costume in the fire in her home, Allenby changes her mind. Instead, she dons it to embody Lisa once more. Allenby then conducts a conversation with herself: literally as Allenby talking to

Lisa. That this is a schizophrenic dialogue is rendered subtly through the cinematography, cleverly creating the illusion of a typical shot/reverse shot pattern that would be used when two people are talking together.

First, Allenby speaks. Then, as she draws a lipstick line on the mirror, we realise we have been watching her reflection (the illusion of a shot). Next, the camera briefly pans right to another, adjacent, mirror from which Lisa responds (her reflection providing the illusion of a reverse shot). Behind her are a frame of light bulbs suggestive of a changing room mirror, to indicate the theatricality of her alternate ego.

In front of two mirrors, Allenby is rendered as schizophrenic (albeit in a clichéd sense of the term), warning (herself) that she should 'watch yourself' around Columbo, before resolving by discussing what 'we' will do in the future. In this moment *Columbo* encapsulates how two versions of history can coexist – one in which Allenby has an alibi, the other in which she is the murderous courtesan, Lisa – a situation rendered as equivalent to 'getting away with murder'. Noticeably such duplication of history is 'theatrical' in its construction of a fictional alternative past, as Allenby's disguise emphasises.

Figure 5.1 The theatricality of performing an alternative identity, or even an alternative history, in *Columbo* 'Sex and the Married Detective' (1989).

To convict Allenby, Columbo realises how she deployed the 'therapy room' in her firm's offices (a noir-ish boudoir for couples looking to rekindle their mutual desires) as though, he states, 'setting a scene'. He describes her using the 'whole room . . . like it was some kind of a stage' within which to murder her husband. Columbo then recreates this staging, including a policewoman in a costume creating a Lisa silhouette, and even unveiling the courtesan disguise (on a mannequin, like a theatrical costume) along with the proof that Allenby purchased it, to secure a confession. This is, then, a stage set three times: firstly as the setting for the scene of David's adultery with Allenby's colleague when he believed her out of town; secondly for Allenby's murder of David (disguised as Lisa) whilst she is supposedly mingling at a party elsewhere; and finally for Columbo's recreating of this history. The 'madness' which this recreated staging of history brings to Allenby (her mentally making-real of the fantasy of being a *femme fatale* seen in the mirror sequence) is thus not only indicative of a stereotypical depiction of a woman murderer less in control of her rational facilities than a man, but also of the pricking of the conscience (à la *Hamlet*) that comes when the realignment of the past shows a false alibi to be a lie.

Yet the iconography of the *femme fatale* associated with the murderous Allenby also suggests that she should be considered sympathetically. The pricking of her conscience also pricks ours. Like many of *Columbo*'s women murderers, Allenby ultimately rebels against patriarchal society and in this her creation of Lisa is not accidental. The *femme fatale* in film noir seeks independence (Place 1998: 56–57). As such, she is depicted as an energetic and energising figure, disruptive of societal norms because of her ability to write her own life story (Del Rio 2012: 162). Indeed, this is as might be expected from a utopian or escapist depiction of woman on television (Geraghty 1991). For many women murderers in *Columbo*, their false alibis for past actions are proposed as 'new' histories which can propel an enhanced future. Their 'false" versions of history reveal a proactive attempt to rewrite the historical past (the official story of history being patriarchal) to liberate them from a structurally unequal position. Allenby's Lisa is a textbook case in point. Hence what is pricked by Columbo's theatrical recreation, ultimately, is as much Allenby's conscience as it is that of the viewer, of US society in general, regarding the inequalities inherent to the status quo.

Columbo's re-enactments are thus the culmination of the aspects of the show discussed in the previous two chapters, combining the performance of paying attention and the ubiquitous nature of recorded reality that renders life akin to a play, film or television show. As early as the second pilot,

Like she was setting a scene, ma'am, yes.

Figure 5.2 'The play's the thing . . .' in *Columbo* 'Sex and the Married Detective' (1989).

'Ransom for a Dead Man' (1971), the woman murderer, high-powered lawyer Leslie Williams (Lee Grant), is entrapped by Columbo, including through the use of re-enactment (of the events surrounding a fake kidnapping, ransom and murder). Initially, Columbo replicates her use of recorded messages, set to a timer to play over the phone to falsely suggest that her husband has been kidnapped and is alive. Williams is most spooked, though, by her adopted adolescent daughter, Margaret (Patricia Mattick), who works in league with Columbo – one might say, takes direction from him – to restage the actual murder. Margaret places Williams in the position of the man she murdered (her husband, and Margaret's father), before taunting her further with a portable beacon and ransom note lettering to complete the revelation of how the staged kidnapping, and the actual murder, were perpetrated. Yet here again the viewer is asked to feel some sympathy for the female killer.

Seemingly, Margaret's role in convicting her stepmother indicates that policing history is essential, or else there is always the danger of her future being taken away from her. After all, Margaret's trust fund was emptied to pay the ransom, leaving her disenfranchised by Williams's cunning technological fakery of history. Williams also cruelly threatens to cut Margaret off from her allowance, and ultimately her inheritance, now that her father is gone. Yet, considering that the patriarch Columbo is instrumental in upholding history, and in manipulatively recruiting teenager Margaret to help him foil another woman's attempt to rewrite it (albeit through murder), we can see it otherwise. Granted, Williams's act of murder is an act of selfish greed as she seeks control of the family law firm. Even so, the manner in which she manipulates the past – using technology to record and (re)play it otherwise than it was – renders the murder she commits representative of why many women murderers in *Columbo* act as they do. They kill because they are beholden to patriarchy's suppression of their wish to write history as they would like to. Counter-intuitively perhaps, if we look past the (stock, generic) sociopathic greed, Williams is actually guilty of setting out to change her fate by rewriting history. She is not content to be a wife and (step) mother. Instead, she wants to be the family's breadwinner and run the law firm alone, whilst her husband effectively retires to the home. Much as the murderer Wade Anders may evoke a counter-intuitive empathy in the viewer in 'Caution: Murder can be Hazardous to your Health' (1991), so too here empathy, perhaps even sympathy, may be evoked by the eventual capture of another non-conformist, Williams.

Columbo is often deflated, or sad, at having caught the murderer. As argued earlier, this can be understood in class terms as his regret for all that they have wasted. After all, why should someone with so much handed to them from birth risk losing it in this way? Yet, another way to see his deflation may be that the way in which Columbo entraps the murderer – by seeing through their faked performance – cannot help but illuminate the unequal nature of late capitalist society (not to mention its broader settler-colonist roots). For many within it, like ambitious career woman Williams, this includes a Kafka-esque assumption of guilt (guilty until proven innocent) due to their non-conformist desires. Ultimately, Columbo the secular priest or shrink may also be sad because he realises that this type of assumed guilt functions to maintain structural inequality.

Historian, Psychiatrist, Conscience . . .
Revenge of the Past, Return of 'Bare Life'

Finally, Columbo's policing of the past in the context of historically-embedded social inequality offers an additional conclusion: Columbo as a figure of justice returning to protect the right to life for all. This is the subject of the remainder of this chapter and the next. It is not by accident that Columbo always involves the murderer in these re-enactments, even if only as a witness, to ensure they realise their guilt. After all, the innocent watch without fear, but the guilty must know fear when history is shown actually to be different from their stated version of it. This discrepancy threatens to undermine their 'story' of their role in past events, and as such, their very identity (or at least, the façade of their innocence). Thus Columbo, performing the role of historian (like Hamlet, reasserting a *historical conscience*), is determined to set the historical record straight. It is this function which explains why, in 'A Case of Immunity' (1975), Columbo briefly joins a protest and carries an otherwise bizarre sign stating: 'Banish the Imposters.' Hence, Columbo can be understood to be an abstract idea or force for justice: *revenge*.

In the 1970s, several US films explored revenge, including rape revenge, as a specific topic: *Straw Dogs* (1971), *High Plains Drifter* (1973), *Death Wish* (1974), *Carrie* (1976), *I Spit on Your Grave* (1978), amongst others (see Glover 1993). Hence the idea that Columbo is a figure intent on revenge – albeit with a much gentler aspect than these gruesome films – does not seem incongruous to the socio-historical context. However, *Columbo* is different to these cinematic contemporaries due to its entanglement of revenge with the need to maintain the veracity of history and to maintain it using theatrical means. The conceit of a play-within-a-play discussed earlier, a theatrical performance designed to catch or kill a criminal as in *Hamlet*, is a feature of English Renaissance revenge tragedy (Clare 2006: 65; Woodbridge 2010: 50). This ties Columbo's policing of history back to societal inequalities in a certain sense, although not to a specific class, gender or racial aspect, but, rather, to the need for justice for the dead. Columbo's policing of history, then, is concerned with maintaining the sanctity of life.

Like the ghost of Hamlet's father, Columbo represents the revenge of history in the abstract: the return of the past like the return of a corpse from a too-shallow grave. But unlike Hamlet's father's ghost, who haunts his son, it is Columbo who 'haunts' the murderer with his persistent investigation. This explains Columbo's appearance only after the murder, as though he arrives to avenge the recently deceased. This is much as his character was originally designed by Levinson and Link, who: 'decided never to show him at police headquarters or at home; it seemed to us much more effective if he drifted into our stories from limbo' (1981b: 27). Thus Columbo is variously aligned with the dead bodies of those he seeks justice for. Murderers may encounter Columbo for the first time where they left the body of their victim: emerging from a walk-in safe in 'Try and Catch Me' (1977), or reclining on an office couch in 'Make Me a Perfect

Murder' (1978) (Catz 2016: 285). Columbo also unnerves suspects by crashing the funerals of murder victims. He conspicuously takes photographs in 'Negative Reaction' (1974), and tactlessly asks questions during a eulogy (by the murderer) in 'Death Hits the Jackpot' (1991). He even appears from behind a huge funeral wreath in 'The Most Crucial Game' (1972), perhaps the most literal example of Columbo being aligned with the deceased whose murder he is investigating. Columbo is not himself the dead, of course, but rather he emerges from 'limbo' to be their walking, talking, snooping, elite-harassing, murderer-haunting, justice-seeking representative on Earth.

By policing history on behalf of the murder victim, Columbo seeks the ultimate in social justice. For those who receive less than everyone else – those, specifically, denied the right to *life* – he seeks revenge. In this respect *Columbo* proffers a similar emphasis on life to that found in a later addition to the wheel, *Quincy, M.E.* Characteristically, Quincy is often depicted emphasising to a sceptic his own belief that – contrary to how things may look – there may have been a murder. If so, he stresses, then it is his duty to uncover it. In this respect, both *Columbo* and *Quincy, M.E.* could be understood as products of the same specific historical moment in which US society was haltingly embracing a different idea of what might characterise life. This was evident, for example, in a movement away from the death penalty,[13] but more broadly in the era's mass political movements agitating for greater equality.

Columbo's engagement with social justice, at its basest principle the right to life for all, becomes more evident through another flashforward. Comparison with the contemporary show which covers a similar terrain, *Mindhunter* (2017–), is useful in this respect.[14] *Mindhunter* explores the FBI's interest in the psychology of serial killers in the wake of such high-profile events as the Tate-LaBianca murders (committed by the Manson family) in 1969. It focuses on the emergence of criminal profiling in the late 1970s, dramatising the interviewing of serial killers like Edmund Kemper and David Berkowitz (aka Son of Sam). *Mindhunter* thus investigates the psychology of people living in the era in which *Columbo* emerged.

Although very different shows, there are several clear resonances between *Mindhunter* and *Columbo* – both around the recording of history, and performance. *Mindhunter* foregrounds how, in this historical

---

[13] Throughout the 1950s and 1960s executions declined, with the death penalty suspended, for a time, in 1972 (Banner 2002: 230–231).

[14] My thanks to the anonymous reader who suggested this productive comparison with *Mindhunter*.

period, there was a realisation of the importance of understanding that serial killers perform their identities in a calculated way to fit into society. Performing the self in a certain way can effectively hide their criminal intent. Moreover, instrumental in lifting this mask is the attention they crave for their murderous acts. Again, as in *Columbo*, entrapment is used to police such a complex psychological terrain, including a calculated play to the murderer's ego. Part and parcel of this is the use of audiotape recording technology to not only capture a history of criminality, but also to skilfully edit it where necessary to establish guilt (without the FBI revealing that such a 'confession' was obtained using methods outside of those legally permitted).

Yet there remains a telling difference between *Columbo* and *Mindhunter* which throws into relief the emphasis *Columbo* places on social justice. *Mindhunter* stresses the causally linear, biographical, familial dimension of the criminal's psychology in a very Freudian manner; for example, troubled relationships to parents, or childhood practices around animal killing which develop into murder in the adult. Childhood provides the first cause and linear drive behind the criminal actions of adulthood. By contrast, *Columbo* indicates how, whilst the family is always with us in the world of work (several murders are committed amongst family members due to struggles for control of family businesses, whilst Columbo constantly refers to his absent family, some of whose lives are, on occasion, threatened due to his being a policeman), nevertheless the shaping power of the broader social milieu is seen to have a much stronger influence on the murderer's actions.

The murderers in *Columbo*, of course, are motivated by very different desires than those of serial killers. As previously discussed, they are very often driven by an underpinning self-belief in their exceptionality. More immediately, though, they are prompted to act by a desire for self-advancement, whether in a family business or more generally; or at least by the preservation of what they have achieved for themselves (therefore often murdering to cover up a past misdemeanour to stop it from coming to light). Although Columbo may attempt to get murderers to face the reality of their past in the manner of a secular priest or shrink, nevertheless, in *Columbo* acts of murder are rarely seen to be straightforward products of troubled childhoods or 'deviant' sexual drives, as they often are in *Mindhunter*.

Whereas *Mindhunter* offers a depiction of serial killers seemingly divorced from their broader social milieu, in *Columbo* the murderers are typically seen to be products of the structurally unequal capitalist system within which they hope to retain or advance their position. In terms of social justice, the murder in *Columbo* is a wrong which must be righted because it is a deadly illustration of how one person can gain personal advantage at the expense of another (albeit only if their historical role in so doing is successfully covered up). This is, precisely, how a history like that of the USA functions, after all, with its celebrated settler-colonial heritage resting atop the obscured histories of genocide and enslavement enacted against indigenous and African Americans. Noticeably in this respect, whilst the serial killers in *Mindhunter* crave attention for their deeds – even sending letters to the press detailing their activities – the murderers in *Columbo* attempt to erase their part in the historical event.

The actions of the murderers in *Columbo*, then, are explained more by social circumstances than character psychology. Even though Columbo may approach some suspects rather like a psychiatrist, for Columbo to seek revenge on behalf of those who were denied the right to life is not to engage with the personal psychological motivations of the murderers nor to address the personal tragedy of the family that has lost a loved one. It is, rather, to address the inequality *inherent to the act of murder*, which steals life from one to ensure the improvement of another. This is seen to be directly linked to the privilege, itself stemming from the USA's colonial history, which enables such acts to take place and then be edited from the past by a false 'story' of history. Rather than explore the psychology of the killer, then, *Columbo* emphasises the right to life for all, thereby providing a closer representation of the era of various large-scale movements seeking civil and other rights than *Mindhunter*'s macabre depiction of a society apparently most vulnerable to the stalking menace of individualistic serial killers.

Columbo's presence haunting murderers in search of confession is thus the pestering return of the past to recall a debt that must be paid to one who has been wronged. On a personal level this is clearly the obligation of the murderer to their victim. However, there is a broader, social level also involved, which indicates the greater debt to society owed by those who profit from the exclusion of others. Columbo's haunting presence indicates that the debt people owe to each other is that of life. Or, put another way, he is a reminder that a commitment not to kill is essential if there is to be any degree of equality to a community. To illuminate this further, in the final chapter the idea of Columbo as defender of social justice is explored in depth. Specifically, how *Columbo*'s engagement with neoliberal globalisation is manifest in the changing depiction of the show's setting – Los Angeles a city built on WASP privilege but now increasingly diverse. The Conclusion then addresses how Columbo's actions might be understood to be, in the sense of defending the same right to life for all, democratic – and ethical.

CHAPTER 6

Locating:
Bare Life in LA

Columbo is set in LA But where exactly is *Columbo*'s particular televisual version of LA located? If we think about the many and varied LAs which have graced the large and small screen, there are many virtual Los Angeles. Hence one might configure the question addressed in this chapter as: what does *Columbo*'s LA looks like? Why is *Columbo* set in the areas of the city that it is and not others, and what do these areas tell us about the show's depiction of LA? We might go further and consider what these areas indicate with respect to broader concerns around, say, class (as explored in the previous chapter). However, with repeated viewing this does not seem the most useful approach. Rather, the question refines itself not to *which* LA (as it were), but, more precisely: *where* (in the world) is *Columbo*'s LA?

The answer which crystalises is that *Columbo* subtly engages with the reshaping of Los Angeles in the late twentieth century. That is, the city's transformation from western outpost of the nation (integral to the US defence industry) to global gateway city (connecting trade with the Pacific Rim). This urban transformation is evoked across *Columbo*'s lifespan as part of a broader exploration of the city's attention industries. In this way, *Columbo* also indicates that a parallel transformation is taking place in the entertainment industry – the movies giving way to the power of television – as is occurring in LA's urban reorientation from nation to globe.

Importantly, although Columbo mostly mingles with the elite, it is those at the lower end of the wealth divide that accompanies LA's transformation with whom Columbo is aligned. He is ultimately figured as an unlikely defender of those reduced to the most meagre existence under neoliberalism. Columbo defends those who, for Giorgio Agamben, are brought down to the position of 'bare life' by globalisation ([1995] 1998). Those whose lives are deemed expendable under late capitalism. Thus, whilst playing *Columbo*'s complex memory game the attentive labourer is also involved in the supplementary process of *locating* themselves within the globally polarised society of late capitalism which LA starkly manifests.

This is why *Columbo*'s depiction of Los Angeles as a global gateway city is important: the *where* of *Columbo*'s LA.

Way Out West

NBC's *Mystery Movie* wheel provided viewers with various recognisable points of entry by setting its shows in different US cities (Morris 2017: 88). *McCloud* in New York, an existing show, was joined by *McMillan & Wife* in San Francisco and *Columbo* in LA. Later additions would include *Banacek* in Boston, and so on. *Columbo* immediately establishes its version of LA in a specific way. In episode one of series one, 'Murder by the Book' (1971), an idealised view of prosperous Californian life immediately emerges. As the episode opens, the killer and his soon-to-be victim meet in a high-rise workplace overlooking the impressive urban sprawl. The view of LA seen through the glass-fronted office practically fills the screen. This is an evocation of LA's long-established trademark 'sublime vista' shot, which provides 'an elevated angle of the cityscape sprawling across the frame' (Shiel 2012: 8). This iconic image of the city features to this day in LA-set detective shows like *Bosch* (2014–). In 'Murder by the Book' this urban location, once established, is then quickly shown to be within easy driving distance of the natural beauty of San Diego. There countrified leisure is available to the successful professional who makes it in LA.

Evocative of a long history of LA boosterism stretching back to the nineteenth century this familiar 'imaginary' seems to position *Columbo*'s Los Angeles as a traditional one, at least amidst the various imagined on-screen incarnations of the city before and since (Mattes 2016: 22–23). This might not seem surprising considering that it was in the late 1960s that Los Angeles re-emerged on film and television screens as a featured location, playing itself[1] for the first time since the immediate post-war height of film noir. For several decades previously Los Angeles had performed, 'chameleon-like', as a surrogate for other destinations (Webb 2014: 156). Even so, across *Columbo*'s lifespan a more complex relationship to the city's situatedness emerges: LA as at once a prominent national urban centre and a globally connected gateway.

Throughout its run, *Columbo* consistently positions Los Angeles as a nationally connected city. This is as befits the city's prominence in the USA by the 1970s as 'America's second largest urban region and its third largest manufacturing centre' (Webb 2014: 158). Characters fly to and

---

[1] This turn of phrase pays homage to Thom Andersen's videoessay, *Los Angeles Plays Itself* (2003). My thanks to William Brown for bringing it to my attention.

from Los Angeles for business in other cities (e.g. New York or Chicago) or to a holiday destination (usually heading south). LA is thus very often positioned as a western outpost of the USA. In 'The Most Crucial Game' (1972) the establishing shot of the airport is presented from an elevated position, with a pull back and then a panning shot, to emphasise its size. The cinematography thus gives the impression of a transport hub impressive in its magnitude, at least for its time. However, this is only done to show the arrival of a social high-roller's specially chartered flight from tourist Acapulco. It is not intended to indicate, say, LA's role in international trade. Moreover, the aerial establishing shots of the stadium at the centre of the episode – which so effectively indicate the size of LA and its population – consolidate this focus on the nation. The stadium being the LA Memorial Coliseum, with crowd dutifully standing for the national anthem, suggests that LA's position is integral to an empire (the USA as Cold War global superpower), rather than as a gateway at the nation's edge.

This situating of LA in a national framework is compounded by the repeated foregrounding of the association of LA with the hi-tech defence industries which thrived during the Cold War (Abu-Lughod 1999: 13– 15 and 252). In 'Mind over Mayhem' (1974), Dr Marshall Cahill (José Ferrer) runs computer simulations of World War III for the military at a think tank ('Cybernetic Research Institute'), complete with futuristic Robby the Robot. As the Cold War draws to a close, in 'Columbo Goes to the Guillotine' (1989) CIA and Pentagon officials are interested in the research taking place at a government-funded scientific institute studying para-psychology (whether telepathy is possible) due to their stated competition with the Soviet Union. Even as the post-Cold War world emerges, not much changes in respect of LA's contextualising nationally. In 'Agenda for Murder' (1990) the radio coverage of the presidential race – playing over the fluid helicopter and crane shots of LA's massed freeways and glistening grey glass and steel skyscrapers – again links California to the nation as opposed to the globe.

Yet despite this, two LA's come to coexist throughout *Columbo*'s run. Los Angeles as a nationally important city, as above, but also LA as a global gateway city. Typically, one or other is more prominent in different episodes. Yet it is the latter, LA as global gateway city, which specifically illustrates how the attention industries shape our contemporary lives. Indeed, understanding how *Columbo* negotiates this link between globalisation and attention (locating the viewer in a global context) unlocks other aspects of the show, such as its tongue-in-cheek referencing of film noir and its obsession with taking the viewer backstage in the film and television industries.

Gateway City

Los Angeles experienced various phases of development during the twentieth century (Lent 1987). *Columbo*'s lifespan, though, coincided with a time of great transformation, as LA redeveloped into a hub for trade with the Pacific Rim. Mike Davis notes that from the early 1970s onwards, under the leadership of Mayor Tom Bradley in particular, LA vastly developed its infrastructure around port facilities, railways and airports to benefit from Pacific Rim trade ([1990] 2006; vi). Thus LA began to emerge as a gateway city when *Columbo* hit the screen. This development, along with increased overseas investment (such as the Japanese financing of skyscrapers in Downtown LA in the 1980s), offset the reduction in the aerospace economy which accompanied the end of the Cold War (Davis [1990] 2006: 135–138; Soja 1996: 442–443). In particular, the major landmarks of the Central Business District appeared since *Columbo* began in the early 1970s (Soja 1989: 238). When *Columbo* returned in the late 1980s, much of the 'prime properties' in Downtown were owned by foreign corporations (Soja 1989: 215), their development having included investment from the Pacific Rim (Soja 1989: 215, 1996: 442–443).

By the early 2000s, when *Columbo*'s run was ending, these changes meant that LA's ports and airports were the third busiest in the world, and its economy rivalled that of many nations (Erie 2004: xi and 4–5). Hence Soja evocatively considers the securing of the Pacific Rim the 'manifest destiny' of LA (1989: 225). Simultaneously, though, this transformation exacerbated the city's unequal wealth distribution, juxtaposing extreme wealth with homelessness, incarceration and gang violence (Davis [1990] 2006: 223–322). *Columbo* is thus set in a sprawling urban space which, for Soja, has historically epitomised the 'dynamics of capitalist spatialization' (1989: 191). More than this, the growth to global stature of LA from the closing out of the Cold War onwards, ensured that this location made *Columbo* representative of the emerging new world which its viewers were just getting used to.

Whilst neither the NBC nor the ABC runs of *Columbo* directly engage with the reasons for the Los Angeles riots of 1992, the economic and societal shift created by Los Angeles's transformation informs the way that *Columbo* depicts the city. Especially, it shapes *Columbo*'s exploration of how globalisation channels attention.

Much of what has been observed of *Columbo*'s negotiation of the transformation of the USA in the late twentieth century is intertwined with the city's development as a conduit for globalised trade. Take Columbo's mastery of numerous trades, discussed in Chapter 4, for instance. This flexibility demanded of the post-Fordist worker is extremely pronounced in *Columbo* due to the Lieutenant's milieu. Unlike other large US cities, LA did not grow due to Fordist mass production industries. Rather, for Edward Soja and Allen J. Scott,

> it is a compound of enormously diverse, flexible production sectors, including financial and business services, high technology industry, and various craft, fashion, and cultural products industries ranging from clothing and jewelry to motion pictures and music recording. (1996: vii)

Hence the celebration of Columbo's ability to master a new trade and associated technology every episode reflects the show's setting with respect to LA's diverse service industries. Columbo as both a dynamic (global) citizen of neoliberal USA and a denizen of LA has the dynamism and irrepressible thirst to encounter the new of an adaptable attentive labourer. Specifically Columbo's engagement with technology speaks to Los Angeles's development as a 'technopolis', from the Silicon Valley innovations in electronics to the military-industrial hardware of the defence industries (Soja 1989: 229). Thus if its LA setting is so integral to *Columbo*'s engagement with late capitalism, how does the show locate the city globally?

Columbo typically indicates that Los Angeles is a city interfacing with the wider world in three ways. Firstly, characters appear in LA who are connected to locations known for their conflictive Cold War pasts, places which, due to US foreign policy, helped usher in the new neoliberal age. As noted in Chapter 2, 'Identity Crisis' (1975) commences with a liaison between two CIA operatives who previously worked as double agents interfering in democratic nations overthrown by military dictatorships: their references to Tupamaros indicate Uruguay, and they state La Paz (Bolivia) in 1967, alluding to the execution of communist revolutionary Ernesto Che Guevara. It was due to such US interference in Latin America that some of the first experiments with neoliberalism were established in countries like Chile, in spite of the popular massed support there for socialist or other left-wing politics (Klein 2007). The murderer, CIA agent Nelson Brenner (Patrick McGoohan) also has awards in his home indicating his involvement, militarily, in Thailand and Korea (where Columbo also served [or so he claims in 'Swan Song' (1974)]). Noticeably in episodes where such international foreign policy ties are evoked Columbo sometimes finds that his jurisdiction is questioned. The national, it seems, may in some sense be superseded by the global. These references to the Cold War and other indications of the USA's global role as post-war superpower render LA a global, as much as a national, space. But it is the other two ways which indicate LA's newer aspect as a gateway city.

Secondly, then, foreign trade and investment is repeatedly referenced. In 'Murder under Glass' (1978), TV chef Paul Gerard (Louis Jourdan) takes his former teacher Mr Kanji Ousu (Mako), who is visiting from Japan, out for sashimi; Columbo interrupts a meeting between Japanese businessmen and English magnate Sir Harry Matthews (Alan Scarfe) in 'Columbo Cries Wolf' (1990); there is discussion of Korean knitwear being bought and sold in 'Ashes to Ashes' (1998); and Korean TV reports on events in LA, again in 'Columbo Cries Wolf'. *Columbo* also includes urban development in its settings: skyscrapers under construction as *mise-en-scène* for murderous activities in 'Blueprint for Murder' (1972) and 'Columbo and the Murder of a Rock Star' (1991); real estate development as motive for blackmail in 'Double Exposure' (1973); or as location for the action in 'Rest in Peace, Mrs Columbo' (1990). *Columbo*'s *mise-en-scène* thus situates LA as a transforming urban environment in a context in which foreign business investment – especially from Northeast Asia – is particularly evident. Whilst there is no suggestion that this building work involves foreign capital – as the actual transformation of LA into a gateway city did – nevertheless the concurrence of urban development and international trade is readily apparent.

Thirdly, over its lifetime *Columbo* gradually acknowledges the multicultural nature of the Los Angeles population via the growing presence of non-English languages. From the late 1960s, Los Angeles was perhaps 'the world's most ethnically and racially diverse metropolis'; and from 1970 to 1990, as the gateway city emerged, LA shifted from 70 per cent Anglo to 60 per cent non-Anglo (Soja and Scott 1996: 14). It is unsurprising, then, that Columbo is addressed in Japanese by a masseuse ('Blueprint for Murder' [1972]), CIA operative Brenner knows Asian languages ('Identity Crisis' [1975]), and more than once Columbo encounters Latin Americans who speak Spanish (e.g. 'Murder in Malibu' [1990]). These conversations indicate the everyday language use of the multicultural urban environment that LA has become, both due to its long historical link to Mexico, but also to several Asian heritages, especially now that it is a Pacific Rim gateway. As explored in the previous chapter, Columbo's alignment with other demographics, via such devices as his love of chilli, is but a partial and hierarchised form of equivalence. Nevertheless, through the emergence of other languages there is at least a hint of the five million immigrants, of mostly Latin American and Pacific Rim heritages, who created what Soja calls a 'dazzling constellation of global cultures' (1989: 443) in Los Angeles across *Columbo*'s lifespan.

There is a usefulness to analysing *Columbo*'s Los Angeles, then, due to the show's longevity on-screen. It is not that *Columbo* foregrounds its engagement with the transforming Los Angeles from the 1970s onwards. Or, at least, if that had been its aim, it could have done so far more point-edly. Rather, it is almost impossible for the viewer not to notice what is going on through *Columbo*'s continued use of LA as location. Accordingly, with the 'additional' representation of LA as gateway city that *Columbo* offers in mind, the question is, how does this view of the city illuminate what is happening in *Columbo* both with regard to the attention industries and Columbo's role as protector of life?

Policing Bare Life

Columbo's indicators of Los Angeles's increasingly outward-facing geopolitical position contextualise the kinds of lives, and lifestyles, available in the global gateway city – those of both the very rich and the very poor. This illustrates further why, even though *Columbo* does not provide a straight-forward critique of class inequality (see Chapter 5), it still immerses itself in the structural inequality of neoliberal globalisation.

On the one hand there are the various lifestyles of the rich and famous which Columbo encounters: wine connoisseur, writer, architect, fitness instructor, magician, TV chef, polygamous painter, etc. On the other, on two occasions Columbo is equated – in remarkably different ways – with the homeless.

Starting with wealthy lifestyles, as the 1970s was a time of growth for Los Angeles (Soja 1989: 192), we can see *Columbo*'s murders for self-advancement as reflecting the partial nature of the distribution of the new wealth this growth created. During the 1970s LA transformed into a 'technopolis' (Soja 1989: 192), with a wealthy elite of 'engineers, sci-entists, mathematicians, technical experts' alongside a 'growing flow of finance, banking, and both corporate and public management, control, and decision-making functions', making LA the USA's key financial hub for Pacific Rim trade and investment (p. 192). Yet this concentration of wealth was balanced atop a large subclass due to the neoliberal polarisation of the labour market (p. 204). Transforming LA into a technopolis created vast wage differentials, by re-focusing capital upwards towards super profits whilst reducing the power of labour (Soja 1989: 204–205). What, then, of Columbo's alignment with the very poor?

Most apparently, despite the transformation of the city and the wealth which accumulated for many, Columbo wears the same suit and raincoat for thirty-five years. The 'everyman' detective is certainly not upwardly mobile in this burgeoning context. More telling, though, are the two occasions on which Columbo is aligned with the homeless. In 'Negative Reaction'

(1974), Columbo visits a homeless shelter (St Matthew's Mission), where an enthusiastic nun (Joyce van Patten) mistakes him for a homeless person due to his dog-tired, unshaven face (established previously to be a result of long hours working the case, his workaholism rendering him metaphorically homeless) and his scruffy seven-year-old raincoat. When Columbo reveals his identity as a police officer the nun humorously misunderstands him to be working undercover on Skid Row. The *mise-en-scène* thus aligns Columbo with the homeless as he eats their beef stew, as much at home in the soup kitchen with a wino as he is in the fancy restaurants where he dines with the elite.

Nearly twenty years later, in 'Butterfly in Shades of Grey' (1993) Columbo is again mistaken for a homeless person. Or rather, in a telling contrast, for an extra playing a homeless person in a soap opera shoot. What is noticeable is how the earlier attempt to recognise something of the degradation suffered by the city's underclass (Columbo's visit to a mission) has been replaced by his accidental discovery of the spectacle, for

Figure 6.1 Columbo is indiscernible from the homeless
in *Columbo* 'Negative Reaction' (1974).

Figure 6.2 Columbo is indiscernible from an actor playing a homeless person in *Columbo* 'Butterfly in Shades of Grey' (1993).

commercial ends, of homelessness as an atmospheric aspect of the televisual image.[2]

As the shoot breaks up due to Columbo's interruption of the action, the extras playing the homeless meander slowly back to their marks. One pushes a shopping trolley containing meagre belongings.

This unusual metafictional moment illustrates something of the global redesign of public spaces, including in LA, to deny homeless people the opportunity to rest (Crary 2013: 26–27). Very precisely in this instance it indicates the displacement forced upon LA's homeless by wealth-segregation-oriented urban redevelopment. During the redevelopment of LA the homeless were, as Davis observes, transformed into 'urban bed-ouins ... pushing ... possessions in purloined shopping carts' ([1990] 2006: 236). This new situation in the gateway city contrasts with the former fixed location of a mission providing a resting place for the homeless in the mid-1970s. For the homeless, the very idea of a place to rest has

---

[2] This is eight years prior to the satirising of this market-oriented shift in view of homeless poverty in *Zoolander* (2001).

been replaced under neoliberalism by either permanent displacement or the mass incarceration of the underclass (Wacquant 2009). In LA specifically, the extent of wealth polarisation was such that by the end of the 1980s, just prior to 'Butterfly in Shades of Grey', alongside condos worth US$11m (which came with a free Rolls Royce) coexisted 'the largest concentration of homeless people in the country' (Soja 1989: 210).

The contrast between the depictions of homelessness in the two examples obliquely indicates how LA's transformation – and accompanying accelerated wealth contrasts – has been mediated by the entertainment industry. *Columbo* provides a degree of critique of the way in which LA's transformation has removed the audience's attention from the plight of those cast out of society. The homeless have been shunted out of sight, now appearing only as a dramatic backdrop to television drama. The contrast *Columbo* creates between the vibrant lifestyles of wealthy murderers and the depravation of homelessness on these occasions indicates how supposedly meaningful lives (exciting and wealth-creating lifestyles) rest atop bare existence (the homeless providing its most extreme example, in the absence of any acknowledgement of those working as enslaved or sweatshop labour [Soja 1996: 445]). The homeless must remain unacknowledged, *Columbo* subtly reminds us, rendered at best a backdrop to a soap opera story, such that our attention remains focused on the wealthy lifestyles to which we must aspire.

Columbo's brief inclusions of the homeless throw into relief that attention and a deficit of attention (inattention) are entwined. For the extra attention needed to benefit the wealthy, insufficient attention must be paid to the poor. This is a mutually informing relationship which fosters, and is fostered by, structural inequality. Typically, *Columbo* replicates the focusing of our attention towards the rich and famous fostered by neoliberalism. Yet on these standout occasions when the homeless feature, *Columbo* also fleetingly reminds us of this structuring absence: that to which we are not encouraged to pay attention by the design of contemporary urban geography, or television shows like *Columbo* itself.

These occasions on which *Columbo* is aligned with the homeless also indicate something more of Columbo's personification of the idea of vengeance (as outlined in the previous chapter) for those denied life by the criminals he seeks to police. The thinking of Giorgio Agamben can help illuminate this more concretely. For Agamben, there is a distinction between a fully integrated, productive life within society – 'a qualified life, a particular way of life' – on the one hand, and 'bare life' on the other ([1995] 1998: 1–4). Agamben argues that contemporary Western civilisation uses the category of 'bare life' to define the boundary or limits of civilisation. Bare life is that which is excluded from participation in political life (p. 7). By definition, bare life is not recognised in the same manner as the life of a citizen of a nation. Rather, it is not a life worth living. Thus the label of bare life indicates people who 'may be killed' without their death being considered a homicide (pp. 8 and 82–83). The examples Agamben provides of bare life range from the Jewish people who were reduced to the level of bare life by National Socialist Germany's propaganda – equating them with vermin, to be exterminated (p. 114) – to contemporary refugees denied the right to participate in the political life of the nations they escape to (pp. 126–131). Whilst the concentration camps of Europe prior to and during the Second World War marked the external limit of society – the location in which bare life can be killed with impunity – under neoliberal globalisation this threshold is evident in detention camps where refugees are held, and in the treatment of the homeless who are shunted out of sight of the wealthy.

The role of Columbo as a figure of revenge, acting on behalf of the dead, plus his alignment with the homeless, ultimately positions him as the protector of bare life. This is clearest once the transformation of LA to take advantage of globalisation is considered. Columbo as representative of the newly deceased polices the sanctity of life, its right to exist even if some would reduce its defined status to that which can be killed with impunity (bare life). Put another way, Columbo polices the right to have a citizen's life: at least a minimal existence without the overhanging threat that another may kill you without justice being done. A love of life is, after all, what Porfiry Petrovich advocates for Raskolnikov in Fyodor Dostoevsky's *Crime and Punishment*. When the young murderer queries what value there might be in confessing to murder, Porfiry replies: 'Life! . . . Join in with the ordinary current of life, and it will take you somewhere yet!' (Dostoevsky [1866] 1994: 364). Not coincidentally, it is also what Falk/Columbo the fallen angel advocates to the other angels in *Wings of Desire* (1987), extolling the joys of everyday simple pleasures (see Introduction and Conclusion). Columbo, the cop forever harping on his ordinary family, is, likewise, the seemingly vitalist policeman of the sanctity of life, or rather, of the right to a meaningful life for all.

Neoliberalism seeks to render exclusive citizens' rights to those who can afford them. Hence Columbo's policing of LA's rich who are getting richer reflects the times' restructuring of society via economics. As noted in Chapter 5, Columbo polices the excesses of the social elite because it is they who have the ability to take a life and eradicate this crime from history. Similarly, it is they who would deny citizenship to those on the lowest rungs of society, wiping them out of history to enhance their own position.

This is apparent in 'A Friend in Deed' (1974), in which Los Angeles's polarised society is foregrounded by the alternation of the action between the wealthy Bel Air district (home to the Deputy Commissioner of police), and a downtown dive bar frequented by former convicts. The wealthy Deputy Commissioner, after killing his wife, attempts to set up an ex-con as the fall guy. This culminates in the spectacle of police helicopters leading squad cars on a manhunt for the ex-con amongst wealthy suburban dwellings. The apartheid-like situating of Global North and Global South adjacently in the same city, the episode illustrates, requires a growing militarily equipped police force to patrol the border between rich and poor.

Contrary to this militarised enforcement of such wealth inequalities, though, Columbo does not convict the ex-con patsy. Rather, he pursues the Deputy Commissioner. Noticeably, the sting Columbo sets up to catch him involves renting an apartment in a 'lesser' part of town, which the Deputy Commissioner is tricked into believing belongs to the ex-con. Everyman Columbo, then, is both aligned with the underclass (he places his belongings in the rented space and they do not seem out of place) and positioned as their champion (he catches the Deputy Commissioner and protects the right to a citizen's life of the former convict). Thus Columbo's alignment with the homeless, the ex-con, and the justice he seeks for the dead, indicates his role as a champion of life, of everyone's potential to be a useful citizen.

Even so, how unique is Columbo's treatment of LA? To play devil's advocate, were other shows of the time not similar? Take The Rockford Files (19740–1980). Jim Rockford (James Garner) is coded as being from blue-collar origins, via his truck-driver father with whom he shares a dilapidated trailer. The pilot, 'Backlash of the Hunter' (1974) sees Rockford seeking justice for a homeless man, even whilst he brushes up against the wealthy Californian elite who are pursuing their self-serving machinations. Again, although The Rockford Files was partly filmed on sets, Sue Turnbull notes that 'the series made considerable use of the "real" Los Angeles' in its location shooting (2014: 107). For example, originally The Rockford Files emphasises the automobile travel so necessary in LA, punctuating its punch-ups with exciting car chases and helicopter shots of the sprawling freeways as Rockford transitions between locations. When The Rockford Files returned in the 1990s, the LA riots even feature as a backdrop to 'I Still Love LA' (1994). So, as in Columbo, a strong sense of Los Angeles is present in The Rockford Files over the thirty-year span.[3] Yet it is not solely

---

[3] My thanks to Colin Gardner for suggesting The Rockford Files as a possible comparison for these reasons.

this emphasis on LA's wealth divide which stands out in *Columbo*. Rather, the clear difference between the two shows is *Columbo*'s engagement with attention in this socially unequal context. *Columbo*'s geopolitical critique of structural inequality in LA, global gateway city, then, functions in tandem with Columbo's engagement with the attention industries in this very same space. To realise this we must attend to *Columbo*'s fascination with Hollywood's history, especially film noir.

Heritage Noir

Many of the murders in *Columbo* take place in LA's richer neighbourhoods. Reyner Banham, writing at the time of *Columbo*'s first run, identified these areas as forming one of the four defining 'ecologies' of LA: the 'foothills' (1971). Whilst it is true, as Soja noted in the late 1980s, that it is possible to find in Los Angeles a wealth of diverse locations – a 'rust-belted Detroit or Cleveland ... a Boston ... a Lower Manhattan and a South Bronx, a São Paulo and a Singapore' (1989: 193) – nevertheless these distinctive Los Angeles's do not typically feature in *Columbo*. This begs the question of why the foothills are so important.

On the one hand, Columbo's policing of the country houses of the foothills – along with, in the 1990s revival episodes, LA's exclusive beach communities – indicates that his job is a policing of privatised spaces: the 'walled in residence' of Anglo LA (Soja 1996: 428). This returns us to the idea of Columbo policing the few rotten apples which threaten to spoil an otherwise prosperous WASP culture (see Chapter 5). After all, Los Angeles was, by the 1960s, the largest US city with the 'highest percentage of native born Protestants' in a city then 80 per cent Anglo and suburban (Soja 1996: 428). Historically, Los Angeles's WASP heritage was firmly established through the settler-colonialism of the late nineteenth century (Soja and Scott 1996: 4–5), which was attracted by boosterism promoting 'an idyllic Los Angeles to Protestant America' (p. 5). Upon this base, the large-scale suburbanisation of LA in the twentieth century's post-war decades created the milieu within which a country house drama could comfortably sit. This informing context works for *Columbo* both in terms of the wider changes it encapsulates (post-war suburbanisation in the USA was not specific to Los Angeles after all) as well as by reflecting the very specific development of Los Angeles.

On the other hand, there is another dimension to the show's emphasis on the foothills which can shed further light on this specificity of place. This additional dimension works along with *Columbo*'s foregrounded play with the importance of the recorded image of the past and what this can mean for the present. Namely, the foothills are so important because they are steeped in Hollywood history. They were both home to the residences of former stars of the classical era and/or provided locations for many film noirs involving private eyes investigating the misdemeanours of the wealthy (Banham 1971: 101). In this sense, LA's connection to Hollywood history informs *Columbo*'s investigation of the importance of the attention industries for the city, due to their role in the creation of what Guy Debord famously dubbed the society of the spectacle: a spectacle designed to be at once the focus of all attention and the mediator of social relations (1967: 12). Debord's view of the inspirational nature of (the spectacle of) celebrity lifestyles, for example, resonates with *Columbo*'s own emphasis on the lifestyles of wealthy Angelinos (pp. 38–39). If our attention is focused on such elite professionals, it follows that there is little left to contemplate the reality of social inequality except in the terms mediated by the attention industries (e.g. the homeless as scenic backdrop to a soap opera story).

The most complex example of this investigation of the film and television industries occurs in 'Blueprint for Murder' (1972), the only episode Falk directed. It sees a plan hatched by architect Elliot Markham (Patrick O'Neal) to dispose of a dead body in the foundations of an under-construction skyscraper. What is interesting for this discussion is that integral parts of the episode were filmed on a construction site in Century City. This location caused Falk myriad directorial problems as it was an active building site which kept changing (necessitating constant re-blocking of scenes) and he had to contend with the swirling dust of construction (Levinson and Link 1981b: 66–67). This setting creates a spectacle of LA's development, especially in the scenes where a foundation pile is dug up. The size and scale of the operation, using cranes and jackhammers, is visually impressive of the transforming city's potential. But more than this, it is in terms of Hollywood history that these skyscraper construction sequences reveal *Columbo*'s emphasis on the importance of LA's attention industries.

Century City, as the name evokes, was formerly Twentieth Century Fox land. It was sold off for development after debts incurred on expensive flops like *Cleopatra* (1963), and as the studio restructured in line with the emerging global shift towards a post-Fordist economy (Webb 2014: 31–34). The Century City redevelopment would be incorporated into the 'downtown business complex', as part and parcel of the 'internationalisation of the Los Angeles regional economy and its insertion into the expanding development of the Pacific Rim' (Soja and Scott 1996: 11–12). This marks the moment of the filming of 'Blueprint for Murder', the episode's finale

Figure 6.3 Century City evoking a television set as LA
transforms, in *Columbo* 'Blueprint for Murder' (1972).

commenting on the way in which the filming of *Columbo* therein is integral
to the city on three related levels.

Firstly, Falk incorporates a metafictional touch, using bright lights
to illuminate the building site when the murderer, Markham, has been
tricked into his entrapment. This renders the space reminiscent of a film
or television set.

It is a Fellini-esque move by Falk to comment on his directorial experiences thus. When the building site is suddenly lit up to reveal the murderer attempting to dispose of the body, it is as if the shot proclaims:
'I, Columbo am the director of this little drama', yet another theatrical flourish as per so many *Columbo* denouements (see Chapter 5). Also,
though, and secondly, it declares: 'I, Falk, am the director of the television
show in which the play is taking place.' Thirdly, the development of that
part of LA is imbricated with the city's history as the – for many decades –
capital of the global film industry. In this process a former site of filmmaking is recast as a set for television.[4] The major force in the entertainment

---

[4] The completed Fox Plaza later featured as Nakatomi Plaza in *Die Hard* (1988).

industry is, much like the city, transforming: 'I, LA am no longer movies, but, literally, television.'

After all, whilst historically the Hollywood studios were integral to the development of Los Angeles as a city (Shiel 2012: 128–210; Jacobson 2015: 168–200), when the economy shifted from Fordist to post-Fordist (and as the urban environment shifted from national to global gateway city), their lots increasingly produced content for the major television networks (Anderson 1994: 4–5; Curtin 2004: 278–279). As discussed in Chapter 1 it was precisely at the time of the emergence of *Columbo* in the late 1960s and early 1970s – with the networks commissioning their own made-for-television movies rather than purchasing them from Hollywood – that the power of the movies was ceded to television (see also Londoner 1985: 606–608).

Tellingly, the body which architect Markham attempts to bury in the foundations is that of a wealthy Texan rancher and horse trainer, Beau Williamson (Forrest Tucker). With cowboy hat and boots, and six shooter car door handles, Williamson is very deliberately figured as a 'cowboy'. Actor Forrest Tucker, indeed, played in various westerns on both big and small screen. Thus this *Columbo* episode seems to suggest that television will protect the national memory of the USA's settler-colonist culture (immortalised on-screen in westerns as its cowboy past), even as the urban redevelopment of cities like LA proceed with a more global focus. Markham, notably, is seeking to use Williamson's finances to develop a new complex in the heart of LA, literally built over the body of the 'cowboy' who (unwittingly) paid for it. In this respect the episode also subtly reassures viewers concerning the shift in television's industrial emphasis at that time – the move away from rural- to urban-centred television shows, including *Columbo* – which were 'burying' the western as a genre 'underneath' the detective show. Somehow the 'righteousness' of this heritage seems assured through Columbo's ability to obtain justice for the murdered cowboy. Hence this drama takes place on former Twentieth Century Fox land just as television rises to dominance over film in LA, and the cop show over the western, precisely through shows like *Columbo*.

This is not the only occasion when *Columbo* indicates the usurping of film's role by television via the concealing of a body on studio land now of more value for television. In 'Requiem for a Falling Star' (1973) Norah Chandler (Anne Baxter), a veteran actor of the silver screen now working in television, murders her personal assistant. Chandler fears her assistant might divulge to a soon-to-be husband, Jerry Parks (Mel Ferrer) (a reporter-cum-muckraking biography-writing sometime-celebrity-blackmailer) that Chandler murdered her philandering husband twelve years previously. A former studio boss thought to have mysteriously disappeared in 1960, he was actually buried in the back garden of Chandler's bungalow. The bungalow, unfortunately for Chandler, was on the studio's lot. As the years passed, the lot's redevelopment rendered her home an anomaly amidst the huge buildings used for shooting. The studio head, Mr Fallon (Frank Converse), explains to Columbo that the movies are in decline, and the studio wants to restructure its available space but is hampered by Chandler's refusal to sell. Here, again, LA's urban redevelopment is mirrored in the entertainment industry's similar reorganisation of its spaces of production to accommodate the greater power of television.

Noticeably, 'Requiem for a Falling Star' (1973) directly draws our attention to the importance of television in this context. It opens in the middle of a shot being filmed, only the shout of 'cut' revealing that we have not been watching the opening murder of *Columbo*, but a show-within-a-show. This produces both a reminder that television is very much a working industry, and a metafictional meditation on televisual constructions of reality. The casting of Oscar-winning Hollywood star Anne Baxter, famous for memorable roles in the 1950s (e.g. *All About Eve* [1950], *The Ten Commandments* [1956]), as a fading Hollywood star now working in television, is similarly self-referential: it mirrors her real-life career. Beyond the self-referential, though, the casting of Baxter again emphasises the relative decline of the movies in comparison to television. Chandler's character echoes Baxter's role as the calculating Eve Harrington in Joseph L. Mankiewicz's much-fêted *All About Eve*, advancing herself as an actress at the expense of all others (and likewise embroiled with a manipulative journalist). If such a story is to be told nowadays, we are shown, it will be by television, not the movies. In *Columbo*, television uncovers that the movies are 'dead' in comparison. The death of cinema is a secret which has been hushed up, like a body buried in the studio lot, which *Columbo* brings to light. In realising how it does this, Columbo's relationship with film noir is key.

To speak of noir in relation to *Columbo* requires careful qualification. Typically, *Columbo* incorporates its allusions to noir with tongue firmly wedged in cheek, maintaining thereby the show's light, often comic, tone. Columbo himself, for example, whilst so evocative of the raincoated LA private eye or gumshoe, is also a loveable and comical figure. Indeed, *Columbo* avoids any sense that Columbo is in danger of becoming imbricated in the dark worlds he polices, as per so many unfortunate noir (anti-) heroes. This is a very different sense of noir being referenced to, say, the neon-lit investigations of organised crime, violent deaths, cops-gone-bad, and the seedy New York underworld in *Kojak* (1973–1978), or again the complex conspiracies of early 1970s noir revival movies like *The Long*

Goodbye (1973) and *Chinatown* (1974). Yet, even in *Columbo's* 'noir-lite' mode, as it were, repeated emphasis on its generic affiliation to film noir not only indicates the cultural heritage enshrined in LA as filming location but also that television has taken the driving seat in advancing this heritage.

Television's noir heritage stretches back to the 1950s and 1960s when movie industry personnel – many with film noir experience – transitioned to television, taking with them noir's 'themes, styles and moods' (Sanders and Skoble 2008: 4–5). *Columbo* was informed by this heritage. Don Siegel, who directed noirs like *The Big Steal* (1949) and the remake of *The Killers* (1964), was initially involved as *Columbo's* possible first producer. As discussed in Chapter 1, the aesthetic look of *Columbo* is thought by some to be that of a B-movie, as were many noirs: across the show's lifespan the attentive viewer cannot help but notice that *Columbo* recycles everything from sets to plot points. A comparison with *Dragnet* (1951–1959 and 1967–1970) is again useful, this time to bring into focus *Columbo's* specific noir-ish aspect. Due to its own roots in noir, *Dragnet* sought to return a stricter, more conservative view of law and order to the televisual streets of LA (Mittell 2004: 121–152; Sharrett 2012: 165; Ousborne 2016: 32–33). *Columbo's* very different return to noir can be seen as a reaction against this strictness. *Dragnet* stands opposed to noir's revelling in the steamy, lurid permissiveness of aspects of West Coast society, and as such produces a negative view of a dangerous, illicit LA (Lent 1987: 344; Sharrett 2012: 171). This is a 'black and white' vision of the city's morality. In *Columbo*, as the preceding chapters have shown, where the line of the law ultimately lies is much more nuanced, if not at times downright ambiguous. A detective series set in Los Angeles, then, *Columbo's* trademark combination of wealth, ambition, greed, murder and an ambiguous thin blue line makes it the perfect vehicle for recycling noir. Only, in contrast to *Dragnet*, what was previously black and white is here returned to its original noir-ish shades of grey, albeit to inhabit this more dangerous LA for a primetime television audience *Columbo* takes a purposefully more light-hearted approach.

What is most distinctive about *Columbo's* 'noir-lite' LA is found in its use of the city's noir heritage to indicate television's newfound 'advantage' over film in this location. This is evident in two ways. Firstly, *Columbo* stresses that television now has the distribution platform which can most effectively capitalise on the archive that the movies created (Hollywood having sold its film libraries in the 1950s and 1960s [Lafferty 1990: 239–245]). Not only can television repeat movies (see Chapter 1), but so too can it reference them in ways that keep their memory alive. This is television as, for Amy Holdsworth, a 'privileged site of nostalgia' which uses the archive to engage in a dynamic play between past and present (2011: 97). This is evident in numerous ways. In 'How to Dial a Murder' (1978) the killer's home, stuffed with movie memorabilia, is a treasure trove of Hollywood props. It includes the curved pool cue of W. C. Fields, and the sled from *Citizen Kane* (1941). Again, in 'Forgotten Lady' (1975), Janet Leigh is pictured watching one of her own former movies for Universal, *Walking My Baby Back Home* (1953). The final credit, 'A Universal – International Picture' is visible on the screen as the film ends. Both instances are, effectively, examples of private archives. More broadly, in 'Requiem for a Falling Star' (1973), consider the sight of Columbo moving around the studio lot amongst all the props and costumed extras evocative of Hollywood's Golden Age genres (from cycling headdress-festooned Native Americans from the western, to dancing girls from the sword and sandal film).

This cluttered *mise-en-scène*, deliberately framed to emphasise the depth and diversity of available props, renders the movies an archive, now with the more explicit indication that from this archive television produces its own content.

Secondly, television, known for being an 'everyday' medium is of necessity a nimble medium. Both because of the intimacy it offers through its

Figure 6.4 Television showcases its appropriation of Hollywood's archive, in *Columbo* 'Requiem for a Falling Star' (1973).

focus on the ordinary and the everyday (Langer 1981: 354 and 362) and also because its 24/7 continuous flow makes drama an intrinsic part of quotidian life (Williams 1990: 59–60 and 94). For example, it can react rapidly to new audience tastes, such as that indicated by the emergence of neo-noir movies in the 1980s (see further below).

Take the first of these, the archive. *Columbo*'s revivification of film noir is especially evident in recycled plots and stars. The second pilot, 'Ransom for a Dead Man' (1971) is a homage to *Double Indemnity* (1944). It recreates the film's central father-daughter relationship, with the stepmother looking to murder her husband (effectively robbing her stepdaughter of her inheritance), along with the surety of the daughter seeking justice for her murdered father. Interestingly, the original noir also contained a character rather like Columbo: a cigar-smoking, minutiae-intrigued hard-working man – albeit an insurance claims investigator, rather than a detective – who smokes cheap cigars (but is forever patting his pockets for an elusive match) whilst obsessively poring over the past to uncover the flaw in the (faked) retelling of history. Finally, in case you did not spot the homage, the movie even *plays on a television* in the *Columbo* episode, watched by the daughter of the murdered man. Film noir, the second pilot rather literally indicates, is now available on TV, in *Columbo*.

Numerous further examples can be cited. *Sunset Boulevard* (1950) is loosely remade in 'Forgotten Lady' (1975), complete with devoted stuffy butler and fading movie star losing track of the distinction between her old movie roles and reality. 'Rest in Peace, Mrs Columbo' (1990) offers an extended homage to the distinctive flashbacks-at-a-funeral of *The Barefoot Contessa* (1954). There are further aesthetic nods to classic noirs like *The Big Heat* (1953) in 'Agenda for Murder' (1990), and to *The Big Sleep* (1946) in 'Columbo and the Murder of a Rock Star' (1991). Various guest stars known for their film noir roles also appear: from Ida Lupino of *On Dangerous Ground* (1951) in 'Short Fuse' (1972); to Jane Greer of *Out of the Past* (1947) in 'Troubled Waters' (1975); and Janet Leigh of *Touch of Evil* (1958) in 'Forgotten Lady' (1975). In this way Universal's role in noir heritage – the studio made such notable noirs as *The Killers* (1946) and *Touch of Evil* (1958) – is also alluded to. Most direct in this respect, in 'How to Dial a Murder' (1978), there is a prominently displayed, spot-lit poster in the home of Dr Eric Mason (Nicol Williamson) of the Universal noir *The Suspect* (1944), the plot of which – involving a murdered wife – is very loosely reworked to provide the backstory to this episode of *Columbo*. Indeed, *The Suspect* is something of a Columbo predecessor in as much as it focuses on an investigation into a suspicious death, by a Scotland Yard

inspector called Huxley (Stanley C. Ridges), who trails and tricks his suspect into confessing, just as Columbo so often does.[5]

Clearly television is able to situate itself in relation to the public's memory of classical Hollywood, then, with *Columbo* offering a primetime contemporary reworking of the archive to create nostalgic pleasure via noir.
This is a heritage integrally connected to Los Angeles as setting. If *Sunset
Boulevard* was Hollywood self-consciously replaying its past with tongue-
in-cheek nostalgia, then *Columbo* shows the potential television now has to
regularly re-engage with this noir heritage in a similar way.

In this nostalgia, the initial *Columbo* run was not unique. The 1970s saw,
Derek Kompare observes, a nostalgic revelling in televisual heritage due to
the mythological re-evaluation of the 1950s as the medium's first Golden
Age (a period coinciding with the supposed 'economic and cultural sta-
bility' of the USA). This was evident in the popularity of 1950s reruns
at that time (Kompare 2005: 109–110). Yet, whilst not necessarily unique
in its activation of nostalgia, *Columbo* is a little different nonetheless. In
its allusions to noir, *Columbo* returns to a slightly earlier era, and with a
more jaundiced eye. Noir emphasised the disposability of the everyman
and pointed the finger at elite corruption. It was a fitting choice, then, for
a series about an overworked everyman cop investigating the crimes of the
wealthy in the era of Watergate.

However, when *Columbo* returned at the very end of the 1980s and into
the 1990s, there was a slightly different evocation of the past again. As
noted in Chapter 1, *Columbo* initially ensured that its appeal included
older audience demographics, through the nostalgia created by cameos or
guest appearances by former stars of the silver screen. In the *Columbo*s of
the late 1980s and 1990s, by contrast, the nostalgia involved was evocative
of a slightly different precedent. Now, for the viewers who remembered
being part of the show's original audiences the experience was of being
reminded of the *Columbo* of the 1970s. In the episodes for ABC, then,
the nostalgia which emerges 'out of the past', to coin a noir phrase, is no
longer for cinema, but television. The later *Columbo*s offered the chance to
relive, in the 1990s, the experience from the recent past of the 1970s, and
all the associated memories this might revive.

This is very evident in 'Uneasy Lies the Crown' (1990) in which
Columbo stumbles upon a group of poker players which includes the television actors Nancy Walker and Dick Sargent. When Columbo arrives, he

[5] This connection is noted on websites like the Internet Movie Database, under trivia
related to the episode.

tries to guess who they are, and the shows they starred in. As this is the second time in the episode in which the group has appeared, Columbo's dredging through his mental archive of old shows and their stars replicates the process that many viewers will have gone through during the group's unexpected appearance the first time. Noticeably, Columbo identifies Nancy Walker from what he calls 'the Rock Hudson show', alluding to *McMillan & Wife* (1971–1977), one of the original companions to *Columbo* in the NBC *Mystery Movie* programme. Columbo is also prompted to remember other iconic shows (such as *I Love Lucy* [1951–1957]) before Sargent reminds Columbo, and viewers, that he starred in *Bewitched* (1964–1972). If there was any doubt that it is specifically the heyday of the television era which produced the original *Columbo* which is being nostalgically evoked, this is firmly emphasised by the appearance of Ron Cey of the Los Angeles Dodgers in the poker group, the player who starred for the team during the 1970s on its way to the World Series in 1981. Television, it seems, has now at least equalled if not supplanted the movies in our cultural memory banks.

Watching familiar faces from television who were famous from the 1960s and 1970s, on *Columbo* in the 1990s, is also a different experience to that of watching them in the *Columbo*s of the 1970s. Especially the return of famous guest murderers like Patrick McGoohan and William Shatner. The intervening years have cemented these actors in the viewers' memory as iconic of the 1960s and 1970s. This is not only because of the roles they played in *The Prisoner* (1967–1968) and *Star Trek* (1966–1969) respectively, but also because of their appearances in the original *Columbo* run[6] alongside other well-known televisual faces of the era playing murderers, like Martin Landau (*Mission Impossible* [1966–1973]) and Leonard Nimoy

---

[6] Along with the guest appearances and cameos of former television stars this nostalgia may have included a chance to return to the pre-Reagan era, prior to the social transformation enacted by the adoption of neoliberalism as global orthodoxy (Berardi 2009b: 111–114). What is immediately different about the *Columbo*s of the late 1980s and 1990s is how the wealth and associated privilege of the murderer is ostentatiously *displayed*. Sex, in particular, is used to attract attention. Witness the sex therapist with her own radio show in 'Sex and the Married Detective' (1989), the privileged polygamous painter in 'Murder, a Self Portrait' (1989), the salacious men's magazine central to 'Columbo Cries Wolf' (1990), or pornography in 'Caution: Murder Can be Hazardous to Your Health' (1991): sex, it is emphasised, sells. This new gaudiness surrounding how attention is capitalised upon contrasts with the 1970s *Columbo*s humorous passing acknowledgements of the Lieutenant's desires in his bashful or occasionally furtive perusal of the human form: a nude model ('Suitable for Framing [1971]), nude sunbathers ('Lovely but Lethal' [1973]), an erotic art book ('The Conspirators' [1978]); or his enthralled captivation by belly dancers ('Identity Crisis' [1975]; 'Try and Catch Me' [1977]).

(*Star Trek* and *Mission Impossible*). In its revival run, then, *Columbo* – after all, a complex memory game designed to hone attention (see Chapter 2) – provides the additional dimension of nostalgia (for previous television shows) to the pleasures it offers. What is key to understand is that, in the 1990s the archive which television can draw upon in effecting nostalgia also includes television: not only the cinematic past, but now the televisual as well. Indeed, television would now seem to hold pride of place in this virtual history.

The second of these points, the nimbleness of television, was also evident when *Columbo* returned with ABC. Here the references shift to neo-noir seemingly in response to the popularity of recent, steamy movies like *Body Heat* (1981) and *Fatal Attraction* (1987) which were influenced in part by the growing market for home video: a new form of film viewing on television. In 'Sex and the Married Detective' (1989), for example, sex therapist Dr Joan Allenby (Lindsay Crouse) dresses as a noir femme fatale (all in black, with fedora), to ensnare her husband in a sexual scenario before murdering him.[7] Just as neo-noir 'bonkbusters' like *Basic Instinct* (1992) and *The Last Seduction* (1994) (Feasey 2003: 167) are distinguishable from their predecessors of the 1940s due to their recognition that what it means to labour has changed in the intervening decades (Freedman 2009: 71), so too this particular noir-esque femme fatale. Allenby, after all, is not only a sex therapist by trade but also a popular author and radio celebrity. With herself as her brand, her knowledge diversified into various content forms to garner the widest attention, Allenby creates a perfect neo-noir femme fatale – a fully-functioning attentive labourer working across the attention industries.

Situated atop this Hollywood heritage, *Columbo* emphasises repeatedly, is the vast entertainment complex which keeps alive the Debordian society of the spectacle on which the attention industries thrive. Not only do we witness numerous films and television shows being made, so too do we attend ball games, classical musical concerts – including at the Hollywood Bowl – gospel gigs, fashion magazine photo shoots, political rallies and the Universal Studio Tour. LA is thus rendered integral to the attention industries' creation of the spectacle to which we must all labour to pay attention: the innocent, after all, watch. But it is a spectacle which threatens to distract from the disenfranchisement of many, the proliferation

---

[7] The next episode, 'Grand Deceptions' (1989), seems to have been influenced by television shows like *The A-Team* (1983–1987), with which it shares some rather gentle military pyrotechnics, and perhaps also the popularity of films like *First Blood* (1982) and two *Rambo* sequels, *Commando* (1985) and *Predator* (1987).

of bare life under neoliberalism. Indeed, this distraction enables the prolongation of a very particular, settler-colonist, view of the history of Los Angeles.

Democratic Detective?

To conclude this chapter, let us firstly recap. Columbo polices the right to a meaningful life for all in the global gateway city. The transformation of Los Angeles exacerbated the distinction between a meaningful existence in society and bare life. *Columbo*'s emphasis on the crimes of elite WASP society in LA's wealthier neighbourhoods, then, perpetuates Los Angeles's historically preferred (white) cinematic and televisual image. Importantly, it also illuminates the function of this image: the 'suppression and appropriation of the earlier histories of Native American, Spanish and Mexican Southern California' (Shiel 2012: 8) in the maintenance of settler-colonist society. This is the tradition, after all, which explains film noir's anxiety over the presence of 'foreigners' in the city, evident in the genre's depiction of LA through the eyes of the white, male detective policing the underbelly of the (white, Protestant) Californian dream (Klein 1997: 80). For Columbo to police this space is, inherently, to engage with the Orwellian history-making of the European settler-colonist culture. It is that, as outlined in Chapter 5, which eradicates all other histories not deemed to belong to the nation, and through this history-erasure reduces all such demographics to the position of those who can be killed with impunity: bare life. By correcting the histories of those murdered, Columbo chooses instead to protect the right to life for those from whom it is unfairly taken.

As a result, it is not too much of a stretch, as the Conclusion will examine further, to consider Columbo's policing as being related to the upholding of a democratic right. This, even if as noted in Chapter 5, *Columbo* is far from inclusive in its depiction of the USA's various citizen demographics. I am not the first to draw such a conclusion regarding *Columbo* and democracy. In 1991, celebrating the return of *Columbo* to television screens in the UK, the journalist Frank Johnson observed that Columbo's policing of the elite was only possible in a democracy:

> The belief that wealth or fame confer power is very American. But American, too, are the institutions which alone can curb that power – police departments, the rule of law, courts. Only in a country where shabby men in dirty raincoats, if enough of them vote the same way, can defeat presidents and senators, can they also defeat those whose superior position makes them think that they can get away with murder. Before democracy, when inexpert militias dealt with crime, which criminals went to the gallows was a matter of luck, or ill-luck. Few of Columbo's murderers would

have met such an end. Instead, they would have used their position to make sure that the suspicious Columbo did. (1991: 15)

Whilst the USA played its role in ensuring that democracy was restricted for many of its own citizens historically, not to mention for people in various other parts of the world during the Cold War, Columbo's defence of a right to life is, whilst limited in its inclusivity, even so, democratic in intent. Doubtless this would have been more apparent in 1991 when Johnson was writing, after the previous decade had seen the fall of many authoritarian governments that gave way to the return or emergence of democracy (in many countries across Latin America, for example) and then, ultimately, the fall of the Berlin Wall in 1989. This democratic impulse, inherent to Columbo's policing of the right to life, I develop further in the Conclusion.

Conclusion:
Paying Attention 24/7

This book has investigated many manifestations of Columbo the attentive labourer. These have included: Columbo the theatre critic unmasking badly performed alibis; Columbo the Kafka-esque low-level functionary of the law (the LAPD as state surveillance); Columbo, conversely, as techno-savvy 'everyman' innocently watching the watchmen (sousveillance); Columbo as class-conscious policeman of history; Columbo as Renaissance-style figure of revenge (ghostly representative of the murdered); Columbo, finally, the protector of the democratic right to life for those cast out by society (the homeless, or 'bare life'). Having come this far, one further interpretation can be added to these various Columbos by way of summation: Columbo as 'fallen angel of history'.[1]

As noted in the Introduction, Columbo is a *zeitgeist* figure. In *Wings of Desire* (1987), fallen angel Falk/Columbo appears as a personification of the seemingly welcoming post-war global spread of capital under US leadership. The other angels he meets are connected to Berlin's inhabitants' memories of the past,[2] or seemingly even to the memories of the city itself (in both instances through the insertion of archival footage of the destruction and ruins created by the Second World War), rendering them strangely evocative of Walter Benjamin's description of Paul Klee's painting *Angelus Novus* as the 'angel of history' (1968: 257). The angel of history, for Benjamin, has its back to the future and as such can only see the destructive results of the ongoing march of time piling up unceasingly in front of it. The aftermath of the 'storm' which we mortals perceive as progress appears to the angel 'a single catastrophe which keeps piling wreckage upon wreckage and hurls it in front of his feet' (pp. 257–258).

---

[1] My thanks to Andrew Jarvis for noting this helpful Benjaminian resonance.

[2] The angels supposedly inhabit an eternal, spiritual realm, unconstrainted by linear history, yet their focus is typically the past (and present) rather than the future.

For his part, however, Falk/Columbo the fallen angel seems to face the future rather than the past. Or at least, he is more concerned with the simple pleasures of living life in the present. He recommends such down-to-earth pastimes as taking coffee, or pencil drawing, to the teetering angels when trying to tempt them into joining him. Yet, curiously, Columbo himself (if we return to the actual television show) remains the one with his attention on the past. At least in the sense that his policing function is to ensure the veracity of the recording of history. Columbo as *fallen* angel of history, then, is evocative of both the 'heavenly' benefits of living in the present (once again, as per Dostoevsky's Porfiry Petrovich's extolling of life for Raskolnikov), but also the attendant historical damage of the advancement of capitalism (a past containing destruction and murder which Columbo must uncover, even though some would rather he, and we, forgot). Indeed, the former seems integrally intertwined with, if not predicated upon, the latter.

On such a view, Columbo is far from a reassuring figure to have as a (fallen) guardian angel. He may wish to welcome the world to late capitalism but joining him seems to entail a heavy price. Columbo the fallen angel of history, then, captures well the ambivalence of *Columbo* found in the many possible Columbos noted above (both good guys and bad guys). Columbo may protect the veracity of history to provide a baseline right to a citizen's life equally for all, but he does so in a society in which some citizen's lives are – to coin the Orwellian phrase – more equal than others. What should we make, accordingly, of the complex memory game of *Columbo* which trains viewers in how to pay attention, along with supplementary lessons on how to perform, learn, police and locate themselves in an all-surveilled society? This is a society, after all, perpetually paying attention to its citizens such that their lives become self-consciously performed as though on live television, and, simultaneously, requiring of them their 24/7 attention as a key driver of the economy. What is at stake in *Columbo*, as is crystallised in Chapters 3 and 4, is what it means to be guilty or innocent under such conditions, Columbo's ambiguous relationship to this, as seen in Chapters 5 and 6, illuminating precisely the inequalities associated with our contemporary global milieu. As such, what the viewer takes away from *Columbo* in terms of how best to perform, learn, police and locate themselves may well depend upon which of Columbo's ambivalent aspects they prefer: whether they focus on Columbo as state surveillance, say, or as sousveillance. This, by turns, may change depending on the episode and how the viewer interprets it. To conclude, then, let us try to understand, and, finally, to look beyond, such ambiguity and ambivalence.

The Ideal Attentive Labourer

In the initial pilot, 'Prescription: Murder' (1968), Columbo is described by psychiatrist Dr Ray Flemming (Gene Barry) as 'the textbook example of compensation'. Columbo has an amazing ability to use his unassuming appearance and manner to lull suspects into mistakes. Yet, were *Columbo* still on the air, what might Flemming's diagnosis be now?

Falk's biographers, Richard A. Lertzman and William J. Birnes, believe that both Falk and the character of Columbo 'displayed many elements of' Obsessive Compulsive Disorder (OCD), in the latter case especially in his emphasis on the minutiae which 'bother' him about his cases (2017: 283–284). They may be right. In 'Lady in Waiting' (1971), Columbo notes that his wife considers him 'compulsive' in his need to tie off the loose ends which trouble him. Even so, Columbo's behaviour does not necessarily correlate completely with OCD. For instance, it seems to lack an initial sense of insecurity or fear (potentially even catastrophic thinking), coupled with anxiety that if something bad were to happen it would be because of his action (or inaction) (Kennerley 2014: 103–111). It is this which obsessive behaviour may be intended to allay, as is apparent in the rituals that accompany OCD (for example, repeatedly checking and rechecking to see if a door is locked). Even if initially designed to neutralise fear, instead such rituals may develop into an obsession. Columbo, though, does not seem to suffer in this way. Where his pencil is, for example, he never knows. Someone with OCD might well know this, and perhaps might also check, even repeatedly, the place where they had put it, for reassurance. Columbo is more generally concerned with much wider issues – the veracity of history, the sanctity of life.

An alternative interpretation, then, would be that Columbo displays symptoms of Generalised Anxiety Disorder which are typically caused by 'persistent feelings of anxiety, constant concerns and "What if . . .?" thoughts' (Kennerly 2014: 98). As Helen Kennerley explains: 'It is not unusual to hear Generalized Anxiety Disorder sufferers say . . . "I can never relax, something is always troubling me"' (2014: 98). The echo of Columbo's patter about how little details bother him is very apparent. In addition, a prevalent issue with Generalised Anxiety Disorder is worrying over uncertainty. Sufferers 'keep worrying about things, hoping that they will come up with some solution or knowledge that will make the difference' (p. 101). Columbo's anxiety seems induced by the possibility that a technologically manufactured false construction of the past will deny justice to one already deprived of a fair chance in life. Thus, what makes Columbo anxious, it would seem, is the constant attention required of him by the social injustice attendant upon late capitalism, itself the latest phase in the history of inequality stretching back to the colonisation of the Americas (Mills 1997; Mignolo 2000). What causes Columbo's generalised anxiety is thus not specific to his biographical past. If we flashforward to the present, this is in stark contrast to Columbo's anxious successors in *Monk* (2002–2009) and *Elementary* (2012–2019). These later shows in a similar mould also feature obsessive detectives, but their anxious behaviour has been very specifically compounded by recent traumatic life events: the death of Monk's wife, Holmes's drug addiction. *Columbo*, rather, reveals the impact of neoliberalism on the contemporary *societal* state of mind.

That Columbo's anxiety reflects a broader societal rather than autobiographical root is perhaps unsurprising. For Franco 'Bifo' Berardi, the proliferation of damaging mental health conditions like 'panic, anxiety, depression' are 'the effects of the economic mobilization of attention' (2009b: 134–135). Specifically, the demands of 24/7 capitalism – including the penetration of the private sphere by advertising (in the era of *Columbo*, on television, but nowadays via the internet) – has created this 'constant mobilization of attention' (p. 107). The toll that such constant attention takes is evidenced by, for example, engagement with social media being linked to mental health issues (Moore 2017; Pinker 2017; Barr 2019).

The ambiguity arises, though, over whether or not Columbo's anxiety is genuine, or, as Dr Flemming intimates, a cunning *performance?* To flashforward again, this time to a popular contemporary show starring a former *Columbo* murderer, is Columbo a little like the protagonists of *The Americans* (2013–2018)? For the Soviet sleepers, Philip (Matthew Rhys) and Elizabeth (Keri Russell) Jennings, their everyday lives as deep-cover spies in Reagan-era USA are lived under the constant anxiogenic threat of surveillance and discovery, forever performing disguised identities. In the episode 'Comint' (2013), in the first series, Elizabeth Jennings summarises her perpetual anxiety, saying: 'You know what I wish, as I fall asleep every night? That I'll wake up and not be worried.' When asked 'About what?' she replies 'Everything.' Or is it simpler than this? Is Columbo playing at anxiety, faking it, whether to outfox his suspects, or perhaps to outwit ubiquitous surveillance? There is no clear answer because television functions by holding such contradictions in place (Mellencamp 1992: 149).

For Patricia Mellencamp, anxiety is television's affect (1992: 80) as it attempts to regulate the way shock is experienced under modernity. It creates shockwaves by reporting on disasters or catastrophes that indicate modernity's precarity (from tsunamis to collapsed buildings), and then smooths over such anxiogenic events with its reassuring technological presence at the scene. Thus, there seems no straightforward answer to the question of whether Columbo is performing or genuine (is a good guy or a bad guy). This is because *Columbo*, like television more broadly, simultaneously begs the question of whether it might all be an act, just as it soothes us that, of course, it is all genuine. Holding this tension in place, Columbo performs the characteristics of Generalised Anxiety Disorder which we can understand to be for some – due to the coincidence of the show's run with the shifting of how attention is channelled towards the close of the twentieth century – a feature of this transforming historical period.

Columbo, then, illustrates that living and working during the latter decades of the twentieth century may entail a long life of 24/7 attentiveness, accompanied by perpetual worry about work. Columbo's final case, 'Columbo Likes the Night Life' (2003), was investigated when Peter Falk was seventy-six, and the character Columbo (who admits to being over forty in 'Double Exposure' [1973]) about the same age. Despite the rigours of such a life, though, Columbo remains the ideal attentive labourer because he never suffers from attention *deficit* (Doran 2017: 6). As noted in Chapter 4, Columbo's attention to the latest advances of modernity indicate as much as anything the perpetual threat posed by inattention (which is identified as rising in tandem with the advance of industrialisation during the nineteenth century [Crary 1999: 13–14]). Indeed, with inattention stigmatised for this reason, it is unsurprising that Columbo – who is introduced in the second pilot looking for his lost pen – is initially misjudged by many as a bungling incompetent. Yet it is Columbo's indifference to mundane realities, his absent-mindedness when it comes to paying attention to where he left his pencil (or when he last filled up his car, or shaved, or changed his clothes), which enables his obsessive level of attention to the case itself.[3]

This is not the only manner in which the necessary pay-off between inattention and attention is played out in *Columbo*. Take Columbo's passions, such as his love of playing pool ('How to Dial a Murder' [1978]), or of cooking ('Murder Under Glass' [1978]). On the one hand these may seem like generic ways of rounding out a character to make them more relatable. Pool, for example, is something which Joe Mannix (Mike Connors) excels at in *Mannix* (1967–1975), and cookery (and the enjoyment of food from sashimi to spinach soufflé) is Frank Cannon's (William Conrad) hobby in *Cannon* (1971–1976). Although such passions are a generic way of showing a well-rounded approach to work/life, in *Columbo* they actually indicate how adept the Lieutenant is at the self-care involved in staying sane with an

---

[3] My thanks to Carl Lavery for inspiring this realisation in conversation.

incredibly unhealthy work/life imbalance. After all, in spite of his obsession with work and resulting perpetual dog-tiredness, on numerous occasions Columbo specifically mentions how much he loves his work. This is why, in 'Murder by the Book' (1971) the first episode of the first season, the closeness between Columbo's passions and his work (their mutually entwined relationship) is foregrounded. Columbo's introduction to viewers quickly sees him offer to cook for the wife of a seemingly kidnapped man. This he does in the second scene in which he features. Columbo returns with the distraught woman to her home, and although declaring himself 'the worst cook in the world', prepares her an omelette. Columbo seems entirely at home in a stranger's kitchen, and whilst cooking is also able to discern – by talking with the soon-to-be-widow – the relationship between the disappeared (in fact, murdered) man and his writing partner. Work may be omnipresent, even invading home life, but when work and hobbies entwine so easily, why wouldn't a person love their work?

There are several standout moments in which Columbo's care of the self is thus highlighted. In an unexpected scene in 'Last Salute to the Commodore' (1976) Columbo joins in the transcendental meditation practice of a young woman working as a naval architect and marine engineer. The attentive productivity of 24/7 capitalism requires that individuals attend to themselves if they are to labour perpetually. As the extremely busy, professional young woman's meditative calm illustrates, so-called mindfulness practices are thus increasingly prevalent in the post-Fordist workforce. And if, ironically, practices like transcendental meditation are often co-opted from Eastern meditative traditions (Doran 2017: 1–7) – without emphasising the alternative way of life to capitalism that a religion like Buddhism indicates is necessary for an ethical attentiveness to one's place in the world (pp. 15–24) – once again television proves adept at holding in play such ambiguities. *Columbo* at once critiques the exhaustion of 24/7 attention whilst reassuring that everything can be managed with just a little cooking and family downtime (or transcendental meditation, for the younger generation).

Moreover, *Columbo* reassures that perpetual work can still somehow enable a private life. Even though Columbo dedicates himself to his attentive labour 24/7, eradicating any distinction between the public and private spheres of his life, curiously he still protects the sanctity of the private in subtle ways. Whilst he says that his first name is 'Lieutenant' because he is entirely at one with his job (see Chapter 3), this also ensures that he retains his actual first name for his personal life. Again, whilst Columbo is forever harping on his family, because we never see his home nor can be sure how much (if any) truth there is in his familial anecdotes, this *all* might even possibly be a fictional smokescreen to protect his actual family. This seems plausible, considering that: the CIA bug his house in 'Identity Crisis' (1975); in 'Rest in Peace, Mrs Columbo' (1990), Columbo's wife becomes the target of an attempted revenge killing solely by virtue of her relationship with the Lieutenant; and the newly-wed bride of Columbo's nephew – who is also LAPD – is kidnapped from the bridal suite by a deranged stalker in 'No Time to Die' (1992). Even against such apparent threats, a private life can, apparently, be protected.

The complex memory game that *Columbo* encourages its viewers to play thus seems designed not only to hone attentive skills, but equally to ensure that attention deficit is minimised. Viewers must learn to be excellent attentive labourers. Even if this may induce anxiety, viewers are reassured that some self-care should ensure continued work can proceed 24/7. Indeed, this attentive labour is branded as innocent, even though it is integral to society's compulsory and all-pervasive self-surveillance. It thereby promotes a more passive, rather than involved, form of citizenship (as explored in Chapters 2 and 4). Against such a bleak interpretation of *Columbo*, however, is there yet a way to see things from a different, more optimistic perspective?

Thou Shalt Not Kill

A further flashforward can shed new light. The contemporary dystopian television series, *The Purge* (2018–), based on the popular film franchise of the 2010s, explores the premise that once a year the rule of law is suspended in the USA. During this time criminal activities are legitimised. The show dramatises Giorgio Agamben's point, made in the wake of laws like the Patriot Act, after 9/11, that the aim of contemporary politics is to make permanent the 'state of exception' in which the social contract is suspended and democratic rights put on hold (2003: 1–7). This terrifying state of affairs was previously used in many countries under military rule during the Cold War to violently 'purge' societies of their left-leaning populations (the potential opposition to the socially divisive neoliberal ideology also being introduced at that time).

Despite how dissimilar the two shows are, *The Purge* shares various commonalities with *Columbo*. Both programmes explore the stark class and wealth contrasts of neoliberal society, the all-consuming nature of work, the pervasiveness of spectacle (even the violence of the purge is televised), the thorny question of who (if anyone) is watching the watchmen, the difficulty women face in business when breaching the glass ceiling, and the notion that women in particular have to murder to receive the promotion their labour deserves. However, there is a crucial difference. In *The Purge*, during the state of exception all life can be killed with impunity. All life is reduced to the status of bare life by government decree. By contrast, and against such a dystopian direction to twenty-first century society, in *Columbo* we find a policeman – albeit living and working along with the exacting demands of late capitalism – who is nevertheless engaged in a 24/7 attentive struggle to protect the democratic right for all to a citizen's life. Herein lies a contrast which can point past the aforementioned ambiguity, offering, finally, a more positive way to interpret *Columbo*.

As noted in Chapter 6, the epitome of bare life in *Columbo* would be the homeless, with whom Columbo is aligned twice, or the ex-con he saves from false arrest by the Deputy Commissioner of police. In 'Ashes to Ashes' (1998), though, the category of bare life is extended even further. Here, an unusual scene occurs in which a puppy is discovered which has been left cooped up overnight without food or water. Columbo, entirely out of character due to his usual obsession with detail, stops everything surrounding the investigation and becomes totally focused on feeding and watering the failing puppy. The original bloodhound, Columbo, is brought to a halt by a dog, such that he almost forgets where he is, or why. His full attention focused on the animal; Columbo will only return to the case once he has provided for the dog's immediate and ongoing well-being. This seeming anomaly, late on in the show's run is, in fact, entirely in character. As Columbo's role is to police the sanctity of life, this sudden intrusion of the animal into a show normally focused on human life and death (murder, specifically) indicates that this sanctity extends beyond the human. Perhaps this is not a surprise considering that all along Columbo's only 'partner' (as per the generic norms of the cop show) is his basset hound. As its name is Dog, moreover, the impression is that Columbo is dedicated not only to his pet (one dog), but to fostering equality with another species altogether (Dog, or *Canis familiaris*). Towards the end of Columbo's run, then, his policing of the sanctity of life seemingly extends beyond the human.

Even so, as explored in Chapter 5, the *epitome* of those excluded in *Columbo* is not the homeless, nor the ex-con, and we can now add, it is not even the animal: it is those who have been murdered. Columbo, protecting life, seeks justice for the dead. This is exactly what is denied those who die during the state of exception in *The Purge*. True, on the one hand Columbo is the ideal neoliberal citizen: he works 24/7, perpetually paying attention in a way that maintains existing class hierarchies and vast social inequality. On the other hand, though, there is nothing ambiguous here. Columbo does this to protect the very minimum right to life which neoliberalism would deny the average citizen, as seen in *The Purge*. This helps explain Columbo's seeming moral ambivalence in his dedication to the law. Columbo, after all, apparently cares little whether motives are selfish or selfless. He will as soon convict a ruthless sociopath seeking material gain as he will a loving mother protecting her daughter from a violent predatory man. Nor indeed does he seem to care whether the act of catching a murderer perpetuates the status quo or challenges it. The moral/amoral position Columbo holds is rendered as such as early as the second pilot, 'Ransom for a Dead Man' (1971). Sociopathic murderer Leslie Williams (Lee Grant) is introduced as a brilliant lawyer, negotiating the line of the law without any moral conviction. In an early courtroom scene, Williams defends an insurance company, ensuring that an injured African American, working-class claimant (a punch press operator) does not receive full compensation for the partial paralysis he sustained in an apartment house insured by the company. This, even though Williams knows, personally, that the building is not up to safety standards. If her amoral pragmatism were not clear enough, Williams is later seen, in the Los Angeles County Courthouse, pointedly coaching another client to cry under questioning. The law, it seems, is less an ass, as in the famous saying, than an *act*. This Columbo himself acknowledges in the exact same courtroom setting when he questions whether the reactions of Williams to the news of her husband's death are exactly in character. For her part, Williams can see through Columbo's act as a detective so perceptively because she herself is such a skilled performer when acting professionally as a lawyer.

The contrast between the two characters, though, is outlined to show that whilst Columbo may be amoral in his pursuit of justice, he is also, paradoxically, to some extent moral. Or, more moral than the murderer at least. Not only will Williams deny the African American claimant his right, she will even kill to enhance her own position. Columbo, for his part, will see justice is done, regardless of whether the outcome is 'fair' or not. The contrast is that Columbo is not – as Williams is – without conscience. This is the insight Columbo uses to entrap Williams.

In case this seems a rather fine distinction, further clarification can be added. Distinct from the murderers he chases, Columbo, like many noir characters before him, is guided by an honour code. Once this code is understood, Columbo's apparent moral ambiguity (good guy? bad guy?) no longer appears perplexing (Sanders and Skoble 2008: 9–11). Columbo follows a clear line throughout all his cases – if a life is taken, there must be reckoning. In 'A Deadly State of Mind' (1975) this process is illustrated very literally when Columbo visits a scientific research centre that studies human behaviour. Dr Anita Borden (Karen Machon) explains that the lab: 'is concerned with the measurement and manipulation of human behavior, on all levels . . . Things like peer group adaptability and anxiety catharsis through hypnotic suggestion.' Columbo's arrival coincides with an explanation of the experiments being conducted, on the voiceover, in which it is explained that a rat called Willy has to learn to follow a partic- ular coloured line to make its way through a maze to find food. Columbo enters the building, and asks how he might locate his suspect, Dr Mark Collier (George Hamilton). Columbo is directed to find his way to Collier by following a blue line on the floor, a test which he successfully completes in spite of the many winding corridors he traverses. Thus, Columbo, the attentive labourer, is equated with a lab rat in a giant experiment con- cerning human behaviour in which his role is to follow the 'thin blue line' (clearly, of the law) with a single-minded dedication. Following this thin blue line, for Columbo the murderer must be caught so that history will be put right: *thus there can be no state of exception.* Whether the history which is put right by uncovering the fake alibi is one which belongs to a fair and just society or not, does not seem to interest Columbo. Or at least, even if it should prick his conscience, he functions as a policeman irrespective of this. Policing the right to life is his only interest, and this is seemingly what shapes his honour code.

Importantly, this is not due to any personal vendetta, it is a societal issue: a right. As discussed previously, unlike *Monk*'s Monk or *Elementary*'s Holmes, Columbo's dedication to policing is not related to a trauma in his personal life. For all his talk of his family, we do not know much, if any- thing, concrete about Columbo's personal history. Certainly, no biograph- ical root cause is given for his actions. To flashforward once more, this is in stark contrast to, say, Hieronymus 'Harry' Bosch (Titus Welliver) in *Bosch* (2014–). *Bosch*'s Bosch has a peculiarly alienating and rather indi- vidualistic sense of justice which determines how he conducts himself as a policeman. In some ways it seems as uncompromising as Columbo's. Yet Bosch's particular honour code is specifically traced back to a biographi- cal root: the murder of his prostitute mother when he was a boy, and the subsequent abuse he suffered whilst growing up in a children's home. What distinguishes the two equally workaholic LAPD detectives Bosch and Columbo, then, is that whilst Bosch's honour code is deeply personal, Columbo's is not, it relates to a societal principle – the democratic right to a citizen's life for all – which he has dedicated himself to policing.

In this rather moral/amoral position, Columbo values a right to life even for those whom society would cast out into the category of bare life. By policing the right to a citizen's life for all Columbo seeks to ward off the state of exception which is rendered so real in *The Purge*. As it is the rich who are most likely to be able to afford to protect their lives when all killing can be conducted with impunity, Columbo's at times unorthodox, even unlawful, methods police the baseline conditions for an inclusive democracy. Hence the role of the preservation of an accurate historical record remains key (see Chapter 5) because the state of exception is, politically, designed to exclude (if not eradicate) not only a section of the population, but also their existence from history. As Hannah Arendt notes, the state of exception is, effectively, an attempt to return society to the 'state of nature' which is thought to precede civilised society: if you will, a (fictional) 'year zero' from which to then restructure a new social contract (1963: 9–13). This may happen in a way which strengthens the existing and by definition unequal hierarchy (e.g. in the twentieth century when US-backed military dictatorships across various continents eradicated left-wing political opposition during the Cold War). Or it may happen in a manner which creates a different, but likely also unequal, hierarchy that privileges those currently left out of the society's riches (e.g. in the twentieth century when communist revolutions in various countries stripped the richest of their wealth and privilege). Whatever the political perspective, what is crucial to warding off the state of exception is the maintenance of existing history such that those in danger of exclusion at least retain some acknowledgement of their (marginalised) existence. This existence is not only threatened by such dramatic historical events as military coups (from the right) and armed revolutions (from the left), but also by more insidious, everyday attempts to rewrite history using different technologies.

For this reason, Columbo must use his attentive skills to guard against what Jayson Harsin has elucidated as the 'anti-democratic' potential of the attention economy. Harsin is referring, in particular, to its provision of 'a felicitous playground for strategic professional political communication (and some amateurs) that aims to distract, distort, confuse, and demobilize; most recently encompassed by the popular terms fake news and posttruth' (2019: 99). Hence Columbo's preoccupation with the correctness of history, including in cases which implicitly link the manipulation of how events are recorded and political election. For example, 'Agenda for Murder' (1990) concludes with the arrest of a lawyer and political advisor, Oscar Finch (Patrick McGoohan), at the point of what seems will be a strategically important electoral victory for his colleague, Congressman Paul Mackey (Denis Arndt). Finch had killed, precisely, to ensure that a crime in the past – an act of political corruption, involving both Finch and Mackey – was not uncovered. The murder in the present, by Finch, was committed to stop this revelation from the past from ruining the congressman's chances in the election. History, then, is what is to be recovered or lost in this democratic function of Columbo's policing.

What Columbo polices, then, is not a Nietzschean 'beyond' of good and evil (as per Dostoevsky's policing of Raskolnikov's murderous action by Porfiry Petrovich), even if Columbo does ultimately police 'exceptional' individuals of this sort (Nietzsche [1886] 1973). Rather, Columbo polices a baseline expectation of an underpinning right to life for everyone. He polices, in other words, good and evil, as though the prohibition against taking a life is the first decision, already made, on where right has been divided from wrong. Rather than a Nietzschean approach, then, Columbo upholds the responsibility to respect the life of an other more in the manner of Emmanuel Levinas. It was Levinas who propounded ethics as first philosophy, our duty to our neighbor being to recognise them: in the sense of acknowledging them and their equal right to life so as to shake us from our own egocentrism ([1961] 1969). In this *Columbo* offers at once a *warning* (protecting this right to life for all is a 24/7 job, increasingly demanding under late capitalism, requiring constant attention) but also, more hopefully, a *reminder* that a democratic society remains possible as long as this baseline is maintained. This is what is at stake when an ethical position recognising the other is upheld in the face of an ideology that seeks the opposite of this: when neoliberalism's war of all against all promotes competitive egocentric individualism (thereby discouraging recognition of the equality of the other), and as its logical conclusion seems to propose the state of exception as norm. To protect such a baseline, though, an everyman cop like Columbo may have to give up on being a good or bad guy. This, *Columbo* seems to indicate, may be a luxury which can only be enjoyed if the baseline upon which such judgements can be made (the extension of the right for all to a citizen's life) is policed in the first place. Hence Columbo is so ambiguously moral/amoral in his singular purpose.

In line with Levinas's ethics, *Columbo* is – just as Dostoevsky's *Crime and Punishment* is, just as the Father Brown novels are – a working through of a very old idea rendered historically as a commandment: thou shalt not kill. This is not in itself a revelation of course. Columbo is a homicide detective after all. Even so, *Columbo*'s engagement with what it means to uphold such a standard during the latter decades of the twentieth century indicates that what might be built on top of such a baseline may be a society democratic in name but so unequal that the right to life is all that many have left to cling to. This the social unrest of the period immediately prior to and during the show's first run indicated much more clearly than (the mostly white) *Columbo* ever does, especially the civil rights and indigenous rights movements along with second-wave feminism. Hence a lingering doubt remains when analysing *Columbo* as to whether life here is understood to be quite the same right for absolutely everyone in such an unequal society. This compounds the sense that it can be hard to determine whether Columbo is an uneasy-making or reassuring policeman (good guy? bad guy?). At the close of 'The Conspirators' (1978), Columbo intercepts smuggled rifles bound for the Irish Republican Army. Unlike his national (albeit not necessarily his literal) forefathers, who fought against the British Empire to gain independence for what would become the USA, ultimately Columbo is no revolutionary (see Chapter 5). Even so, Columbo justifies his actions in terms of saving lives. He points out to the Irish poet and gunrunner Joe Devlin (Clive Revill), that his fundraising in the USA was done under false pretenses: 'you pretended to raise money to help the Irish victims, and all the while you were planning to make more victims'. A right to life for all, once again, regardless of the societal conditions of the life lived. Thus, the same overarching question always re-emerges: should this society be upheld in the form it is, further propelling all the inequalities it fosters (themselves the legacy of the USA's long history of settler-colonisation), or should it be changed, even if such a revolution might well mean the loss of life? Put another way, can a moral/amoral position be justified, or does it just excuse the maintenance of inequality?

One way to answer this question is to consider Columbo's role as the leveller of the mythical status of the murderer as an 'exceptional' person (Downing 2013). The murderers are all reduced to the reality of their guilt by the banal, ordinary, everyday everyman. In this respect it is Columbo's abilities as an always engaged attentive labourer which are celebrated. This is clear in a speech which Columbo gives in 'The Bye-Bye Sky High IQ Murder Case' (1977). Columbo, speaking to a murderous genius (a member of an elite club for intellectuals), observes:

> All my life I kept running into smart people . . . In school there were lots of smarter kids. And when I first joined the force sir, they had some *very* clever people there. And I could tell right away that it wasn't going to be easy making detective as long as they were around. But I figured if I worked harder than they did, put in more time, read the books, kept my eyes open, maybe I could make it happen. And I did. And I really love my work sir.

Thus, the same paradox remains as has been explored in previous chapters, that in order to guard against abuse of the system, Columbo must effectively become one with the system which demands that he pay attention to work, even to love work, 24/7. By keeping his 'eyes open' and policing the (Nietzschean) 'exceptional' murderer, though, Columbo at least seems to be protecting a basic democratic right. Indeed, noticeably, in the timing of *Columbo*'s release, this Nietzschean idea of the exceptional person has a very particular meaning. Socio-historically it corresponds with the neo-liberal view of the centrality of the individual in the midst of a war with all others.

This idea, of the strong (the exceptional) ruling over the weak is, as Franco 'Bifo' Berardi notes, ingrained in the dominant economic doctrine of late capitalism which posits that the only law to be followed is that of the market. The murder committed for self-advancement – as is typical of *Columbo* – is, ultimately, an action against equality, an act of Social Darwinism (Berardi 2015: 33–41). This mistaken belief in Social Darwinism is firmly established in the first two pilots and repeated by many murderers thereafter. This also may be why Columbo often seems more sad than satisfied after catching a murderer (see Chapter 5). What pleasure is there to take in policing this selfish doctrine of exceptionalism after the horse has bolted? What pleasure if it has already led to murder in the mistaken belief that it is one person's right to prevail over 'weaker' citizens, an attitude integral to the maintenance of an unequal society?

Columbo's moral/amoral position, then, offers a degree of reassurance that, at the very least, 24/7 attentiveness can police the excesses of neoliberalism's Social Darwinism. In a similar vein, new light can also be shed on *Columbo*'s function as a game designed to hone viewer memory, with respect to its emphasis on maintaining democracy. As noted in Chapter 2, this complex memory game could be (perhaps a little cynically) tied to the idea of television as a medium for the focused delivery of advertisements. On the other hand, though, it could provide practice for viewers in the skills needed for being attentive to democratic rights under neoliberalism: how to perform, learn, police and locate ourselves so as to ensure our rights as citizens.

With hindsight, *Columbo* reveals the late twentieth-century emergence of the conditions upon which would later be established the 'surveillance capitalism' of our current moment (as so astutely identified by Shoshana Zuboff [2019]). Columbo's adeptness at paying attention is positioned amidst ubiquitous, technologically enhanced, total societal surveillance, a situation increasingly electronically managed in the years since *Columbo* ended. In contemporary society, the role of not only television but also the internet in influencing democratic elections has become apparent since the US presidential election and the UK's referendum of 2016 on its place within the European Union (Webster 2014: 146; Doyle and Roda 2019: 3; Zuboff 2019: 507; Cadwalladr 2020). Surveillance capitalism has provided a way of not only predicting people's behaviour – a futures market in foreseeing consumer trends at heart and one which also has a direct political application if utilised in that way – but even of directly influencing their behaviour (Zuboff 2019: 8–9). This threat to democracy offered by today's surveillance capitalism is what Columbo is involved in policing in utero, paradoxically it may seem, through his own at times invasive surveillance of the everyday. Although Columbo may seem moral/amoral, his defence of democracy positions him against the 'radical indifference' which, for Zuboff, tech companies take towards the distinction between truth and falsity in the contemporary era (2019: 509). This is the indifference which enables 'fake news' to be deliberately touted as equal to actual news via social media platforms intent on maximising profit, a potentially perilous situation for democracy.

Were there to be a remake of *Columbo* now, we might imagine Mark Ruffalo or Natasha Lyonne – or my own personal pick, Joaquin Phoenix – playing the Lieutenant, investigating not the millionaire filmmakers of Hollywood but the tech billionaires of Silicon Valley. Policing surveillance capitalism with his own form of 24/7 surveillance of the everyday, Columbo would sift through the false history of the killer's alibi much as internet users nowadays vigilantly sift through fake news to find the truth. Perhaps, in an updating of the subliminal cut episode, 'Double Exposure' (1973), Columbo might even turn the expertise of the murderer against him- or herself by running an advert to target them using their own algorithmically known preferences, thereby tricking them into giving away their guilt. As before when *Columbo* was new, the richest are those who seek to profit the most by altering how the past is recorded. Thus the updated list of possible murderers is as long as ever; whether it is political consultants, space travel entrepreneurs, green energy suppliers, investment bankers, hedge fund managers, or, with the audiovisual more to the foreground, virtual and augmented reality innovators, videogame designers, animation artists, voiceover actors, former film star politicians, reality television family members, VJs, news website proprietors, social media service providers, the list goes on. Playing these killers, we might find the return of, for example, later *Columbo* murderers like Ian Buchanan or Matthew Rhys, appearing again as per the show's former casting of recurring murderers (Patrick McGoohan, Robert Culp, Jack Cassidy, George Hamilton and William Shatner). There might also be some supporting roles or cameos from other previous murderers, such as Lee Grant, Dick van Dyke, Joyce van Patten, Faye Dunaway, Shatner or Hamilton. Alternatively, perhaps some of the many outspoken celebrity fans of *Columbo* might feature, such as Andrea Riseborough, after her unforgettable role as the reluctant but ruthless killer in the 'Crocodile' [2017] episode of *Black Mirror* [2011–] [Olley 2021], or Stephen Fry after his deadly General Melchett from *Blackadder Goes Forth* (1989), beneath whose respectable bluster is a scarcely submerged dead-eyed maniac sending thousands to their deaths without a care in the world.

That Columbo would police these well-to-do professionals in the same manner is still, as before, not a class issue per se, but relates to the social justice due to those who have less, and may even be murdered, so that the elite can have more: the need to adhere to a certain baseline right for all, that of the chance to live a meaningful life as a citizen. That this updating of *Columbo* is so easy to imagine illustrates why the show continues to remain as relevant today as it was when it first hit the screens, in the era that also saw the emergence of neoliberalism, the economic doctrine that continues to shape our globalised world.

Ultimately, the exhausting 24/7 nature of everyday surveillance in the defence of life against the machinations of surveillance capitalism and the structural inequality of neoliberalism, a fight precisely for democracy (Zuboff 2019: 61), is what remains so pertinent about *Columbo* for our contemporary era. To hold on to the rights of a citizen, to ward off the state of exception as norm (which seeks to reduce all to bare life) requires that we perform, learn, police and locate ourselves accordingly. This may take us into an ambiguous grey area akin to that within which Columbo's actions appear moral/amoral. Nevertheless, this is what requires us, in the twenty-first century, like Columbo before us, to pay attention 24/7.

Bibliography

Abu-Lughod, Janet L. (1999), *New York, Chicago, Los Angeles*, Minneapolis: University of Minnesota Press.

Acland, Charles R. (2012), *Swift Viewing*, Durham, NC: Duke University Press.

Agamben, Giorgio [1995] (1998), *Homo Sacer*, trans. Daniel Heller Roazen, Stanford, CA: Stanford University Press.

Agamben, Giorgio (2003), *State of Exception*, trans. Kevin Attell, Chicago: University of Chicago Press.

Allen, Robert C. and Annette Hill (eds) (2004), *The Television Studies Reader*, London: Routledge.

Alvey, Mark (2004), 'Too Many Kids and Old Ladies', *Screen*, 45: 1, pp. 40–62.

Anderson, Christopher (1994), *Hollywood TV*, Austin: University of Texas Press.

Andreeva, Nellie (2018), 'Steven Spielberg On His Friendship With Steven Bochco That Spanned 47 Years', *Deadline*, 1 April, https://deadline.com/2018/04/steven-spielberg-steven-bochco-remembrance-columbo-1202356722/ (accessed on 29 April 2020).

Anon. (1968), 'U's "Murder" on TV Kills All Competition', *The Film Daily*, 4 March, pp. 1 and 3.

Anon. (1972), 'Strong Sunday (Disney, Falk) Lifts NBC-TV to Fifth Week Rating Win', *Variety*, 268: 11, 25 October, p. 33.

Anon. (1995), '*Columbo* Leads the Way through French Primetime', *Variety*, 358: 1, p. 46.

Anon. (1996), 'Paris Honours TV's Columbo', *The Times*, 2 March, p. 16.

Anon. (2018), 'Steven Bochco, Creator of Hill Street Blues, Dies at 74', *The Guardian*, 1 April, https://www.theguardian.com/tv-and-radio/2018/apr/02/steven-bochco-creator-of-hill-street-blues-dies-at-74 (accessed on 29 April 2020).

Aoyama, Gosho (2005), *Case Closed 7*, trans. Joe Yamazaki, San Francisco, CA: VIZ Media.

Arendt, Hannah (1963), *On Revolution*, London: Penguin.

Armstrong, Lois (1976), 'Over the Tube', *People Magazine*, 9 August, pp. 21–24.

Banham, Reyner (1971), *Los Angeles*, London: Allen Lane.

Banner, Stuart (2002), *The Death Penalty*, Cambridge, MA: Harvard University Press.

Baron, Cynthia and Sharon Marie Carnicke (2011), *Reframing Screen Performance*, Ann Arbor: The University of Michigan Press.

Baron, Cynthia and Yannis Tzioumakis (2020), *Acting Indie*, London: Palgrave.

Barr, Sabrina (2019), 'Six Ways Social Media Negatively Affects your Mental Health', *The Independent*, 10 October, https://www.independent.co.uk/life-style/health-and-families/social-media-mental-health-negative-effects-depression-anxiety-addiction-memory-a8307196.html (accessed on 22 April 2020).

Bell, Julia (2020), *Radical Attention*, London: Peninsula Press.

Beller, Jonathan (2006), *The Cinematic Mode of Production*, Hanover, NH: Dartmouth College Press.

Benjamin, Walter [1942] (1968), 'Theses on the Philosophy of History', in *Illuminations*, trans. Harry Zohn, ed. Hannah Arendt, New York: Schocken Books.

Benshoff, Harry M. (2016), *Film and Television Analysis*, London: Routledge.

Berardi, Franco 'Bifo' (2009a), *Precarious Rhapsody*, trans. Arianna Bove et al., Wivenhoe: Minor Compositions.

Berardi, Franco 'Bifo' (2009b), *The Soul at Work*, trans. Francesca Cadel and Guiseppina Mecchia, South Pasadena, CA: Semiotext(e).

Berardi, Franco 'Bifo' (2015), *Heroes*, London: Verso.

Bergfelder, Tim, Erica Carter, Deniz Göktürk and Claidia Sandberg (eds) (2020), *The German Cinema Book*, Second Edition, London: Bloomsbury.

Blum, Richard A. (1984), *American Film Acting*, Ann Arbor, MI: UMI Research Press.

Blum, Richard A. and Richard D. Lindheim (1987), *Primetime Network Television Programming*, Boston, MA: Focal Press.

Bochco, Steven (2017), *Truth is a Total Defense*, UK: Amazon.

Boddy, William (1990), *Fifties Television*, Urbana and Chicago: University of Illinois Press.

Bok (1971), 'NBC Murder Mystery (Columbo)', *Variety*, 264: 6, 22 September, p. 24.

Brecht, Bertolt (2014), 'Short Description of a New Technique of Acting That Produces a *Verfremdung* Effect', in B. Brecht, *On Theatre*, eds M. Silberman, S. Giles and T. Kuhn, London: Bloomsbury, pp. 184–195.

Brooks, Tim and Earle Marsh (1995), *The Complete Dictionary to Prime Time Network and Cable TV Shows 1946-Present*, New York: Ballantine Books.

Brunsdon, Charlotte (2000), 'The Structure of Anxiety: Recent British Television Crime Fiction', in E. Buscombe (ed.), *British Television. A Reader*, Oxford: Clarendon Press, pp. 195–217.

Bruzzi, Stella (2007), *Seven Up*, London: BFI.

Buckland, Warren (2006), *Directed by Steven Spielberg*, New York: Continuum.

Buckland, Warren (2009), 'Introduction', in W. Buckland (ed.), *Puzzle Films*, Oxford: Wiley-Blackwell, pp. 1–12.

Bueno, Claudio Celis (2017), *The Attention Economy*, London: Rowman and Littlefield.

Bull, Sofia (2012), *A Post Genomic Forensic Crime Drama*, Doctoral Thesis, Stockholm University: Acta Universitatis Stockholmiensis.

Bull, Sofia (2016), 'From Crime Lab to Mind Palace', *New Review of Film and Television Studies*, 14: 3, pp. 324–344.

Buonanno, Milly (2017), 'Introduction', in M. Buonanno (ed.), *Television Antiheroines*, Bristol: Intellect, pp. 1–24.

Buxton, David (1990), *From the Avengers to Miami Vice*, Manchester: Manchester University Press.

Cadwalladr, Carole (2020), 'Fresh Cambridge Analytica Leak "Shows Global Manipulation is Out of Control"', *The Guardian*, 4 January, https://www.theguardian.com/uk-news/2020/jan/04/cambridge-analytica-data-leak-global-election-manipulation (accessed on 29 April 2020).

Calabrese, Omar (1992), *Neo-Baroque*, Princeton, NJ: Princeton University Press.

Caldwell, David and Paul W. Rea (1991), 'Handke's and Wenders's *Wings of Desire*', *The German Quarterly*, 64: 1, pp. 46–54.

Caldwell, John Thornton (1995), *Televisuality*, New Brunswick, NJ: Rutgers University Press.

Caldwell, Sarah (2019), 'In Small Packages', in L. Fife Donaldson and J. Walters (eds), *Television Performance*, London: Palgrave, pp. 22–42.

Cantor, Muriel G. (1971), *The Hollywood TV Producer*, London: Basic Books.

Cantor, Muriel G. and Joel M. Cantor (1992), *Prime-Time Television*, Second Edition, London: Sage Publications.

Cantrell, Tom and Christopher Hogg (eds) (2018), *Exploring Television Acting*, London: Methuen.

Caraway, Brett (2011), 'Audience Labour in the New Media Environment', *Media, Culture & Society*, 33: 5, pp. 693–708.

Carlson, James (1985), *Prime Time Law Enforcement*, New York: Praeger.

Carney, Ray (ed.) (2001), *Cassavetes on Cassavetes*, London: Faber and Faber.

Carr, John Dickson (1967), *The Problem of the Wire Cage*, New York: Zebra Books.

Carrington, Damian (2020), 'Coronavirus: "Nature is Sending us a Message", Says UN Environment Chief', *The Guardian*, 25 March, https://www.theguardian.com/world/2020/mar/25/coronavirus-nature-is-sending-us-a-message-says-un-environment-chief?CMP=share_btn_fb (accessed on 25 March 2020).

Catz, Sheldon (2016), *Columbo Under Glass*, Albany, GA: BearManor Media.

Caughie, John (2000), *Television Drama*, Oxford: Oxford University Press.

Caughie, John (2008), 'Telephilia and Distraction', *Journal of British Cinema and Television*, 3: 1, pp. 5–18.

Caughie, John (2014), 'What Do Actors Do When They Act?', in J. Bignell and L. Stephen (eds), *British Television Drama*, Second Edition, London: Palgrave Macmillan, pp. 143–155.

Cawelti, John G. (1976), *Adventure, Mystery, and Romance*, Chicago: University of Chicago Press.

Chesterton, G. K. (2006), *The Complete Father Brown Stories*, Ware: Wordsworth Classics.

Chierichetti, David (2003), *Edith Head*, New York: HarperCollins.

Chow, Rey (2002), *The Protestant Ethnic and the Spirit of Capitalism*, New York: Columbia University Press.

Christie, Agatha (1931), *Peril at End House*, New York: Pocket Books.

Citton, Yves [2014] (2017), *The Ecology of Attention*, trans. Barnaby Norman, Cambridge: Polity Press.

Clare, Janet (2006), *Revenge Tragedies of the Renaissance*, Tavistock: Northcote House Publishers.

Cohan, Steven (2008), *CSI: Crime Scene Investigation*, London: BFI Classics.

Columbophile (2019), 'Moffat Clarifies Stance on Columbo Following *Radio Times* Interview', *The Columbophile*, 19 November, https://columbophile. com/2019/11/20/moffat-clarifies-stance-on-columbo-following-radio-times-interview/ (accessed on 29 April 2020).

Connor, Neil (2018), 'Chinese School Uses Facial Recognition to Monitor Student Attention in Class', *The Telegraph*, 17 May, https://www.telegraph. co.uk/news/2018/05/17/chinese-school-uses-facial-recognition-moni-tor-student-attention/ (accessed on 3 April 2020).

Cook, Roger F. (1997), 'Angels, Fiction, and History in Berlin', in R. F. Cook and G. Gemünden (eds), *The Cinema of Wim Wenders*, Detroit, MI: Wayne State University Press, pp. 163–190.

Corner, John (1999), *Critical Ideas in Television Studies*, Oxford: Clarendon Press.

Crary, Jonathan (1999), *Suspensions of Perception*, Cambridge, MA: The MIT Press.

Crary, Jonathan (2013), *24/7*, London: Verso.

Creeber, Glen (2006), *Tele-visions*, London: Bloomsbury.

Cremona, Patrick (2019), 'Mark Gatiss Has "No Immediate Plans" to Revive *Sherlock*', *Radio Times*, 18 November, https://www.radiotimes.com/news/tv/2019-11-18/sherlock-return-mark-gatiss/ (accessed on 29 April 2020).

Crisell, Andrew (2006), *A Study of Modern Television*, London: Palgrave.

Cullins, Ashley (2019), '*Columbo* Creators Awarded $70M in Universal Profits Fight', *The Hollywood Reporter*, 1 November, https://www.hollywoodre-porter.com/thr-esq/columbo-creators-awarded-70m-universal-prof-its-fight-1251660 (accessed on 29 April 2020).

Curtin, Michael (2004), 'Media Capitals', in L. Spigel and J. Olsson (eds), *Television After TV*, Durham, NC: Duke University Press, pp. 270–302.

Curtin, Michael and Jane Shattuc (2009), *The American Television Industry*, London: Bloomsbury.

Davenport, Thomas H. and John C. Beck (2001), *The Attention Economy*, Boston, MA: Harvard Business School Press.

Davis, Mike [1990] (2006), *City of Quartz*, London: Verso.

Davis, Mike (2006), *Planet of Slums*, London: Verso.

Dawidziak, Mark (1988), *The Columbo Phile: A Casebook*, New York: The Mysterious Press.

Dawidziak, Mark [1988] (2019), *The Columbo Phile: A Casebook*, Thirtieth Anniversary Edition, St Martin, OH: Commonwealth Book Company.

Debord, Guy [1967] (1994), *The Society of the Spectacle*, New York: Zone Books.

Deleuze, Gilles (1992), 'Postscript on Societies of Control', *October*, 59, pp. 3–7.

Deleuze, Gilles and Félix Guattari (1972), *Anti-Oedipus*, trans. Robert Hurley, Mark Seem and Helen R. Lane (1983), Minneapolis: University of Minnesota Press.

Deleuze, Gilles and Félix Guattari (1980), *A Thousand Plateaus*, trans. Brian Massumi (1987), London: Athlone.

Del Rio, Elena (2012), 'Feminine Energies, or the Outside of Noir', in D. Martin-Jones and W. Brown (eds), *Deleuze and Film*, Edinburgh: Edinburgh University Press, pp. 155–172.

Dick, Philip K. (1962), *The Man in the High Castle*, London: Penguin.

Diehl, Heath A. (2014), '"Listen to the Silence": Dismantling the Myth of a Classless Society in the Fiction of Marcia Muller and Sara Paretsky', in J. H. Kim (ed.), *Class and Culture in Crime Fiction*, Jefferson, NC: McFarland and Company Inc., pp. 49–68.

Dienst, Richard (1994), *Still Life in Real Time*, Durham, NC, and London: Duke University Press.

Doran, Peter (2017), *A Political Economy of Attention, Mindfulness and Consumerism*, London: Routledge.

Dostoevsky, Fyodor [1866] (1994), *Crime and Punishment*, Ware: Wordsworth Classics.

Downing, Lisa (2013), *The Subject of Murder*, Chicago: University of Chicago Press.

Doyle, Waddick and Claudia Roda (2019), 'Introduction', in W. Doyle and C. Roda (eds), *Communication in the Era of Attention Scarcity*, London: Palgrave, pp. 1–6.

Dyer, Richard (1997), *White*, London: Routledge.

Dyer, Richard (2015), *Lethal Repetition*, London: BFI.

Ebert, Roger (1995), 'Diabolique', *rogerebert.com*, 17 February, https://www.rogerebert.com/reviews/diabolique-1995 (accessed on 29 April 2020).

Eco, Umberto (1985), '*Casablanca*', *SubStance*, 14: 2, pp. 3–12.

Eco, Umberto (1994), *The Limits of Interpretation*, Bloomington: Indiana University Press.

Edgerton, Gary (1991), 'High Concept, Small Screen', *Journal of Popular Film and Television*, 19: 3, pp. 114–127.

Edwards, Martin (2016), 'Introduction', in M. Edwards, *Murder at the Manor*, London: The British Library, pp. 7–10.

Ehrlich, Linda C. (1991), 'Mediations on Wim Wenders's *Wings of Desire*', *Literature/Film Quarterly*, 19: 4, pp. 242–246.

Ellis, John (1982), *Visible Fictions*, London: Routledge.

Elsaesser, Thomas (1989), *New German Cinema*, London: BFI.

Erie, Steven P. (2004), *Globalizing L.A.*, Stanford, CA: Stanford University Press.

Falk, Peter (2008), *Just One More Thing*, New York: Arrow Books.

Feasey, Rebecca (2003), 'Sex, Controversy, Box-Office', in J. Stringer (ed.), *Movie Blockbusters*, London: Routledge, pp. 167–177.

Feuer, Jane (1984), 'MTM Enterprises', in J. Feuer, P. Kerr and T. Vahimagi (eds), *MTM 'Quality Television'*, London: BFI, pp. 1–31.

Fife Donaldson, Lucy and James Walters (eds) (2019), *Television Performance*, London: Macmillan International.

Fisher, Mark (2009), *Capitalist Realism*, New York: Zero Books.

Foucault, Michel (2007), *Security, Territory, Population: Lectures at the Collège de France 1977–78*, trans. Graham Burchell, ed. Michel Senellart, London: Palgrave Macmillan.

Freedman, Carl (2009), 'The End of Work', in M. Bould, K. Glitre and G. Tuck (eds), *Neo-Noir*, London: Wallflower, pp. 61–74.

Freeman, R. Austin [1912] (2011), *The Singing Bone*, Wisconsin: Resurrected Press.

Frie (1968), 'Prescription Murder', *Variety*, 250: 2, 28 February, p. 38.

Friedberg, Anne (1993), *Window Shopping*, Berkeley: University of California Press.

Frolkis, Joseph P. (2013), 'The Columbo Phenomenon', *JAMA*, 309: 22, pp. 2333–2334.

Fry, Tony (ed.) (1993), *R. U. A. TV?*, Sydney, Australia: Power Publications.

Fuchs, Christian, Kees Boersma, Anders Albrechtslund and Marisol Sandoval (2012), 'Introduction', in C. Fuchs, K. Boersma, A. Albrechtslund and M. Sandoval (eds), *Internet and Surveillance*, London: Routledge, pp. 1–28.

Fukuyama, Francis (1989), 'The End of History?', *The National Interest*, 16 (Summer), pp. 3–18.

Galpert, Alan L. (2013), *The Colossal Columbo Quiz Book*, Virginia Beach, VA: CreateSpace.

Gambaccini, Paul and Rod Taylor (1993), *Television's Greatest Hits*, London: Network Books.

Ganascia, Jean-Gabriel (2009), 'The Great Catopticon', in *Proceedings of the 8th International Conference of Computer Ethics Philosophical Enquiry (CEPE)*, 26–28 June 2009, Corfu, Greece, http://www-poleia.lip6.fr/~ganascia/Publications?action=AttachFile&do=view&target=GreatCatopticon.pdf (accessed on 9 May 2020).

Gardner, Colin (2012), *Beckett, Deleuze and the Televisual Event*, London: Palgrave.

Gardner, Colin (2018), 'Towards a "Minor" Fascism', in F. Beckman (ed.), *Control Culture*, Edinburgh: Edinburgh University Press, pp. 141–165.

Gardner, Eriq (2018), 'Judge Allows "Columbo" Fraud Lawsuit Against Universal', *The Hollywood Reporter*, 9 February, https://www.hollywoodreporter.com/thr-esq/judge-allows-columbo-fraud-lawsuit-universal-1083344 (accessed on 30 April 2020).

Gazzara, Ben (2004), *In the Moment*, New York: Carroll and Graf.

Geraghty, Christine (1991), *Women and Soap Opera*, Cambridge: Polity Press.

Gianakos, Larry James (1978), *Television Drama Series Programming*, Lanham, MD: Scarecrow Press.

Gilbert, Dennis L. (2017), *The American Class Structure in an Age of Growing Inequality*, Tenth Edition, Los Angeles: Sage.

Gitlin, Todd (1983), *Inside Prime Time*, London: Routledge.

Glover, Carol (1993), *Men, Women and Chainsaws*, Princeton, NJ: Princeton University Press.

Graf, Alexander (2002), *The Cinema of Wim Wenders: The Celluloid Highway*, London: Wallflower.

Graham, Jacob and Tom Sparrow (eds) (2018), *True Detective*, Oxford: Wiley-Blackwell.

Graham, Stephen (2013), 'The New Military Urbanism', in K. Bell and L. Snider (eds), *The Surveillance-Industrial Complex*, London: Routledge, pp. 11–26.

Grant, Lee (2015), *I Said Yes to Everything*, New York: Plume.

Gray, Jonathan and Amanda Lotz (2018), *Television Studies*, Second Edition, Cambridge: Polity Press.

Gwenllian-Jones, Sara and Roberta E. Pearson (2004), 'Introduction', in S. Gwenllian-Jones and R. E. Pearson (eds), *Cult Television*, Minneapolis: University of Minnesota Press, pp. 3–26.

Harsin, Jayson (2019), 'Political Attention', in W. Doyle and C. Roda (eds), *Communication in the Era of Attention Scarcity*, London: Palgrave, pp. 75–111.

Harvey, David (1990), *The Condition of Postmodernity*, Oxford: Blackwell.

Harvey, David (2005), *A Brief History of Neoliberalism*, Oxford: Oxford University Press.

Hassoun, Dan (2014), 'Tracing Attentions', *Television & New Media*, 15: 4, pp. 271–288.

Hastie, Amelie (2017), 'Columbo, Cassavetes, and a Biography of Friendship', *Celebrity Studies*, 8: 4, pp. 493–509.

Hills, Matt (2002), *Fan Cultures*, London: Routledge.

Hills, Matt (2004), 'Defining Cult TV', in R. C. Allen and A. Hill (eds), *The Television Studies Reader*, London: Routledge, pp. 509–523.

Hills, Matt (2012), 'Mainstream Cult', in S. Abbott (ed.), *The Cult TV Book*, London: I.B. Tauris, pp. 67–73.

Hilmes, Michele (ed.) (2007), *NBC America's Network*, Berkeley: University of California Press.

Himmelstein, Hal (1994), *Television, Myth and the American Mind*, London: Praeger.

Hirschhorn, Clive (1983), *The Universal Story*, London: Octopus Books.

Holdsworth, Amy (2011), *Television, Memory and Nostalgia*, London: Palgrave.

Hopkirk, Peter (1996), *Quest for Kim*, London: John Murray.

Hughes, Paul (2018), *The Columbo Case Files*, ebook, Paul Hughes.

Hyatt, Wesley (2006), *Emmy Award Winning Night-time Television Shows, 1948–2004*, London: Macfarland.

Jacobson, Brian (2015), *Studios Before the System*, New York: Columbia University Press.

Jameson, Fredric (1984), 'Postmodernism, or the Cultural Logic of Late Capitalism', *New Left Review*, I: 146, pp. 53–92.

Jancovich, Mark and Nathan Hunt (2004), 'The Mainstream, Distinction, and Cult TV', in S. Gwenllian-Jones and R. E. Pearson (eds), *Cult Television*, Minneapolis: University of Minnesota Press, pp. 27–44.

Jaster, Margaret Rose (1999), 'The Earnest Equivocator', *Journal of American Culture*, 22: 4, pp. 51–55.

Jenner, Mareike (2016), *American TV Detective Dramas*, Basingstoke: Palgrave Macmillan.

Jhally, Sut and Bill Livant (1986), 'Watching as Working: The Valorization of Audience Consciousness', *Journal of Communication*, 36: 3, pp. 124–143.

Johnson, Frank (1991), 'Frank Johnson Welcomes the Return of Columbo, his Favourite TV Detective', *The Daily Telegraph*, 20 February, p. 15.

Johnston, Chris (2018), 'YouTube Top Earners', *BBC News*, 3 December, https://www.bbc.co.uk/news/business-46427910 (accessed on 30 April 2020).

Kafka, Franz [1925] (1977), *The Trial*, London: Pan Books.

Kahneman, Daniel (1973), *Attention and Effort*, Englewood Cliffs, NJ: Prentice Hall.

Karpovich, Angelina I. (2010), '*The Avengers*', in D. Lavery (ed.), *The Essential Cult TV Reader*, Lexington: The University Press of Kentucky, pp. 36–43.

Kennerley, Helen (2014), *Overcoming Anxiety*, London: Robinson.

Kerr, Paul (1984), 'Drama at MTM', in J. Feuer, P. Kerr and T. Vahimagi (eds), *MTM: Quality Television*, London: BFI, pp. 132–165.

Kestner, Joseph A. (2000), *The Edwardian Detective, 1901–1915*, Aldershot: Ashgate.

Kim, Julie H. (2014), 'Introduction', in J. H. Kim (ed.), *Class and Culture in Crime Fiction*, Jefferson, NC: McFarland and Company Inc., pp. 1–10.

Kingsley, Simon (2004), 'Making History', Variety, 394: 7, pp. 6, 8, 12 and 16.

Kipling, Rudyard [1994] (1901), *Kim*, Ware: Wordsworth Classics.

Klein, Naomi (2007), *The Shock Doctrine*, London: Penguin.

Klein, Norman M. (1997), *The History of Forgetting*, London: Verso.

Knight, Peter (ed.) (2002), *Conspiracy Nation*, New York: New York University Press.

Koehl, Christian (2004), 'Hollywood and Rhine', *Variety*, 394: 7, p. 17.

Kompare, Derek (2005), *Rerun Nation*, London: Routledge.

Kouvaros, George (2004), *Where Does it Happen?*, Minneapolis: University of Minnesota Press.

Kwon, Heonik (2010), *The Other Cold War*, New York: Columbia University Press.

Lafferty, William (1990), 'Feature Films on Prime-Time Television', in T. Balio (ed.), *Hollywood in the Age of Television*, London: Routledge, pp. 235–256.

Langer, John (1981), 'Television's "Personality System"', *Media, Culture and Society*, 3: 4, pp. 351–365.

Lanham, Richard A. (2006), *The Economics of Attention*, Chicago: University of Chicago Press.

Lazzarato, Maurizio (2012), *The Making of the Indebted Man*, trans. Joshua David Jordan, Pasadena, CA: Semiotext(e).

Lazzarato, Maurizio (2014), *Sings and Machines*, trans. Joshua David Jordan, Pasadena, CA: Semiotext(e).

Leach, Jim (2009). *Doctor Who*, Detroit, MI: Wayne State University Press.

Lefait, Sébastien (2013), *Surveillance on Screen*, Plymouth: The Scarecrow Press.

Lent, Tina Olsin (1987), 'The Dark Side of the Dream', *Southern California Quarterly*, 69: 4, pp. 329–348.

Lertzman, Richard A. and William J. Birnes (2017), *Beyond Columbo*, Los Angeles: Shadow Lawn Press.

Levinas, Emmanuel [1961] (1969), *Totality and Infinity*, trans. Alphonso Lingis, Pittsburgh, PA: Duquesne University Press.

Levinson, Richard and William Link (1981a), *Stay Tuned*, New York: St Martin's Press.

Levinson, Richard and William Link (1981b), 'How We Created Columbo – And How He Nearly Killed Us', *American Film*, 6: 5, pp. 26–28 and 66–68.

Levinson, Richard and William Link (1983a), 'Dialogue on Film', *American Film*, 9: 3, pp. 20–26.

Levinson, Richard and William Link (1983b), 'Interview with Richard Levinson and William Link', in H. Newcomb and R. S. Alley (eds), *The Producer's Medium*, Oxford: Oxford University Press, pp. 128–153.

Levinson, Richard and William Link (1986), *off Camera*, New York: Signet.

Levinson, Richard and William Link (1992), 'The Rotating Umbrella', in D. Marc and R. J. Thompson (eds), *Prime Time Prime Movers*, Syracuse, NY: Syracuse University Press, pp. 180–194.

Link, William (2010), *The Columbo Collection*, Norfolk, VA: Crippen and Landru Publishers.

Londoner, David J. (1985), 'The Changing Economics of Entertainment', in T. Balio (ed.), *The American Film Industry*, Madison: University of Wisconsin Press, pp. 603–630.

Lotz, Amanda D. (2007a), 'Must-see TV', in M. Hilmes (ed.), *NBC America's Network*, Berkeley: University of California Press, pp. 261–274.

Lotz, Amanda D. (2007b), *The Television will be Revolutionized*, New York: New York University Press.

Lowry, Brian (2018), 'Steven Bochco, Innovative Co-Creator of "NYPD Blue," "Hill Street Blues," Dies at 74', *Variety*, 1 April, http://variety.com/2018/tv/news/steven-bochco-dead-dies-nypd-blue-1202741169/ (accessed on 2 May 2020).

McBride, Joseph (1997), *Steven Spielberg*, New York: Simon and Schuster.

MacDonald, J. Fred (1990), *One Nation Under Television*, Chicago: Nelson-Hall.

MacLean, Nancy (2017), *Democracy in Chains*, London: Scribe Publications.

Mann, Arnold (1984), 'How Costs Got Out of Hand', *Emmy*, 6: 5, pp. 8–10 and 62.

Mann, Steve, Jason Nolan and Barry Wellman (2003), 'Surveillance', *Surveillance and Society*, 1: 3, pp. 331–335.

Marill, Alvin H. (1975), 'Films on TV', *Films in Review*, 26: 1, pp. 41–44.

Martin-Jones, David (2011), *Deleuze and World Cinemas*, London. Continuum.

Martin-Jones, David (2018), *Cinema Against Doublethink*, London: Routledge.

Martin-Jones, David (2019), 'Transnational Turn or Turn to World Cinema?', *Transnational Cinemas*, 10: 1, pp. 13–22.

Mattes, Ari (2016), 'Unlawful Entry', in E. M. Clift, M. Guaralda and A. Mattes (eds), *Filming the City*, Bristol: Intellect, pp. 11–26.

Mellencamp, Patricia (1992), *High Anxiety*, Bloomington: Indiana University Press.

Melley, Timothy (2000), *Empire of Conspiracy*, Ithaca, NY, and London: Cornell University Press.

Meyers, Cynthia B. (2011), 'The Problems with Sponsorship in US Broadcasting, 1930s–1950s', *Historical Journal of Film, Radio and Television*, 31: 3, pp. 355–372.

Meza, Ed (2004), 'Teuton's Commercial Television Titan', *Variety*, 396: 7, pp. B4–B5.

Mignolo, Walter D. (2000), *Local Histories/Global Designs*, Princeton, NJ: Princeton University Press.

Mills, Charles. W. (1997), *The Racial Contract*, Ithaca, NY: Cornell University Press.

Mittell, Jason (2003), 'The "Classic Network System" in the US', in M. Hilmes (ed.), *The Television History Book*, London: BFI, pp. 44–49.

Mittell, Jason (2004), *Genre and Television*, London: Routledge.

Mittell, Jason (2015), *Complex TV*, New York: New York University Press.

Modleski, Tania (2008), *Loving with a Vengeance*, New York: Routledge.

Monaco, James (1977), 'Roots and Angels: US Television 1976/77', *Sight and Sound*, 46: 3, pp. 158–161.

Moore, Barbara, Marvin R. Bensman and Jim Van Dyke (2006), *Prime-Time Television*, London: Praeger.

Moore, Matthew (2017), 'Social Media is Bad for your Mental Health, Facebook Admits', *The Times*, 18 December, https://www.thetimes.co.uk/article/social-media-is-bad-for-your-mental-health-facebook-admits-82vnjlnk5 (accessed on 22 April 2020).

Morley, David (1986), *Family Television*, London: Comedia.

Morris, Nigel (ed.) (2017), *A Companion to Steven Spielberg*, Oxford: Wiley-Blackwell.

Mulhall, Stephen (2001), *On Film*, London: Routledge.

Murgia, Madhumita (2019), 'London's King's Cross Uses Facial Recognition in Security Cameras', *Financial Times*, 12 August, https://www.ft.com/content/8cbcb3ae-babd-11e9-8a88-aa6628ac896c (accessed on 3 April 2020).

Nagib, Lucia and Anne Jerslev (eds) (2013), *Impure Cinema*, London: Bloomsbury.

Nannicelli, Ted (2016), *Appreciating the Art of Television*, London: Routledge.

Napoli, Philip M. (2003), *Audience Economics*, New York: Columbia University Press.

Napoli, Philip M. (2010), *Audience Evolution*, New York: Columbia University Press.

NBC (1971a), 'Mystery Movie Top Rates New Program Among Adults', *Audience Measurement, Special Projects*, 5 October, [NBC Research Highlights] Wisconsin Center for Film and Theater Research, Madison, WI.

NBC (1971b), 'Mystery Movie Top Rated New Show', *Audience Measurement, Special Projects*, 11 October, [NBC Research Highlights] Wisconsin Center for Film and Theater Research, Madison, WI.

NBC (1971c), 'NBC Leads in Adult 25-64 Top Twenty', *Audience Measurement, Special Projects*, 14 October, [NBC Research Highlights] Wisconsin Center for Film and Theater Research, Madison, WI.

NBC (undated-a), 'NBC Mystery Movie 1971–1972 Season', *NBC Program Analysis*, [Microfiche], US Library of Congress, Washington, DC.

NBC (undated-b), 'Master Telecast Report: Mystery Movie, Death Lends a Hand', *NBC Master Books*, [Microfilm], US Library of Congress, Washington, DC.

NBC (undated-c), 'Master Telecast Report: Mystery Movie, Dagger of the Mind', *NBC Master Books*, [Microfilm], US Library of Congress, Washington, DC.

Nelson, Robin (1997), *TV Drama in Transition*, London: Macmillan.

Nietzsche, Friedrich [1886] (1973), *Beyond Good and Evil*, London: Penguin.

Olley, Cat (2021), 'My Cultural Life: Andrea Riseborough', *Elle Decoration*, 17 February, https://www.elledecoration.co.uk/lifestyle-culture/a35534524/andrea-riseborough-interview/ (accessed on 20 February 2021).

Ousborne, Jeff (2016), 'Policing the Crime Drama', *Clues*, 34: 2, pp. 32–42.

Patten, Dominic (2019), 'NBCUniversal Scores New Trial Over $70M In "Columbo" Profits', *Deadline*, 2 December, https://deadline.com/2019/12/columbo-lawsuit-new-trial-nbcuniversal-unpaid-profits-1202798872/ (accessed on 2 May 2020).

Pearson, Roberta (2012), 'Observations on Cult Television', in S. Abbott (ed.), *The Cult TV Book*, London: I.B. Tauris, pp. 7–17.

Pearson-Jones, Bridie and Roisin O'Connor (2017), 'Arnold Schwarzenegger Terminates Troll who Questions Need for Special Olympics', *Independent*, 25 March, https://www.independent.co.uk/arts-entertainment/films/news/

arnold-schwarzenegger-youtube-comment-special-olympics-troll-response-a7649466.html (accessed on 2 May 2020).

Pedersen, Erik (2017), '"Columbo" Architects Sue Universal Over Unpaid Profits From Detective Drama', *Deadline*, 14 November, https://deadline.com/2017/11/columbo-creators-sue-universal-unpaid-profits-1202208380/ (accessed on 2 May 2020).

Perry, Jeb H. (1983), *Universal Television*, London: Scarecrow Press.

Pinker, Susan (2017), 'Does Facebook Make us Unhappy and Unhealthy', *The Wall Street Journal*, 25 May, https://www.wsj.com/articles/does-facebook-make-us-unhappy-and-unhealthy-1495729227?mod=rss_Technology&affc=0d5d423c-1412-471d-9460-6a1f0390cac4 (accessed on 22 April 2020).

Place, Janey (1998), 'Women in Film Noir', in E. A. Kaplan (ed.), *Women in Film Noir*, London: BFI, pp. 47–68.

Plain, Gill (2001), *Twentieth-Century Crime Fiction*, Edinburgh: Edinburgh University Press.

Primack, Brian A., Ariel Shensa, César G. Escobar-Viera, Erica L. Barrett, Jaime E. Sidani, Jason B. Colditz and A. Everette James (2017), 'Use of Multiple Social Media Platforms and Symptoms of Depression and Anxiety', *Computers in Human Behaviour*, 69 (April), pp. 1–9.

Queen, Ellery (1982), *Five Complete Novels*, New York: Avenel Books.

Reeves, Jimmie L., Mark C. Rodgers and Michael Epstein (1996), 'Rewriting Popularity', in D. Lavery, A. Hague and M. Cartwright (eds), *Deny All Knowledge*, New York: Syracuse University Press, pp. 22–35.

Rice, Jerry (2002), 'NBC at 75, The '70s', *Variety*, 386: 6, 25 March, p. 40.

Robinson, David (1969), *Buster Keaton*, London: Secker & Warburg.

Roda, Claudia (2019), 'A Roadmap of Studies in Attention and Digital Technology', in W. Doyle and C. Roda (eds), *Communication in the Era of Attention Scarcity*, London: Palgrave, pp. 7–20.

Rogowski, Christian (2019), *Wings of Desire*, Rochester, NY: Camden House.

Sanders, Steven M. and Aeon J. Skoble (eds) (2008), *The Philosophy of TV Noir*, Lexington: The University Press of Kentucky.

Sarris, Andrew [1962] (2004), 'Notes on the Auteur Theory in 1962', in Leo Braudy and Marshall Cohen (eds), *Film Theory and Criticism*, Sixth Edition, Oxford: Oxford University Press, pp. 561–564.

Schneider, Molly A. (2016), 'Television's Tortured Misfits', *Journal of Film and Video,* 68: 3–4, pp. 30–50.

Sconce, Jeffrey (2000), *Haunted Media*, Durham, NC: Duke University Press.

Sepinwall, Alan (2018), 'TV's Top 10 Detectives', *Rolling Stone*, July, p. 131.

Shakespeare, William [c. 1599–1602] (1980), *Hamlet*, London: Penguin.

Sharrett, Christopher (2012), 'Jack Webb and the Vagaries of Right-Wing TV Entertainment', *Cinema Journal*, 51: 4, pp. 165–171.

Shattuc, Jane M. (2010), 'Television Production: Who Makes American TV?', in J. Wasko (ed.), *A Companion to Television*, Chichester: Wiley-Blackwell, pp. 142–156.

Shaviro, Steven (2011), 'The "Bitter" Necessity of Debt', *Concentric*, 37: 1, pp. 73–82.

Shaw, Janice (2014), 'The Poet Dalgleish and Kate from the Block', in J. H. Kim (ed.), *Class and Culture in Crime Fiction*, Jefferson, NC: McFarland and Company Inc., pp. 31–48.

Shaw, Lou and Peter Feibleman (1976), *Columbo: Fade in to Murder*, PROD #45902, May 25th 1976. Revisions dated 9/7/1976 and 12/7/1976. Teleplay from an original story by Henry Garson. Director Bernard L. Kowalski. Producer Everett Chambers. Los Angeles: Universal City Studios. Housed at the BFI Special Collections, Berkhamsted, UK.

Shiel, Mark (2012), *Hollywood Cinema and the Real Los Angeles*, London: Reaktion Books.

Sicart, Miguel (2014), *Play Matters*, Cambridge, MA: The MIT Press.

Simon, Herbert A. (1971), 'Designing Organizations for an Information-Rich World', in M. Greenberger (ed.), *Computers, Communications, and the Public Interest*, Baltimore, MD: John Hopkins University Press, pp. 38–72.

Simon, Herbert A. [1969] (1996), *The Sciences of the Artificial*, Cambridge, MA: The MIT Press.

Sklar, Robert (1980), *Prime-Time America*, Oxford: Oxford University Press.

Sloan, Michael (2019), *"One More Thing, Sir . . .",* Albany, GA: BearManor Media.

Smythe, Dallas W. (1981), *Dependency Road*, Norwood, NJ: Ablex.

Snauffer, Douglas (2006), *Crime Television*, London: Praeger.

Soja, Edward (1989), *Postmodern Geographies,* London: Verso.

Soja, Edward W. (1996), 'Los Angeles, 1965–1992', in A. J. Scott and E. W. Soja (eds), *The City*, Berkeley: University of California Press, pp. 426–462.

Soja, Edward and Allen J. Scott (1996), 'Introduction to Los Angeles', in A. J. Scott and E. W. Soja (eds), *The City*, Berkeley: University of California Press, pp. 1–21.

Spigel, Lynn (1992), *Make Room for TV*, Chicago: University of Chicago Press.

Spigel, Lynn (2004), 'Introduction', in L. Spigel and J. Olsson (eds), *Television after TV*, Durham, NC: Duke University Press, pp. 1–34.

Stadler, Jane (2017), 'The Empath and the Psychopath', *Film-Philosophy*, 21: 3, pp. 410–427.

Steger, Manfred B., (2008), *The Rise of the Global Imaginary*, Oxford: Oxford University Press.

Stephenson-Burton, A. E. (1995), 'Through the Looking Glass', in D. Kidd-Hewitt and R. Osborne (eds), *Crime and the Media*, London: Pluto Press, pp. 131–163.

Stoddart, Helen (1995), 'Auteurism and Film Authorship Theory', in J. Hollows and M. Jancovich (eds), *Approaches to Popular Film*, Manchester: Manchester University Press, pp. 37–58.

Stoddart, Scott F. (ed.) (2011), *Analyzing Mad Men*, Jefferson, NC: McFarland and Company Inc.

Sturcken, Frank (1990), *Live Television*, Jefferson, NC: McFarland and Company Inc.

Taylor, Ella (1991), *Prime-Time Families*, Berkeley: University of California Press.

Thompson, Robert J. (1996), *Television's Second Golden Age*, Syracuse, NY: Syracuse University Press.

Thompson, William E. and Joseph V. Hickey (2011), *Society in Focus*, Seventh Edition, Custom Edition for Mott Community College, Boston, MA: Pearson.

Toffler, Alvin (1970), *Future Shock*, London: Pan Books Ltd.

Tuchman, Mitch (1978), 'Close Encounter with Steven Spielberg', *Film Comment*, 14: 1, pp. 49–55.

Turnbull, Sue (2014), *The TV Crime Drama*, Edinburgh: Edinburgh University Press.

Viera, Maria (2004), 'Playing with Performance', in C. Baron, D. Carson and F. P. Tomasulo (eds), *More than a Method*, Detroit, MI: Wayne State University Press, pp. 153–172.

Vila, Xavier and Alice Kuzniar (1992), 'Witnessing Narration in *Wings of Desire*', *Film Criticism*, 16: 3, pp. 53–76.

Wacquant, Loïc (2009), *Punishing the Poor*, Durham, NC: Duke University Press.

Walters, James (2019), 'The Enduring Act', in L. Fife Donaldson and J. Walters (ed.), *Television Performance*, London: Palgrave, pp. 61–83.

Wartenberg, Thomas E. (2007), *Thinking on Screen*, London: Routledge.

Wasko, Janet (2010), 'Introduction', in J. Wasko (ed.), *A Companion to Television*, Chichester: Wiley-Blackwell, pp. 1–14.

Watson, Mary Ann (2008), *Defining Visions*, Oxford: Blackwell.

Webb, Lawrence (2014), *The Cinema of Urban Crisis*, Amsterdam: Amsterdam University Press.

Webster, James G. (2014), *The Marketplace of Attention*, Cambridge, MA: The MIT Press.

Wenders, Wim (1992), 'Wim Wenders's Guilty Pleasures', *Film Comment*, 28: 1, pp. 74–77.

Westad, Odd Arne (2007), *The Global Cold War*, Cambridge: Cambridge University Press.

White, Hayden (1973), *Metahistory*, Baltimore, MD: Johns Hopkins University Press.

Williams, Raymond (1990), *Television*, London: Routledge.

Woodbridge, Linda (2010), *English Revenge Drama*, Cambridge: Cambridge University Press.

Zimmermann, Eric and Heather Chaplin (2013), 'Manifesto: The 21st Century will be Defined by Games', *Kotaku*, 9 September, https://kotaku.com/manifesto-the-21st-century-will-be-defined-by-games-1275355204 (accessed on 2 May 2020).

Zuboff, Shoshana (2019), *The Age of Surveillance Capitalism*, London: Profile Books.

Index